W9-CCY-857
VERMONT COLLEGE
MONTPELIER, VERMONT
WITHDRAWN

THE AMERICAN UNIVERSITY

Books by Jacques Barzun

History

THE FRENCH RACE
RACE, A STUDY IN SUPERSTITION
DARWIN, MARX, WAGNER
CLASSIC, ROMANTIC, AND MODERN
BERLIOZ AND THE ROMANTIC CENTURY
THE MODERN RESEARCHER (with Henry F. Graff)

Criticism

OF HUMAN FREEDOM
TEACHER IN AMERICA
GOD'S COUNTRY AND MINE
MUSIC IN AMERICAN LIFE
THE ENERGIES OF ART
JOHN JAY CHAPMAN: WRITINGS
THE HOUSE OF INTELLECT
SCIENCE: THE GLORIOUS ENTERTAINMENT
THE AMERICAN UNIVERSITY

Translations

BECQUE'S LA PARISIENNE
PLEASURES OF MUSIC
DIDEROT'S RAMEAU'S NEPHEW
MIRBEAU'S THE EPIDEMIC
MUSSET'S FANTASIO
FLAUBERT'S DICTIONARY OF ACCEPTED IDEAS
NEW LETTERS OF BERLIOZ
BERLIOZ'S EVENINGS WITH THE ORCHESTRA
FOUR PLAYS BY COURTELINE
BEAUMARCHAIS' FIGARO'S MARRIAGE

THE AMERICAN UNIVERSITY

How It Runs
Where It Is Going

by JACQUES BARZUN

1817

HARPER & ROW, PUBLISHERS
NEW YORK, EVANSTON, AND LONDON

THE AMERICAN UNIVERSITY. *Copyright © 1968 by Jacques Barzun. Printed in the United States of America. All rights reserved. No part of this book may be used or reproduced in any manner whatsoever without written permission except in the case of brief quotations embodied in critical articles and reviews. For information address Harper & Row, Publishers, Incorporated, 49 East 33rd Street, New York, N.Y. 10016.*

LIBRARY OF CONGRESS CATALOG CARD NUMBER: 68–15959

A-T

378.73
B296a

To JOHN W. GARDNER
in friendship and admiration

21880

Contents

In the nature of things, greatness and unity go together; excellence implies a center.

—John Henry Newman

Preface

This book is for the general reader who takes an interest in higher education, either as the graduate of a college or as the parent of somebody who will be one. Among general readers I venture to count also my colleagues in colleges and universities, both faculty members and toilers in administration, for experience shows that nowadays few persons on any campus have the leisure to become familiar with the circumstances of more than one sector, a situation that accounts for many of the misunderstandings and dissatisfactions found at institutions of higher learning.

I need hardly add that what I offer by way of panoramic view is an interpretation based on experience, rather than a report embodying comparative figures and "studies." My studies have consisted of daily work at the problems I describe, supplemented by travel and talk with colleagues and students. Reflections on society, coupled with the details of the position I have long since taken about education, furnish out the rest.

No one who is curious about American universities need fear that statistical research about them is being neglected: well-known educators and anonymous compilers alike are collecting data without cease; every institution at any time can be found filling in or sending out a questionnaire about some important part of its operations. The facts so gathered are often useful, but their significance is determined in the end by the choice among possible directions, attitudes, and purposes.

Now, nobody can choose a direction for the American university as an institution, nor do I believe that its best future can be plotted from figures arising out of practices found in two thousand independent establishments. Practices are not comparable throughout a range as wide as that between the corner garage and the General Motors corporation. All types of school, or nearly all, have their place in our national scheme, and we may be grateful for their abundance and the devotion it brings out and absorbs. But the university is an institution transcending time and geography. When strong and self-aware, the university belongs to civilization rather than to one country, and it elicits from the world a kind of devotion other than that which goes to the local academy, just as it turns its energies to other ends than merely supplying the market with a standard human product.

Since only the university can direct itself, the aim of the public's concern should be to think rather than to do. Thinking on such a subject means attending to significant details, the understanding of which may modify attitudes, and thus indirectly lead to desirable change. Sometimes all that is needed is for public opinion to grasp the *idea* of the university, so that this refreshed conception may reach those in charge of particular universities and remind them of where the true road lies.

In the chapters that follow I have sought to give those significant details and to show their relation to the idea of a university as it might emerge again from the present contradictions and predicaments of our great institutions. The book is therefore description, analysis, and indications of a possible future.

The obligations I have incurred in this undertaking extend far beyond my power to cite or remember. They include what I owe to every colleague, student, and friend I have talked with about education for the past twenty years and to every institution that has honored me with an invitation to visit it. In naming here some of the persons who have told me or taught me memorable things, I am recording only the chiefest objects of my gratitude, while also recalling the cordial associations growing out of my term as dean and provost.

At the head of the list stands the late Harry J. Carman, who as Dean of Columbia College often allowed me to overhear his administrative worries and plans, an experience combining—as so many felt in his presence—instruction and the spectacle of total selflessness.

The same feeling of communion accompanied my work with the chief officers of President Grayson Kirk's "administration"—in the first few years with John A. Krout, later with my close friends Lawrence H. Chamberlain, Stanley Salmen, and Ralph S. Halford. I was fortunate in having also as colleagues at the head of the several schools such deans and directors as Edward W. Barrett, Courtney C. Brown, Charles R. Colbert, Andrew W. Cordier, Jack Dalton, P. Frederick DelliQuadri, John R. Dunning, Wesley J. Hennessy, Richard H. Logsdon, H. Houston Merritt, William A. Owens, John G. Palfrey, Kenneth A. Smith, Gilbert P. Smith, Davidson Taylor, David B. Truman, Clarence C. Walton, and William C. Warren. Without their helpful advice and ready information I should not have penetrated any distance into the intricacies of professional education or the formal conditions of its use in the modern world.

In other domains, and notably in accounting and finance, my ignorance was partly dispelled by the friendly efforts of the late James L. Dohr and of Charles W. Bastable, Jr., reinforced by conversations with the Treasurer of Columbia University, William Bloor, and successive members of the Trustee Committee on Finance.

In the course of many and various transactions, and also at an annual weekend meeting of the most friendly and candid sort, I had the opportunity of comparing notes with fellow provosts and deans, among them: Kingman Brewster, William De Vane, and Charles Taylor of Yale; J. Douglas Brown of Princeton; McGeorge Bundy and Franklin Ford of Harvard; James D. Hart and

Roger Heyns of Berkeley; Mark Ingraham of Wisconsin; and Edward Levi of Chicago. To them all, my grateful regards.

To my staff, which included, besides Harry Boardman, Paul D. Carter, Robert J. Cooper, and Richard L. Plaut, Jr., the members of the Registrar's office, the Admissions and the Placement officers, I can only give my thanks collectively for putting their minute knowledge and experienced judgment at my disposal.

In the preparation of the text I had once again the expert collaboration of my old friends Miss Violet Serwin and Mrs. Virginia Xanthos Faggi, the second of whom helped me read proof, compiled the Check List, and made the Index.

J.B.

110 Low Library
January 15, 1968

P.S.—The completed typescript of this book was in the hands of the publisher six weeks before the student outbreak of April 23 that disrupted the work of Columbia University. I have since then found no reason to change or add to the substance of what I had written months earlier.

J.B.

May 3, 1968

Introductory

> I admit that Plato's world was not ours, that his scorn of trade and handicraft is fantastic, that he had no conception of a great industrial community such as that of the United States, and that such a community must and will shape its education to suit its own needs. If the usual education handed down to it from the past does not suit it, it will certainly before long drop this and try another.
>
> —MATTHEW ARNOLD

> The society of a university may embrace many groups within the state who possess capacity and energy for the serious pursuit of knowledge. . . . It thus becomes "an instrument of the people," placing its resources at the disposal of all members of the state who need its aid.
>
> —J. J. FINDLAY

The North American university is unlike any other. Its structure, management, sources of support, relation to Church and State, and responsibility to the public are unique and set it apart from all other types—English, Continental, or South American. As for the one element that universities share all over the world—teachers and students—it is, despite appearances, less homogeneous in interest and purpose than it used to be, hence cannot be relied on to give a uniform character and destiny to culturally diverse institutions.

In the United States that character and destiny are now a subject of public and private discussion as they never were before, and the reason is obvious. During the past twenty years the leading universities of the country have changed markedly in form and function, carrying with them—part way or altogether—the eighteen hundred other establishments called colleges and universities. All tend to suffer from similar and unexampled difficulties. They spend huge sums and are desperately poor; their students attack them; their neighbors hate them, their faculties are restless; and the public, critical of their rising fees and restricted enrollments, keeps making more and more peremptory demands upon them. The universities are expected, among other things, to turn out scientists and engineers, foster international understanding, provide a home for the arts, satisfy divergent tastes in architecture and sexual morals, cure cancer, recast the penal code, and train equally for the professions and for a life of cultured contentment in the Coming Era of Leisure.

One may be tempted to shrug off these fierce claims as part of the mid-century madness. But they are pressed just the same, and the university must somehow meet them, on pain of being reminded that it lives on charity. There it sits, doors open, overcrowded in city or country, and bound to perform from day to day the miracle of juggling deficits and coaxing donors, of soothing alumni and keeping its scholars faithful, while trying also to outlive the picket lines, sit-ins, teach-ins, and hot or cold articles in the local press.

Not all these miseries, it is true, bedevil all colleges and universities all the time. But the fact remains that the university as an institution has become the object of an endless domestic guerrilla, part organized, part fortuitous. It is perhaps time that this institution, which is still much loved and respected, even by its impatient clients, should be better understood. The subject is complex and variable, but not beyond comprehension. Why, then, is it so poorly known?

To begin with, there are in the country many overlapping kinds

of universities, not equally besought or beset. There are private and public universities (and hybrids like the land-grant colleges); there are new and old, state and municipal, secular and church-governed, urban and rural universities; there are four-year colleges that content themselves with undergraduate instruction and others that venture to give higher degrees in certain subjects; and all these exist side by side with the many colleges and universities in name only—institutions of lesser scope relabeled in the general excitement with some loftier title. This is what we should expect as a result of rapid expansion and limitless answerability, coupled with widespread confusion as to what a university is and can do.

The things that interest newspaper readers about universities besides athletics—the scientific discoveries, art exhibits, "studies" on human and social woes; the new buildings, fund-raising campaigns, and unsatisfactory admissions policies—are but external products. The public knows little, and perhaps cares not at all, about the vast apparatus of men and machines, rules of law and of thumb, duties and ambitions that lie below the externals and that are, like our national culture, in a perpetual state of flux. Yet, without an informed view of this heaving organism, much that affects the national culture no less than the university must remain a mystery.

The new functions it has taken on and the methods it has improvised in a decade-and-a-half have torn apart the fabric of the former single-minded, easily defined American university. A big corporation has replaced the once self-centered company of scholars and has thereby put itself at the mercy of many publics, unknown to one another and contradictory in their demands. It is not surprising that the newspaper reader, like the reporter who supplies him with fragmentary facts, is bewildered.

Indeed, the place is not always clearly seen by those within, so diverse are its activities and changeable its conditions of life. The internal stresses and strains are of course matters of gossip on the campus, but their cause is often a puzzle: Why do we do *this?*—is it the trustees? Why can't we do *that?*—doesn't the administration understand? Why weren't we told?—after all, *we* are the university. Faculty, student body, administration all suffer from a lack of mutual comprehension—and there are times when the lack seems irremediable.

The point is not that idle curiosity remains unsatisfied but that the missing information is essential to right action, individual and corporate. Both the need and the lack are new, as a simple contrast will make clear. Barely twenty years ago the workings of a large university such as Columbia could be sketched in a few strokes. Though the university already comprised a dozen schools, and its student body and faculty matched in size their largest counterparts, its administration presented a spectacle of endearing simplicity. The president, the secretary, a few deans (fewer than there were schools and largely unassisted by subdeans), together with half a dozen understaffed clerical and business offices, kept the show going. The innocence of those days appears from the fact that sixty-seven persons reported to the president—whenever they felt they wanted to. Under a set of statutes quite properly general, each unit or department (there were twenty-eight departments of arts and science) worked by precedent. Lacking any common procedures in written form or any table of organization at any level, a wide diversity reigned, which furnished lunch-table conversation of endless interest. Each group knew it was impossible to carry on teaching and scholarship in any other way than its own, and marveled at the other groups' ability to do the impossible.

Each department was led by a senior member designated "executive officer," lest the title of chairman suggest rules of order. With or without his colleagues' advice he did his best for his little republic under the unpredictable but rare and usually benevolent directions of the president. Privileges or their absence rested upon some bargain made or not made in the dim past. Such discrepancies were accounted for by the different needs of different subject-matters—vastly different, for example, like French and Italian, or like Physics and Chemistry—differences deemed sufficient to explain why, in one or the other department, leaves granted were more frequent or telephones more numerous.

About this same time (the mid-forties), the budget of the university consisted almost entirely of academic salaries, books and supplies, and maintenance costs. The president was supposedly in charge of its preparation, but by statute and in practice he was head of the educational sector only; the treasurer had parallel powers and direct access to the trustees. But conflicts did not arise—or they were kept down. At any rate, it was believed that all the financial affairs of the university were settled at the president's Saturday lunch with the treasurer. Unfortunately, toward the end of that era, despite good intentions on both sides, it often happened that the budget for business affairs was passed before the educational estimates were in hand. The outcome was that education had to make do with what was left, having had no chance to question or review the business side's claims upon the available resources.

These conditions appear in retrospect more alarming than they were, and this is one measure of the distance we have traveled in less than twenty years. Today no university could last a week under such a regime. And the reason why the old order spelled tolerable diversity rather than mad anarchy is that the demands upon the institution were fewer and gentler. There was more time; the interests of the individual as well as of the corporation were less momentous; errors and omissions were more easily repaired; the regularity that was absent from the organization was present in the mores, in the outlook of its members, and in their private circumstances. In short, Columbia University, despite its relative massiveness and reputed riches, was still an enterprise capable of being grasped and run by one man.* The president could deal offhand with seventy or seven hundred people and take care of their infrequent wants, easily knowing what had gone before and

* The changed meaning of "large scale" can be gauged by recalling how John Jay Chapman interpreted the advent of President Eliot at Harvard a hundred years ago: "The circumstances required the construction of a one-man machine. . . . This is the only way in which executive business on a large scale can be done quickly. . . . On the other hand, . . . a true University always rests upon the wills of many divergent-minded old gentlemen, who refuse to be disturbed, but who growl in their kennels."—J. J. Chapman, *Selected Writings,* ed. J. Barzun, New York, 1957, 213.

what he was doing now, to use or not as a precedent the next time.*

Today, the word "multiversity" has gained currency as a description of the changed reality, and it strongly hints that no group of men can do all that is attempted at our universities and still maintain the cohesion that makes an institution.

That point is still to be proved. Meanwhile the situation is rich in paradoxes. The American university has upheaved itself to "catch up" and "modernize," words that mean: has ceased to be a sheltered spot for study only; has come into the market place and answered the cries for help uttered by government, industry, and the general public; has busily pursued the enthusiasms of our utopian leaders of thought, both private patrons and big foundations; has served the country by carrying on research for national goals; has, finally, recognized social needs by undertaking to teach the quite young, the middle-aged, the disabled, the deprived, the misdirected, and the maladjusted.

In this great effort it has been encouraged with money and fair words. But despite this eagerness to help and this quick adaptation to new duties, the university is now receiving the harshest criticisms it has ever had to endure. Never so trusted, never so challenged. Government (both the legislative and the executive branch) is suspicious of its management of research. Foundations accuse it of conservatism and inability to change. Students who attend it regard it as another establishment to be brought down by violence and revolutionized. Benefactors and paying customers shake their heads over rising costs and low productivity. And inside the house the scholars, who repeat that *they* are the university, complain of the work and the pay like wage earners, while declaring that their allegiance is not to the particular place but to their subject of specialization, their "discipline."

It may be that these diverse remonstrances are the sign of a deep attachment, that the critics are only dissembling their love,

* Until the fifties the presidential files for any one year fitted readily into three drawers. By 1956–57, one year filled up fifteen drawers, and the volume has kept multiplying annually ever since.

which will work its legendary miracle if only we give it time. But whatever the future may hold, it is clear that both the anxious state of the American university and its altered life call for immediate attention. The dangers are clear and present—bankruptcy, paralysis, futility.

The causes of disaster have developed with a fatal logic since the Second World War. The new university emerged then as the by-product of its own war effort. It was the Manhattan Project, the V-12 Program, the GI Bill of Rights, following close upon the participation of the academic community in the New Deal, that catapulted the university into its present headlong rush. To that momentum was added, after the war, the impetus of a world power that must continue to mobilize academic men for global advice and activity.

The war, then, is the event that divides past from present in what concerns us here. It was at that time, in 1945, that I published under the title *Teacher in America* an account of university working as it was then. The book was based on a tour of inquiry that I had been asked to make for the guidance of Columbia College in restoring the civilian curriculum. The university was still a traditional institution, the handiwork of a brilliant empire builder in the classical manner, Nicholas Murray Butler. Still in the saddle, "Nicholas Miraculous" had dominated the scene since 1902, having directed all things himself like a virtuoso conductor, without crisis or rebellions.* But by the close of his reign the dislocation caused by war and the drift due to the slackening of his direct control created a need for new plans and a new mode of administration. If the university was to maintain its rank it must be reorganized.

What is to be discussed later makes it relevant here to say a

* So regular had the lack of system become at the end of Butler's time that he could rely on his docile deans and coast as it were by gravity. The departments were similarly inclined. Even when he appointed a full professor without consulting anyone, the growling in the kennels was localized and brief. Today such an act would blow a president sky-high and furnish the papers with congenial matter for weeks.

word about the reasons that moved a thereupto blameless member of the institution such as myself to give up for a time his chosen work and submit to a sentence of hard labor—the long hours and grueling conditions of the executive life, coupled as it is with the overt pity and envious disdain of one's colleagues. The decisive reasons in my case were my long attachment to the university—thirty-two years as student and teacher—and the knowledge that its indispensable modernizing was to be carried out under the direction of a new president, who from the beginning conceived his task in the terms just stated, and who chose his associates because they shared his sense of urgency and his view of what needed to be done. Thoroughgoing reorganization should indeed have begun on Dr. Butler's retirement, but it was not until 1953, after two interim presidencies, that the election of Grayson Kirk as fourteenth president since 1754 and of Dr. John Allen Krout as vice-president gave hope of change.

Even then, another year had to elapse, during which all available energies were bent upon the Bicentennial Celebration of 1954–55. Systematic work was thus postponed until the autumn of the latter year, which was when I joined the administration as dean of the graduate faculties. About the same time, the president appointed a faculty committee to examine the state of the university and recommend changes. The report, published after wide discussion in 1957, and known as the Macmahon Report, provided a chart of the changes deemed desirable in the work of instruction and research. One of the recommendations was the creation of the post of Dean of Faculties, to which I was named in 1958 with the added title of Provost—a term whose meaning will appear in the sequel.

The Dean of Faculties was to provide a unifying force in the work of instruction and research, such as is commonly expected elsewhere from the Academic Vice-President; but it was clear from the outset that few if any of the goals defined by the faculty committee could be reached without recasting or strengthening every administrative agency, codifying procedures, and devising many new ones. This reshaping of the structure while carrying on the daily operations was necessarily a cooperative effort, in which not merely the president and his immediate aides, but the deans of the sixteen schools, the directors of all the institutes and centers, and the chairmen of the forty departments must take part, often changing their long-rooted practices and helping their subordinates to follow suit.

All changes, moreover, must commend themselves to those directly affected, the faculty and students, which meant consultation and discussion—yet not without the tactful imposition of limits if the new machinery was to be in motion before the end of the century. The shift must somehow be made from one-man fitful authority to delegation-with-consensus. Freedom must be salvaged out of the previous lack of system without replacing the anarchy of laisser-faire by that of bad bureaucracy.

Add to this overhaul the need to find and train a much enlarged corps of second-line administrators and to develop ways of adapting all new methods to continually changing requirements—whether imposed by Washington or by the march of mind—and it will not seem that the time taken for bringing order to one large university was excessive; rather, it was surprisingly brief. When I resigned my administrative duties in the spring of 1967, twelve years had gone into filling the outline of the new American university. Not every comparable institution had suffered the long interregnum that put Columbia administratively at a disadvantage in the early fifties, but what had to be done there amounts to a comprehensive agenda of what has had to be done elsewhere or is being done wherever expansion and modernization are in progress. The summary of this effort as I saw it should furnish at once a sketch of the recent upheaval in our American system and a bird's-eye view of the aims, organization, and turmoil that characterize our leading universities today.

1 The New University

> The University is a Paradise, Rivers of Knowledge are there, Arts and Sciences flow from thence . . . ; bottomless depths of unsearchable Counsels there.
>
> —JOHN DONNE

> Ivry great invintion, fr'm th' typewriter to th' V-shaped wedge, can be thraced to this prodigal instichoochion.
>
> —MR. DOOLEY

THE ACADEMIC OMNIBUS

The American university of today is best understood as a *residual* institution. What I mean by residual in this context can be gathered from what I have already said: the university is the last outpost of help, like the government of a welfare state. Whatever the individual and the society cannot do for themselves is entrusted to the likeliest existing agency. Faith in education and faith in the integrity and good will of those called educators have accordingly wished upon the mid-century university a variety of tasks formerly done by others or not done at all. Just as the lower schools must organize transportation, free lunches, dental care, and "driver education," so the university now undertakes to give its students, faculties, and neighbors not solely education but the makings of a full life, from sociability to business advice and from psychiatric care to the artistic experience. Again, every new skill or item of knowledge developed within the academy creates a new claim by the community. Knowledge is power and its possessor owes the public a prompt application, or at least diffusion through the training of others. It thus comes about that the School of Social Work aids the poor, the School of Architecture redesigns the slum, the School of Business advises the small tradesman, the School of Dentistry runs a free clinic, the School of Law gives legal aid, and the undergraduate college supplies volunteers to hospitals, recreation centers, and remedial schools.

While accepting these and a hundred other tasks, the university has lost its quasi monopoly of instruction and research. The latter is now shared with independent institutes and big corporations; the former is shared with ordinary business firms, the army, and the communications media.* There has occurred, in short, a regrouping of the forces once known and kept apart as educational, medical, charitable, artistic, and the rest. Yet the main tendency, when a gap appears in what someone conceives as the beneficial order of things, is to think: we will get the school to do it; we will find the money and urge the university to take it on. As I suggested not long ago to a "seminar" of 1,600 school heads, gathered by Robert Hutchins at Los Angeles: "the nearest equivalent to what the university is becoming is the medieval guild, which undertook to do everything for the town."[1]† The motive of the university is not overweening self-confidence. It is that Alma Mater, like many women, can resist her own feelings better than she can resist the feelings she inspires in others. And the motive of the community in making its requests, I concluded, is "not so much an expression of natural greed as a pathetic desire for light and love. The only thing that the guild used to provide and we do not is Masses for the dead, and if we do not it is because we are not asked."

* In some cities there are now more classrooms on business and industrial premises than in school buildings, and the subjects taught outside the school range from the rudiments of literacy to applied physics.

† Superior numbers refer to Notes, page 303.

EXPANSION AND EXPENSES

One measure of the change brought about by the addition of good works to old-time teaching is the skyrocketing of budgets. In 1953 the annual budget of Columbia University was twenty million dollars; in 1966 it was a hundred and twenty. Inflation accounts for about a sixth of that increase. The rest is explained by the addition and growth of activities—centers, programs, institutes, research projects, exchange agreements, partnerships and affiliations for scientific and social purposes, with all the attendant services and benefits that the modern corporation is expected to provide, *plus* the cost of space and maintenance for the expanded staff. Though still insufficiently large, that regiment of clerks and junior administrators is needed not merely to serve the needs of the proliferating cells but to keep some sort of organic order among them.

Nor is this all. University expansion was at first haphazard and casually treated. But by the end of the first decade after the war it became apparent that the rate of replacement of faculty members on tenure was about 2 to 1, even though the student body remained constant; that is, for every senior scholar who retired or resigned, the regular departments of instruction found themselves requiring two new men of high repute and costly qualifications. These requests cited the rapid splitting up of subject matters into new specialties, but they also spoke of the relief forces needed for men who had taken on as extras the collateral programs, centers, and projects. From that time dates the populousness of the modern university.*

No adequate idea of the incessantly buzzing and booming academic grove, the harsh orchestration resulting from the dis-

* This type of expansion has also occurred abroad. The English are particularly sparing of personnel, but at Cambridge, for example, university officers increased by 48 percent between 1945 and 1958. (See Jasper Rose and John Ziman, *Camford Observed,* London, 1964, 255.)

parate purposes carried on there, can be derived from generalities, however familiar from reports and speeches. Nothing short of enumeration will suggest the size of the structure or the complexity of the effort. And even then, the very act of setting items down on paper introduces an order which falsifies the inevitable confusion.* It is inevitable not for lack of a proper scheme for dealing with the results of deliberate policy; it is inevitable from the simple fact of *number.*† Give five thousand talented people diversified responsibilities under a minimum of hierarchy, yet with intersecting orbits, and their duties and their talents alike will produce daily innovation and impatience, rash promises and unruly acts, resistance to system and forgetfulness of forms.

But what do these people actually do to require the vast expenditure and bring about the permanent confusion? One could truthfully answer that they do what they have always done: teachers teach and do research, and the rest supply various supporting services. It is the changed assumptions behind these activities and the enlarged constituency recognized by the university that generate the new atmosphere. Let us start with the old purpose of teaching. The new assumption behind it is that higher education shall be open to all.‡ Neglecting substance for a moment, let us look at the side effects. The first is a great increase in the number

* See Appendix B: "The Parts of a University."

† A typical distribution runs as follows: professors—1,550; other officers of instruction—1,900; research staff—750; officers of administration—780: total—4,980. This count does not include the floating population of postdoctoral fellows (about whom see below), which runs into the hundreds; nor does it include the students, whose leaders, as everybody knows, contribute their mite to the carnival.

‡ It is not the urge to go to college that is new—or the parents' circumstances: in 1787 General Artemas Ward was confiding: "Dana can't make himself Easy without he goes to Harvard College. . . . If I could obtain my honest dues from the Public . . . I should be able to pay every debt, Educate my son, and have something hansome left. If the President can't consent to let him be absent from College a considerable part of his time the first two years, that he may save something and also Earn something by keeping a School, I see no way that I shall be able to carry him through College. . . . I wish to know who is to be his chamber Mate."—Autograph in *The Month at Goodspeed's* (Boston), vol. 36, no. 8, May 1965, 268–269.

of applications for admission. Judgments of merit become harder to make, tests and application forms grow more complex. The staffs of admissions offices increase, to absorb the paper work and also to travel across the country in search of those students best suited to the particular program, graduate or undergraduate. Meanwhile a faculty committee sits on borderline cases among applicants.

With admissions goes the distribution of financial aid, since many students lack means. Undergraduates submit answers to an exhaustive questionnaire, filled out by the parents and uniform for the majority of liberal arts colleges. The detailed replies furnish an exact view of each individual's need, so that evenhanded justice may be done. These blanks have to be read and judged. For graduates, the members of each department or school take turns examining hundreds of dossiers containing the applicant's record, faculty recommendations, and a sample of written work.* Each year the number of applications mounts and the deadline date advances to permit the sorting to be done in time.

Now follow the admitted students. Most of them are housed and fed on campus. The dormitories are anything but luxurious, yet the rooms must have telephones, the lounges television, and the corridors food-vending machines. On each floor there must be a counselor. The dean's office staff includes not only a dean of students and a proctor, but a group of six or eight psychologists, in addition to the psychiatrists and doctors at the medical office and infirmary. The psychologists take care of the first signs of emotional trouble, and their services are oversubscribed. From the faculty, younger men are chosen as academic advisers, and they too put in long days helping students to fashion the education they want or ought to have. The work of the premedical adviser, given the competition for medical school admissions, is arduous and occupies a small staff.

* These same men also serve on awarding committees for the Fulbright Commission, for many private foundations, and for the federal and state agencies that subsidize research projects. All this useful work is part of the new mobility and strain of academic life.

THE BYGONE SIMPLICITY

Another branch of the dean's office runs a program of extra-curricular activities, which comprise a daily newspaper and an FM radio station, both supported by the university. More important lately have been the students' civic enterprises already mentioned —volunteer work in city slums, schools, and welfare agencies. These opportunities naturally do not arrange themselves, which means another office and much scheduling and going about. In the summer, the same students may go to Washington to serve as interns to congressmen—this too is organized—or they may set up and administer a program for teaching pupils from local high schools, either able ones or near-dropouts, all of which requires typists, telephones, letterheads; housing and catering, and dealing with government—hence an able director with an assistant, since nowadays little can be done without conferring face to face and some responsible person must be in the office when the head is away.

Financial aid to students generally covers but a part of their expense. Those without other resources must take part-time work, which implies a student employment office. The Federal Work-Study program contributes generously to student aid, but the statistics and procedures alone call for a group of six intelligent clerks under a chief schooled in government regulations. Now most of the jobs thus subsidized afford service of one sort or another to the university, and it follows that the professors, librarians, or administrators who employ the students become involved in the paper work. Still other students earn their keep in one of the Student Agencies that provide the campus laundry service, newspapers and magazines, babysitters and bartenders, charter flights, and other miscellaneous goods and services. Like the sizable business that it is (grossing $1.5 million a year), it needs university supervision. The business vice-president and two or three faculty members sit on a board of directors, keep minutes, hire bookkeepers, and argue with Civil Aeronautics about flight regulations.

These details do not exhaust the reality; to some they may appear a trivial clutter. But though only the beginning of the story, they show how far campus life has moved from the ancient seclusion, self-help, modest expectations, and informal—indeed nonchalant—arrangements. Any Columbia faculty member who happens to be also a graduate of thirty years ago went through an admissions office manned (if that word will cover the facts) by two men and a girl. They handled *all* admissions, which now occupy upwards of forty people. The senior of the two men was a professor of logic who gave only part of his time to interviewing. There was little paper lying around to be read. Similarly, the assumptions about who went to college and how the ill-to-do were to get there bore no resemblance to our regimented ways. The Employment Office also consisted of two and a half persons, instead of the present eighteen, and it did not hold meetings and sponsor lectures to help "career planning."

Fifty years ago, George Edward Woodberry, a pioneer of the Great Books movement, recalled his difficult start in life, and he tells us how a student made his way: "I was a 'new boy,' coming a month later than the others—poor and shy; I remember I slept out in the hall in the top story of 'Abbott' the first nights, till two kind-hearted boys took me in with them (three in a bed) till a place could be found for me."[2] This was at Phillips Exeter Academy, not college, but the attitude and magnanimous lack of method held throughout the system.* "Democratic education" meant a reasonable chance, not an organized routine. The young, unknown Woodberry was helped by Charles Eliot Norton and James Russell Lowell because pluck and talent stood out and one man spoke to another. The helping hand was individual. A year before he finished college, Woodberry was borrowing money on his earnings as tutor in order to help a junior boy.

* Comparable conditions are recorded in *The Diary of a Student at Delaware College (1853–1854)*, ed. W. D. Lewis, Baltimore, 1951.

Moreover, except in academic work, what we should call standards were unknown, not even suspected—witness the admission one month late and the sleeping assignment to a hallway. This was the time, just a century ago, when the students at Harvard (among them William James) would resort to a row of partly screened privies behind the president's house, because the dormitories lacked all plumbing. The president had to protect his peace and quiet in person by scolding the boys when they became too noisy.[3]

CONTINUOUS SIDE EFFECTS

Nowadays it is the boys who scold the president, and we shall see that one of their motives is anger at the spread of system as such. Students resent the interlocking of the Registrar's Office with the Selective Service Administration, the certification of their good standing, and the reporting of their course grades in complicated computer form. If they knew that inquiry agents from various branches of the government are virtual fixtures in that same office, studying dossiers, they would be angrier still. The intent to serve the student and the strict control over what is available for inspection by these agents do not alter the feeling of system closing in.

Again, as everybody knows, well-intentioned arrangements by the university for recruiting, whether by the armed forces or by certain unpopular corporations, provoke riots and strikes and petitions. The point here is not the merit of the protests but the ever-present sense on the campus of *arrangements* made or to be made, the oppression of the computered life, felt as inevitable, yet far from smooth in practice as it is in theory. As I suggested at the outset, it is the new assumptions and multiplied relationships of the university that have destroyed the old calm. Teaching students always meant admitting them, aiding the poor, keeping grades, encouraging extracurricular doings, and helping toward employment. *Perfecting* these operations, *improving* the democratic opportunity for education, is what has made them exorbitant in price and claustrophobic in effect.

Passing from paraphernalia to substance we observe a parallel result. In the first place, the subject matter of instruction has split and split again into lesser but larger specialties. What one man would have taught in 1880 required three in 1920 and from ten to thirty in 1960.* The famous H. A. Giles (1845–1935), for example, was in himself a whole department of Chinese Studies. Today, it is not unusual for a scholar to specialize in the first half of a given century of European or American or Eastern history (or language and literature) and to select from that half century only one aspect of the field. If, as is likely, such a man dictates his terms, he can enclose himself in his principality, teach no undergraduates, serve only as specialist: "Better fifty years of Europe than a cycle of Cathay." The assumption here is that the university, as the producer of knowledge, must be composed exclusively of productive scholars, which means specialists who specialize.

Granting the assumption, what are the practical consequences? A department feels an obligation to cover the entire field as before; hence it must hire more persons, each doing less. Not all can be on tenure, so visiting professors become a regular element in the staff. Failing visitors, adjuncts can be borrowed for one course from a neighboring institution, at least for a year or two. Keeping the department up to full strength is therefore a never-ending task. Add the need to replace those who resign or retire, who die or who go on leave, and the *business* of a department, as distinguished from its profession, becomes as anguishing as playing the stock market. The business is at the same time much more expensive than before, owing to the necessary trips, calls, letters, and meetings. For "the department" is no longer the chairman alone but a democratic machine embracing a search committee for beating the bushes and an executive committee for ratifying their choices.

* The earliest professors in American universities combined in their titles four or five related subjects; they were said by a later wit to hold not chairs but settees.

The repercussions are not over when the staff for any one year is assembled. New members have to be taken in, made to feel at home, for this is no longer a natural process. They receive informative leaflets, departmental rules, a faculty handbook about their rights and privileges. They must get on lists, file tax blanks with the controller, be visaed and vetted and insured, medically and otherwise, and become members of the faculty club: two sponsors—a mere formality—but that is where the time goes.

In most large universities, where space is cramped, an apartment or a house must be found for the incumbent by the university.* Office staffs exist to do nothing else, usually with little thanks from the beneficiaries. Of course, if the new recruit wants to buy a house in the suburbs, he applies to the treasurer, through the business vice-president, for a mortgage loan. Before this he has, through the dean, recovered his moving expenses. Scholarship aid for his children (or tuition aid if they are of college age) is obtained through the secretary's office, like tuition exemption for the wife if she wants to take courses for edification or a degree. In short, the full life is in full swing as in other parts of the welfare society.

Back in the school or department, the obvious consequence of the enlarged, more specialized teaching body is a proliferation of courses. How this is compatible with the "flight from teaching" is one of those mysteries impenetrable to the layman and reserved for university theologians, but we shall understand it shortly. These many courses, persons, leaves, and returns cause an unprecedented amount of work—and confusion too—for the registrar, the editor of the catalogues, and the student advisers. For final decisions by leave-takers and visitors are often made late or are incompletely signified, so that both printed page and word-of-mouth are contrary to fact. What *is* fact is that the visiting

* It is an illusion to think that the housing problem exists only for members of city universities. The great midwestern institutions, once lost in the prairie, are now hemmed in as well, and it is a rare faculty member who enjoys the old comfort of living on campus or walking to his work.

luminary whose courses are not "in the book" need expect no students, and the regular man who has left without putting it "in the book" is cursed by those who counted on joining his course.

THE SHINIER SIDE OF THE COIN: RESEARCH

At last, the professors reporting "present" join the melee. Yet, however mindful of their students and of the university, they try to keep a little time open for "their own work." That work is in fact a part of their obligation mentioned in the statutes, though it is difficult to measure and not enforceable. Neither, for that matter, is any specified kind or amount of teaching for an officer with tenure. The modern assumption is that a professorship confers the right of self-direction in teaching as in research, and one hears that right frequently cited as the essence of academic freedom. Somehow, the scholar adapts himself to the demands of lecturing, examining, keeping office hours, serving on committees, reading dissertations and fellowship applications, writing letters of recommendation, and identifying at sight a few useful members of central administration. For the rest, he toils in the library or laboratory under the mantle of his discipline, meaning not the medieval hair-shirt but the silk-lined cloak of professionalism.

In that guise he and his peers constitute the chief asset and heaviest burden of the new university, the prevailing belief being that research is the great justification of the whole enterprise. The analogies at work here are with science and industry. Only research makes science progress; only research and development keep the nation (economy, industry, culture, consumer market) thriving. *New* is the keynote. New products, ideas, ways of doing the same thing, on the chance that they will be better, *newer*.

This is not to say that the universities do not harbor a great many scholars bred in an earlier tradition or inclined to it by temperament—men who study because they love knowledge, who are moved by curiosity and can rest in contemplation. But they are not the active principle in the university of these days, even though they are highly respected and in no way made to feel superfluous. On the contrary, they are a necessary luxury; their ungrudged eminence is the homage that the jet-propelled university pays to the ivory tower, not without some qualms about the better place to be in.

Meanwhile the born activists organize their research. They mobilize equipment and call for more. They summon the library to augment its holding in the field—periodicals in science, books and documents in other subject matters. They respond to Washington requests for the submission of projects—"pure" research, mostly, whose subsidy will help support young graduate students as assistants and will pay for more equipment and more publications. A project director may have one large undertaking or a cluster of projects. Besides the expensive computer installations, space and other facilities have to keep up with this expansion, which the university administration hardly dares to regulate, lacking the competence to judge its worth, and in any case not wishing to lose the good will of an important professor smiled on by Washington science and capable of *Nobel-caliber work.*

Teaching and project-directing do not preclude the acceptance of work as a consultant—to a public body, a private firm, or a foreign government. The researcher is the sole judge of how much he can do.* He often—and justly—argues that consultancies bring him in contact with the latest thought and practice in his field, with the "real world" which the new university acknowledges as kin. But the more activities the scholar takes on, inside or outside, the more difficult he makes life for himself and his colleagues. The trouble is of course legitimate, but when one wants to know why it is that the "simplest things are so hard to get done," the answer is:

* The one-day-a-week maximum mentioned in faculty handbooks is but a mere suggestion, which does not fit the life of a researcher in science.

the extreme mobility of persons on whom one has to depend,* and the doubtful assumption that by hiring more helpers one can multiply one's effective attention indefinitely.

The scholar, almost in proportion to his capacity for juggling claims, soon realizes that he must exert himself harder and harder to maintain the same output. Such is the natural result of modern communications: as consultant to one firm, he attracts the notice of three others, which write him alluring offers. In Washington, his success with one project leads to his becoming a referee on others; within the profession, his discoveries suggest that a group of fellow workers should start a new journal. He must be the editor and see whether it cannot be housed at his university. Meanwhile, right there, at home and unknown to him, notable men in different disciplines have come to the conclusion that the world requires the immediate study of a neglected subject—say, the Social Impact of Science. Nothing less than a new institute will accomplish this, for the work is *interdisciplinary*. Our man is approached, he is interested, he has connections. Before he knows it, he is writing prospectuses, haggling with the university Office of Projects and Grants about proposed budgets, sitting through meetings where the word "angle" in the first draft is thoughtfully changed to "approach" and back again; and not long after he is seen loitering along the corridors of the Ford Foundation.

A few years of this scholarly life drive the teacher-director to certain unshakable convictions: he must go on leave—needs a change of scene. His teaching load is excessive—a large lecture course and five doctoral candidates.† If he cannot get really comfortable working conditions when he returns from his leave, he

* For example, a student needing a signature to authorize some educational purpose may have to come and come again to get it from his sponsor, who is on his travels. The latter is not "neglecting his students"; the travel is not frivolous; but the effort and the irritation of the student, and perhaps also the guilt feelings of the absent one, contribute to the general malaise.

† This number presupposes candidates in a laboratory science. In the social sciences and the humanities an instructor may sponsor an indefinite number. Most men take care of six to a dozen students at various stages of their dissertation.

will entertain one of the many offers that come to him from elsewhere, yes, even if he has to go to a state university not hitherto on the academic map. He will take with him a few younger men, build up the department, and the place *will* be on the map.

Part of this program is the expression of fatigue, but news of it causes instant concern at several universities, beginning with the one that understandingly grants him special leave. For if he does not return to it, replacements will be sought here or there, unsettling as many departments in a "domino effect."

The perennial question of "load" is everywhere revived by his discontent, which can be directly traced to the pull of outside forces. Can salary increases, further fringe benefits, more research help, clerical help, machine help, divine help take care of the obvious necessities of the case, multiplied on all the campuses by fifty, a hundred, or more similar cases? For it is not that the university begrudges its able men good working conditions, but that there are tremendous obstacles in the way: lack of money, lack of space, danger to morale (if among equals some take less of the teaching burden), danger to educational administration (if the teaching is spread among so many that mustering it each term is like rallying the Continental Army at Valley Forge).

By such questions and reflections one comes to understand the gravity of the strain caused by conflicting claims at the point where the world and the university join and divide.

THUNDER ON THE LEFT

So far the trips away from home have been to the regions of government and industry and the agencies of intellectual and scientific culture. There is another and broader country, which starts with the immediate neighborhood and extends over the whole world. The assumptions that take the university to those parts are the ones stated in general form in the Introduction and again, more suggestively, in the mottoes at the head of this chapter. The community, it was said, wants light and love. Eager to provide both, the university has built a new apparatus of agencies and habits to this end.

The traditional form of the desire to serve the community is "extension work," first organized by the English universities in the middle of the last century. Such course offerings have long since coalesced into regular schools, which provide evening instruction to those who are employed during the day and who want to obtain professional training or a liberal degree.

With the advent of different groups desiring undergraduate work on other terms than the usual four-year college affords, the evening schools at universities have set up various special programs—for somewhat older students who missed the chance at seventeen or took it and failed; for married women whose children, grown up, no longer need maternal care; for businessmen or professionals who have chosen the wrong career and want to pursue another—the ad writer who hopes to become a doctor; the fireman who wants to teach; the soldier who needs a bachelor's degree to enter law school; finally, the remedial programs for many kinds of persons handicapped by environment or mischance. In addition, such schools periodically organize conferences, long or short, to which the public is invited for such enlightenment as may be had on current topics or perennial perplexities, like career planning.*

A university with strong professional schools will similarly conduct short courses for working members of the profession who want to learn in brief compass the latest findings in their subjects. These range from business to engineering and library science to periodontics. Such courses may be offered several times during the year and may occupy on each occasion the full time of chosen faculty members. A further innovation, due to the initiative of Professor Frank Tannenbaum of Columbia, is the so-called University Seminars, which bring together for biweekly meetings scholars from various departments of the university and men from business and the professions. The seminar has a continuing

* These categories describe in fact the current offerings of the Columbia University School of General Studies.

topic—The Problem of Peace, The Economics of Distribution, or Population and Social Change; The City, Language and Communications, or The Culture of the Renaissance—which is illuminated by papers and discussion. All members are on an equal footing, qualified by their knowledge. There are no grades and no degrees—and no students, except in the honorific sense.

All these extension programs are inspired by the ideal of public service and have a strong hold on the imagination of their organizers. Whether the public at large views them with the same fervor is another question. Students who benefit often express satisfaction and gratitude, but the common assumption is not that the university is going out of its way to help: rather it has a duty to serve the needs of the world as they arise, and should respond more freely still, to any and every demand.

So long as the cost and effort of running special programs do not lead to any internal struggle over shrinking university resources, the outgoing effort of the institution is taken by university people as normal and they will favor each new program as it comes—e.g., helping to educate nurses to fill the shortage. But when space and talent are overtaxed, and when, moreover, community opinion tends to be arrogantly critical and hostile toward the university, the most benevolent grow discouraged and begin to wonder whether it is right to work so hard for a return in brickbats.

Their spirits might recover if they understood why the new university, never before so hospitable, should be regarded by many with hatred and contempt, like a bad stepmother. The case for these feelings will be made when I discuss the enemies of the university. Here the friction matters for what it tells us about the needs of the university. With some of these every newspaper reader is familiar: universities since 1945 have had to expand physically, and the need to occupy neighboring land and buildings has not yet ceased. Expansion brings the institution in conflict with the immediate neighbors, with city hall, whose plans may differ, and with the local politicians, who see in the opposing claims a good issue to whip up into a heroic defense of the people against powerful vested interests. And no doubt some honestly believe that leaving several hundred citizens undisturbed should prevail over the needs of even a national university.

It is also argued that university expansion means removing valuable property from the tax rolls, and therefore impoverishing communities already hard pressed. But critics forget that all such expansion goes with increased employment and trade. Supposing Columbia University forced out of New York by sheer constriction, the loss of its payroll would be greater by far than that of the Brooklyn Navy Yard. The choice between the interests of town and gown is difficult in any case, as it has always been, and the universities are aware of the hardships they cause—more aware perhaps than state or federal roadbuilders when they dispossess and devastate. But sympathy does not help. If the university is in a big city—Chicago or New York or New Haven—it is likely that the area surrounding the institution is deteriorating and in self-protection the university must take measures that look like waging war on the inhabitants: bringing in the police against crime and vice, hiring special patrols, and buying real estate as fast as funds and the market permit.

To mitigate the resulting hardships the institution will doubtless set up a community office where the displaced tenants, who receive a relocation payment to begin with, will also get help in finding a new dwelling. That office often grows into a kind of settlement house, giving out advice and comfort in legal, marital, parental, and other difficulties. The university quickly finds itself in the unaccustomed business of running a welfare agency.

The logical next step is to furnish these remedial services on a larger scale and systematically. If the university knows so much (the argument runs), why does it not help government in curing the urban blight? Why does it not study the minority problem, take the lead in fashioning a decent society? Many of the leading universities, public and private, have since 1950 established centers, seminars, and programs looking to the many aspects of this national problem.* Until the Ford Foundation decided to spur these efforts by widespread grants, the programs were limited by the particular talents and resources of the several schools. Now these universities are expected to devote themselves to urban and minority betterment as a permanent and comprehensive goal.

The task falls into three parts: conducting research, training professional workers, and running so-called action programs—direct help on the spot. The first is of course well within the university tradition, though original thinkers on this vast predicament are scarce. Training courses might be supposed to follow easily upon research, but turning theory into an applied art is always more difficult than appears at first. Finally, university supervision of centers of action means finding a new group of persons whose abilities will, by definition, be other than academic and thus cause the university to bid for them against governmental and private welfare agencies. Once found, they will present difficulties of assimilation into the system—schedules, titles, salaries, leaves, and the like—which is already strained by disparities and eroded by exceptions. Even the university-wide organization of such a three-part program creates tangles of jurisdiction and coordination that tend to loosen useful ties. But necessity knows no law, and if society summons its *residual* institution to perform, it must turn to and do the best it can.

OUTPOSTS AND EXCHANGES

Not less frequent or more muted cries for help come to the American university from all corners of the globe. Some of these requests are the natural outcome of published research: an expert is sought out by a foreign government or bank or institution of learning. Other calls are routed through the State Department and

* These postwar innovations differed in aim and scope from the earlier instructional work in urban planning, usually associated with the school of architecture.

become quasi official, almost command performances—to serve as science attaché at an American embassy or delegate to an international congress. And then there are the exchanges. Exchanges toss back and forth between universities: scholars, students, books, microfilms, works of art, labor leaders, entrepreneurs, and government officials. Senator Fulbright's invention made usual what before had been exceptional—the Theodore Roosevelt professorship at the University of Berlin before 1917 or the Harmsworth chair in American history at Oxford. Now Fulbright instructors and students are as common as daisies. University arrangements for these temporary absences are taken in stride, though they signify another alteration in the character of the university.*

More complicated by far are the exchanges sought by a single institution and meant to continue indefinitely. A university in Hungary or Japan, Africa or the Argentine, feels the need to expand its horizons by the regular addition of an American scholar or scientist. The obvious device is the offer of an exchange, which may involve students and scholarly materials as well. The plan is more easily conceived than executed. Most often the calendars do not jibe. In this country young scholars do not want to prejudice their advancement by leaving their home institutions. Older scholars are tied down by earlier commitments, and moreover do not like to uproot themselves for just one year. And longer absences are usually not allowed by the university, except for urgent national service.

The decisive obstacle is the disparity of currencies: the cost of living here, the salaries abroad, do not permit anything like an even exchange.† The American side must provide a heavy subsidy, for travel and livelihood to its own man as well as for administer-

* Persons who deplore the brain drain from Europe might put in the balance the annual outpouring of talent from these Western shores, most of it for a fixed term, to be sure, but aggregating many lifetimes when totaled up. If it were computed from 1945, the start of the new era, it would be interesting to see who was now the debtor in the balance of trade.

† So far all efforts to use the $4 billion of American "counterpart funds" for such purposes have run into great technical difficulties.

ing the scheme, which is much more complex at this end. Invariably, when such an exchange has been discussed at length with the proposers and potential participants, the upshot is an application to a foundation. It sometimes succeeds, but the guarantee has a five-year limit, and the cycle of desire and frustration begins anew. Occasionally an industry will foot the bill, for solid practical reasons —as in the subsidy of a geologist to work at a foreign university sitting upon an oil field. Again, the federal government has money for lectureships in business, economics, and health sciences in South America and other parts. But exchanges (as against single visits) in the humanities and social sciences depend either on fugitive gifts or on extreme sacrifices.

Easier to support are the programs that American universities, north, east, south, and west, have opened in foreign countries. They serve as centers of instruction and residence for undergraduates who wish to take a term or a year abroad, for graduates who elect a summer session in the foreign country, and for natives attracted by lectures and seminars on American literature or history. In short, these are links between cultures, serving chiefly the home school in its teaching of foreign languages and civilizations, but also affording (as does Reid Hall for Columbia University in Paris) communication with the heads of foreign university systems, who are these days much interested in American mass education.

The maintenance of centers abroad for special research is more costly, because they are not endowed and the student fees cover much less than half the outlay. Staffing is an endless trial of strength and luck, for the reasons given in connection with exchange programs. On this account there exist cooperative arrangements—for example, in Taiwan—which divide the burden among five or six universities and multiply the clientele. Similar combines support the outposts scattered over the world, the Etruscan digs and desert camps, the observatories, deep-sea installations, institutes for tropical medicine, and the like. No one can accuse the modern American university of being provincial or isolationist.

OPPORTUNITIES VERSUS MEANS

The readiness of the new university to meet claims and seize opportunities is sufficiently apparent from even so sketchy a survey as the present one. The only question is whether there are rational limits to the readiness. Not a day passes in any university without a fresh suggestion being made, by a faculty member or by an eager stranger, for adding another outrigger, sideshow, or three-day rodeo. To refer to proposals in this way is not to disparage them, but simply to suggest the relation they necessarily bear to the central function and motive of the "old" university. The words "great opportunity to do something new and useful" are a powerful lure, but opportunities do not automatically generate means. For example, in a large city such as New York a university has a great opportunity to teach many of the less familiar languages, because native informants (as they are called) are not hard to find. Columbia University offers courses in fifty-eight languages altogether, including Urdu, Korean, Iranian, Turkic, and many others not commonly available. The demand for them is genuine but fitful. Student fees do not even pay for the costs of instruction. The result is that this lavish offering, or a large part of it, is that familiar burden, a necessary luxury.

Likewise with the new professions that come into being, the new lines of research that are opened up every month—or so it seems. No finite institution can take a vow to fulfill the infinite.

But if that is true within the realm of scholarship and education, it must be all the more true in the realm of good works. In the former realm, the bounds are marked by available money and men; in the latter, by the very same restriction and by an additional one: the diminishing power of an institution to absorb and coordinate new groups and functions when what is already complex and sizable overshoots a certain mark—the Babel index.

While describing the university's present load, still cheerfully borne, I referred in passing to the new offices that had to be created within the last fifteen years to furnish the new services. But in its transformation the university has developed other imponderable needs and must serve them too: public relations and image-nursing; continuous fund-raising; systematized contact with alumni; "listening posts" close to federal, state, and city governments, as safeguards against ill-informed legislation; health and safety inspection against radiation and other dangers incidental to scientific research; regular consultation with comparable universities on the common problems, particularly tuition rates and the rules of the U.S. Budget Office; increased occasions for sociability (to counteract both confusion and system) and for psychiatric aid (when sociability is not enough); continuous surveys and audits of all current operations through an Office of Facts and Figures; perpetual codification and amendment of rules and procedures; greatly increased printing, to make known the university to its constituents and prevent error and self-deception on their part; control over the few or many loosely tied institutes, laboratories, and centers matured since the war; continuous study of electronic and other novelties reputed to "revolutionize education" every few months; staff and committee work to cope with the influx of art in all forms and to manage exhibits, concerts, plays—the whole cultural showcase, as the Mayor of New York calls it; finally, the creation of a planning group, with an architectural office attached, to chart the course and study the conditions of future growth.

Unsympathetic observers who have noted the recent mushrooming of officialdom in our universities have often concluded that the growth is but another illustration of Parkinson's law. The supposition would be correct if that law, plausible at first, were a little more in accord with the facts. What happens when a new office is opened—say, to administer the government's NDEA fellowships and loans*—is that the administrator and his typist are overwhelmed by applications and inquiries, puzzles and errors, as soon as word gets around that the new benefits exist. The trouble

* NDEA = The National Defense Education Act of 1958, Public Law 85-864.

grows faster than the office force. One simply tries to keep up and make the deadlines.

Meanwhile the administrator finds that the *government's* requirements increase in volume—more statistics, closer screening, more frequent reports. This occurs because more and more institutions want a portion of the inelastic appropriation; the Washington agency needs more data. The university officer may seem to be building an empire because he now has six assistants and three typists; the reality is that the new service *equals* just so much paper and manpower. This example holds throughout—in the library, the medical office, the registry of off-campus housing—everywhere. And the reason for the phenomenon is so plain that there is no point in imagining little bureaucratic Caesars plotting aggrandizement.

Nor should it be imagined that the many types of administrative work to be done on the campus find a host of eager applicants well qualified to carry on. The opposite is true. Talent is scarce everywhere, the university can rarely pay salaries as large as does business; and most important, dealing even occasionally with an academic community is an art which, if not inborn, comes only after long apprenticeship and severe bruises. Generally speaking, the university has to administer itself, that is, the bulk of its managerial manpower must come from the professorial ranks or from recent graduates who have not yet forgotten what a teacher is like. This axiom may seem extraordinary, but it is true—and it puts one more limitation on what the university as Lady Bountiful can promise or perform.

The new university thus presents a spectacle on three levels, like a medieval sculpture of the Last Judgment. On one plane is an administrative apparatus struggling to keep instruction, research, and community services in balance and the corporation solvent. At the center is the faculty, solicited from every quarter (including the university itself) to impart its knowledge and yielding (or not) to the temptations and summonses possible and impossible. In the third realm is the student body, fraternizing with its young instructors, often turning away from the education it seeks, and tending to lump the once-revered university with the social evils to be reformed. The new American university goes back scarcely twenty years; the "old" university is less than a century old. If the new deserves to be saved, the salvation can come only from within, from those who continue to say that they are the university. And their self-reformation can occur only if they fully understand what they have come to be doing and the setting in which they do it.

2 Scholars in Orbit

In an ideal state, gentlemen who were immersed in abstruse calculations and discoveries would be forced by Act of Parliament to talk for forty-five minutes to an ostler or a landlady . . . ; they would be examined in the colours of omnibuses . . . ; they would be taught to become men of the world. . . .

—G. K. Chesterton

. . . Bid the professor quit
His fraudulent pedantries, and do i' the world
The thing he would teach others.

—G. B. Shaw

THE FACULTY: ITS PROVENANCE AND PROMOTION

After an imaginary tour of the new university and a reading of the daily papers, there is no mystery in what professors do and where they go; but where do they come from? Who are these people? How does one get to be full professor at Harvard, Princeton, Columbia, so as to qualify for Washington, Karachi, and the front page of the *New York Times?* The simplest answer is to describe appointment procedures. They tell us what merit consists of, merit once defined influences the direction that talent and young ambition take, and the outcome exemplifies the modern idea of the university.

Professors are made from graduate students—graduates in arts and science or in the several professions that are taught in university schools. Graduate students come out of colleges, where the later professions and specialties are anticipated by appropriate courses, early "research," and a more or less elaborate system of student advising. The new university is of course strong on professional training, but the main theater of its recent upheaval has been the so-called nonprofessional sector, the forty to sixty departments of instruction covering the arts and sciences—English, Chemisty, History, Mathematics, and the like.

In these departments the road to a professorship opens with a student's indicating that he "intends to go into teaching." This is the standard phrase and it may be true. On learning of this purpose, one of the young man's instructors may appoint him his research assistant—to fetch books from the library and verify footnotes. Or, without this preliminary, the beginner may be given a section of an elementary course to teach. At Columbia, no such teaching appointment is allowed until the candidate has passed his oral examinations in subject matter, halfway to the Ph.D.* Elsewhere, first-year graduate students are sometimes relied upon for all "section work" in freshman courses. But the choice among candidates is based largely on the capacity to do research. The presumption holds that anyone who possesses certified knowledge and is not a deaf-mute can teach. No formal attempt is made to impart to the novice any notions of lecturing, examining, grading, or conducting a discussion group.†

* But laboratory assistants in the sciences are first- or second-year graduate students.

† In some universities, such as Harvard, an elective course in teaching problems and methods is offered to graduate students who are intending teachers. When that Harvard course recently attained a registration of 100, there was much rejoicing over the triumph. That peak number amounted to 1 in 18 graduate students. At most other universities such a course would be considered superfluous. Accordingly, some graduate professors take occasion to give their students, in passing, a few tips about teaching.

College and university teaching is thus the only profession (except the proverbially oldest in the world) for which no training is given or required. It is supposed to be "picked up." But it is only fair to add that many who start are eliminated by the end of their first year. Though teaching is hard to test, their inadequacy somehow gets to be known: their student victims or their young colleagues talk. For those who survive a trial appointment, the next step is to "get on with the dissertation"—an easy resolve hard to act on: teaching three courses each term makes writing a book a heavy task.* Yet it must be done and an examination passed upon it within a specified time, usually seven years from the beginning of graduate work; that is, some three or four years after the end of course-taking and preparing the subject orals.

Fortunately, the old monumental, life-sentence, eiderdown-quilt dissertation, which I described and deplored in *Teacher in America,* is receding into the past. Most departments approve only manageable topics and set limits to the number of pages that may be catapulted at a sponsor. The change has come partly in response to repeated urgings by graduate deans† and partly in self-defense: the sponsor is swamped; he needs a pitchfork to turn over the papers on his desk, and he therefore views with a lackluster eye the student who has chosen to tell all in twelve hundred typed pages.

The dissertation over, the graduate-student-instructor turns overnight into an assistant professor, with an increase in salary of possibly $1,000 or $1,500. The great change from as recently as ten years ago is that the beginning grade of instructor hardly counts; it is regularly by-passed. The shortage of able men is acute,

* Hence the introduction at Columbia of the grade of preceptor, charged with a two-thirds load and supposedly overseen by an older colleague who encourages the production of the thesis. Not all departments like preceptors: they want whole men, for administrative convenience. But then they are also surprised and sorry when the full-time instructor "doesn't get on with his book."

† See Appendix D, Nos. 39, 44, 55, 57, 68, and 69.

and anyone completing the Ph.D. at one university and invited by another now goes there as an assistant professor from the outset, instead of ripening several years as instructor.*

SEEKING THE RARE BIRD

The next hurdle in the path is the ad hoc committee that determines tenure, ordinarily linked with the rank of associate professor. The procedure varies at different universities, but all the self-respecting ones go through a fixed series of steps. When a vacancy, natural or contrived, occurs in the tenure ranks of a department, the chairman names a search committee, which is charged with surveying the cosmos for the best possible candidate. That committee reports its findings to the executive committee of the department (i.e., the tenure members), which names a first choice, followed by one or more alternatives. The list may include the assistant professors already in the institution. The chairman then goes to the dean for reassurance that the empty salary line will be kept in the next year's budget or augmented to meet rising rates.

If the departmental choice is the man on home ground, the promotion ordinarily lifts him to the lower level of the scale set for associate professors. If the choice is for an outside man, or if the home product is being bid for by another university (or government or industry), the dean is asked not for a fixed salary but for a bargaining range. Bargaining goes on not only about salary but also about teaching load, fringe benefits, and possibly special perquisites, such as extra leaves, research assistance, laboratory space and equipment, or an allocation to the university library for the purchase of books at the incumbent's pleasure. With outsiders

* "Instructor" is both a rank and a generic term designating anyone who teaches in the university. "My instructor" may well mean "my professor." Similarly, "officer of instruction" applies to anyone entrusted with teaching duties, regardless of rank.

the dickering is often viva voce, each party desiring to take a good look at the other. When the hunted man is an undoubted catch in this matrimonial market, the passionate offer may be made by the chairman in person at the pursued's own university. Or, again, the president of the suitor institution may invite the man and his wife for a few days' visit, preferably at the presidential house. The headiest form of flattery so far devised is to receive as the opening bow-and-scrape a letter from the president *handwritten.* It implies: "We love you! We mean it!"

This courtship must be kept in mind if one is to understand the workings of the ad hoc committee which is the gateway to tenure professorships, as has been said. Not all candidacies, of course, call forth the full deployment of lures and bribes. The more common ones take the form of an inquiry from the chairman to find out whether the scholar would move from his present post. This starts a conversation that may take most of an academic year. When the original plan is not realizable on any customary terms, it is because the brilliant scholar has just done something spectacular and is being bid for by two, three, or even five great universities simultaneously. The etiquette then gets complicated and the terms flamboyant. Feelings get hurt if responses are not candid or prompt, but no one is shocked if the scholar asks for the moon.

A very usual demand is to have the wooing university also offer positions to one or two of the man's protégés. They then move in a team—a "package deal." The justification is that they are jointly engaged in some important research, or else that the senior man, a great specialist, "needs somebody to talk to." An algebraic topologist, for example, would expect to wither if he were alone of his kind in a mathematics department. The modern university needs—or at any rate the modern scholar wants—clusters of talent. Genius itself no longer wants to be *sui generis.*

Equally common is a type of offer which seems to imply exactly the opposite principle, and which has caused much criticism within the university and outside. I mean the offer of a professorship without teaching or other duties.* "Come to us and grace our campus." In practice this usually means "grace our catalogue," for the only reason why anybody should accept such an offer is to give all his time to research, and specialized research can hardly invigorate an institution or a department. The eminent but solitary scholar goes abroad or hides in the library or directs his own laboratory, with few or no other contacts. Yet when foundation gifts or state university budgets provide the money for such professorships, it is usually in the hope that a great man will start or strengthen "new centers of excellence." What has generally resulted is the demoralization of those already in the department at salaries half the "distinguished" salary—the rabble who not only teach but do the dirty work. Nor has it always been good for the star to end his career as a remote luminary, barely perceptible to his resentful colleagues, and badgered not by students but by a bevy of research assistants asking for something to do.

We now approach the consummation of the bargain. If the terms do include special privileges and allow the new recruit to maintain a golden silence, it is likely that the chairman has been assisted in the negotiations by the graduate dean, the dean of faculties or provost, the academic vice-president, or even the president. It is—has been—major business. Any deal that shatters the salary norm must also have been approved by the budget committee, of which more later. When all is cleared, the dean of faculties (or vice-president) appoints an ad hoc committee to review the candidate's qualifications. Details of its working may differ, but the principle is uniform, namely, that a group of tenure

* To cite a pair of examples: "We will pay you $10,000 more than your present salary. You need not teach. You will have $12,000 for research assistants and books. You may be away from the campus every third term. If you do want to teach, you will receive additional compensation at the rate of $1,000 for each semester course."

Or again: "Your salary will be $32,000 (an increase of $11,000). You can order the library to buy all the materials you want, for we are building it up from scratch. Your own research account can in addition be drawn on up to $30,000 a year. We should like you to teach, but that is at your discretion."

faculty members, other than those in the department involved, shall give their assent to promotions and tenure appointments.* The effect is that instead of putting the choice of new professors in the hands of the candidate's future colleagues, backed by the administration, the choice is ratified by five additional judges having the power to seek opinions wherever they like.

TRIAL BY ONE'S PEERS

The procedure for ad hoc committees is elaborate and therefore described in the *Faculty Handbook.* The chairman of the department that asks for the new man procures copies of his works in print, or a representative sampling. This material is read by the members of the committee, together with letters from scholars outside the university detailing the candidate's good points. (Adverse remarks in writing are rare.) On the day, the chairman appears before the committee and makes a case for the appointment or promotion. The dean of faculties (or graduate dean) is present, but as a referee only. He does not vote or express opinions. The chairman answers the committee's questions, then withdraws, and discussion begins. The candidate's biography and writings, and his character as it emerges from the letters or the direct knowledge of members of the committee, are scrutinized.†

The hoped-for end is a unanimous vote for or against, and it is generally obtained. A division of 3 to 2 often means that the department has put up one of its younger men prematurely. In the

* At Columbia, the system was instituted in 1954, after a university committee had decided that departmental decisions by themselves were not a sufficient guarantee of excellence. In some of the professional schools, notably Law, Architecture, Medicine, and Social Work, such a guarantee is obtained by requiring the entire tenure faculty to vote on tenure posts.

† In a valuable work, *The Academic Marketplace,* now somewhat out of date, the sociologists Caplow and McGee produced evidence that the practice of ad hoc committees does not always conform to the theory, especially in the matter of reading the candidate's scholarly works. But such variations are only to be expected in an environment where impatience with "administration" and a dislike of taking oneself solemnly sometimes tempt men of integrity to neglect their obligations.

view of some "he hasn't published enough," as when an ingenious young scholar produced nine long articles, in three languages, which turned out to be three articles slightly altered at head and tail to fit the needs of foreign journals: $3 \times 3 = 9$.

Again, a man from outside may be deemed a poor choice, because too far along in his career. Faculty members tend to want incompatible merits—great fame and the intellectual vigor of youth. Hence the differences of opinion in certain ad hoc cases: "He's not likely to do much more at his age"; or "He sounds good but hasn't produced much yet."

Everybody honestly wants to "strengthen the department"—in scholarly eyes departments and faculties are always anemic—but does strength consist in productivity or in prestige? There is a touching faith that scholarly reputation, which naturally betokens past achievements, will attract good students. In some close-knit or highly specialized fields, such as mathematical statistics or molecular biology, this is no doubt true. But over the whole range, students go here or there for other considerations, often more practical than intellectual. Even when they know a "great name" from his books or public acts, they maintain a wise skepticism about his ability to teach or the likelihood of his being in residence when they appear.

When the ad hoc committee has decided, it reports its findings, often in great detail, to the dean of faculties, who is supposed to verify the procedure and forward his recommendation to the president. Since the dean has gauged the candidate's merit, in person and through reading, well before naming the ad hoc group, what happens is that a unanimous approval by the committee is simply recorded as a final judgment, which the president is notified of in due course. If the committee is split 3 to 2 and the reasons given are such as to suggest a poor choice (or a possible source of faculty dissension), the dean declares the majority inadequate to pass the candidate. If the dean is doubtful all on his own, he naturally advises the president. From beginning to end the administration plays the role of midwife only. No unanimous decision by the committee, whether positive or negative, would nowadays be flouted by a president or his academic second. In a word, the faculty recruits itself.*

And that is how Ph.D.'s wind up sitting in chairs.

SEVEN TYPES OF ASSIDUITY

The climb upward is naturally hedged about by many unwritten rules, and there are professorships and professorships. A four-year liberal arts college wants good teachers as well as respectable scholars; whereas a great university, while it may sincerely want good teachers, will compromise and take the great inaudible expert whom it would be cruelty to both sides to put in front of a class. The related issue popularly known as "Publish or Perish" is almost always confused, because the disputants see different aspects of an improbable goal—the multiple perfection that all desire in other men. The "grand teacher" whom students idolize seems to his departmental colleagues an indifferent asset—he publishes mediocre articles or too few or none at all. "He has tenure, we're stuck with him—one of our mistakes." It is part of the settled order of Nature that every department of every university has at least one such member.

Another academic type is that of the man who has a public reputation for writings that his fellows deem "not scholarship"—"He's a critic or worse, a journalist." Sometimes—as was true of Veblen—the discredited works turn out to be epoch-making. Next come the men of action, who may once have been excellent scholars but who have discovered the knack of reassuring statesmen and comforting industrialists, who devise projects smiled on by foundations, who foment conferences and lead an airborne existence. Universities seeking "visibility" have a penchant for such men and sometimes look for them among ex-ambassadors, deposed heads

* In England, as Mr. Bruce Truscot (pseud.) reminded us some years ago in his excellent book *Red-brick University* (London, 1943–1945), an election to a professorship may entail the approval of several thousand people, most of them, of course, giving only a formal "aye" in a routine agenda.

of foreign states, international bankers with government experience, or artists of renown, all of them supposedly image-enhancing.

Whatever the new university may wish to be, its administration has a duty to maintain a balance among types of talent. And first of all it must ensure the continuity of teaching: a nonteaching university is a contradiction in terms. Still, contradiction has never stopped corporate bodies from forgetting their purpose. At Columbia, the ad hoc procedure states in black and white that promotion to tenure may properly be given to a scholar who does not publish much (or at all) if evidence shows that he is indeed a scholar. A teacher who lives on old notes and earns popularity by being always accessible for a chat may add to the warmth of college halls, but in the long run he causes more harm than good. A scholar-teacher (as the hopeful phrase goes) is a man who loves teaching, does it well, and continues to study his subject.*

It usually takes a stubborn tradition to make room for such men in the vicious rivalry of the new university. Just because the bidding is feverish, choosing the right headliners takes experience; it is easy to be deceived by glitter and vogue and to pay a ruinous price for them. This is true equally when the man sought is a public-affairs extrovert and when he is a touted authority on an abstruse new field. In this last situation the chances are that faddishness reigns and genius is proclaimed on slender grounds. Use mathematical symbols to discuss French irregular verbs and your fortune may be made—for a while. But it does not take divination to recognize the profound scholar in an established field. The question for the university then is what it wants him for. Is it to impart knowledge? Is it to give him sanctuary for his remaining years? Is it to show him off?

These aims are not incompatible, but if one clearly predominates it should be acknowledged, particularly if the university is tying up one of the fattest stipends in the department for eight or

* A notable example at Columbia College was the late Professor Andrew Chiappe, who never published between his Ph.D. dissertation and some essays on Shakespearian romance, which are to appear posthumously. But for twenty years his several courses on Shakespeare were fruits of deep scholarship and performances of high originality.

ten or twenty years. One thing is plain: the man's glory will not be transferred from the institution where he did his great work to that which has bought him. The risk then is: will he retire on salary? It is the duty of a dean of faculties, at the cost of his own popularity, to make vivid these possibilities and repeatedly put Benjamin Franklin's question—do you want to give all your money for that whistle?

The question is particularly cogent when the candidate is from a foreign university. The other side of the Atlantic is always greener; the very names of foreign universities suggest scholarship incrusted; and it seems like a coup to detach a man from Leyden or Munich or Paris or Oxford, even for a visiting professorship. All the same, recruits from the Continent must be closely scanned. Can they speak English? And, even more important, will they accept American ways of higher education—frequent lectures, accessibility to students, a heavy schedule of examinations, departmental and university committee work—a hundred things that the free-floating foreign professor knows nothing of and may well resent as infringing his independence.*

That independence extends to the course offering, and American chairmen, in their eagerness to land the foreign catch, are inclined while negotiating to slur over the department's expectations. The great scholar may do "just what he wants." Yet if, as once happened, the visiting professor offers American students courses ostensibly on the history of medieval trade but actually on the condition of the roads in Flanders during the twelfth century, the students will attend a few times, then withdraw until the return from leave of the wider-ranging American historian. Meanwhile, the deserted foreigner enjoys an unintended sabbatical of his own. The department rationalizes the event by saying that the great man's presence, at lunch and in the corridors, was "extremely stimulating."

The upshot of such mistakes and misunderstandings is that conscientious deans, who are themselves academic men but who see

* One such scholar, reared and trained in Germany, was found after a few semesters to have ingeniously excluded all women students from his classes.

more cases of disillusionment, draw up guidelines for both appointments and course offerings. With luck and cunning these documents get adopted, become part of the lore. They set forth not only the conditions under which replacements for those on leave are allowable but also the traps surrounding the recruiting of foreigners—the dangers of overripe fame, the treacherousness of narrow fields and vague understandings by letter; together with warnings about visa regulations, the cost of moving household goods, and the need to announce new courses.

THE SPORT OF BUCCANEERS: RAIDING

The reverse face of recruiting is raiding. When university A is attempting to recruit Mr. X, his university, B, is being raided. The act flatters both the man and his institution, but he enjoys it more. For he is now in a position to bargain with his chairman, dean, and president, and they must ask themselves: what is he worth to us? Of late years—say, the past ten—raiding at (or against) the best universities has been continuous. No institution is so high on Olympus as to be immune from aggression. As the government, the foundations, and other patrons have spread the wealth to spread the talent more evenly across the country, the tenders of salary and privilege have overcome the former feelings of devotion to one place, to say nothing of inertia and the pleasure of linking one's name permanently with that of an ancient seat of learning.

The rejoinder to a raid is a counteroffer, which comes after asking the incumbent what would make him happy where he is. Some increase in rank or salary is inevitable and taken for granted; one "matches" the opposition. But there has grown up since 1950 a vast menu of fringe benefits that cover almost all the needs of man, from parking and children's schooling to travel and moving allowances, major medical insurance, faculty apartments, corner offices, summer grants, and reduced teaching load.*

* An admirable critical survey of their kinds and forms has been compiled by Professor Mark H. Ingraham: *The Outer Fringe: Faculty Benefits Other Than Annuities and Insurance,* University of Wisconsin Press, 1965.

We saw above some examples of munificent offers designed to alienate the affections of the most loyal. Those bids were made to senior men of wide repute. But there is also raiding in the lower ranks, for at the present time the greatest shortage of talent occurs in the generation of men between 28 and 38. The assistant professor is at a premium and is correspondingly coddled.

This cherishing usually takes the form of a one-year leave, early in his holding of the rank, to enable him to write his "first real book."* The dissertation, so important twenty months before, is now dismissed as prentice work, and he is expected to produce something earth-shaking enough to justify his prompt promotion to tenure. He can only remain an assistant professor five years, and it takes a full year to go through the promotion procedure. Add to this the one-year advance notice required if there is no intention to promote, and it follows that judgment on him must begin in his third year.†

What creates these stringent conditions is not solely the competition for young men, which has greatly lowered the age at which tenure is allotted. It is also, and mainly, the pressure put on colleges and universities by the American Association of University Professors, which has decreed that anyone teaching full time for seven years at any rank in a given institution obtains automatic tenure.[1]‡

In addition to the paid year's leave, the young scholar is at many institutions eligible for a summer research grant of about

* With this end in view Columbia College established for its younger faculty members the Lawrence H. Chamberlain Fellowships, which combine honor and stipend.

† In order to lengthen the chance to do scholarly work and have it fairly judged, the faculties at Columbia decided in 1965 to permit assistant professors to hold the rank for seven years, provided their first appointment at the university was at that rank.

‡ The only latitude afforded by the Association is that the strict observance of an eight-year rule (ten years in medical schools) is accepted as evidence of good faith. Since no administration likes to tangle with the AAUP and incur well-publicized odium on the charge of "exploiting young men," the rule of up-or-out in eight years is observed at all reputable schools.

$1,500, which permits him to turn down the summer teaching post he would otherwise seek. He submits a project to a faculty committee on research and, unless he is grossly careless or badly advised, he gets his grant. For everybody understands like the Psalmist that "promotion cometh neither from the east nor from the west nor from the south," but research is the test.*

It is obvious that all this fueling of research works in one respect against the university. For when the young scholar brings out his monograph, he becomes "visible" to other institutions and begins to be wooed. He is "one of four in the country that everybody wants." It is prestige-cashing time and he develops a severe itch of the overnight bag. Tagged as brilliant on the strength of perhaps one long article, he assumes rather independent airs, is handled with kid gloves by his chairman and warmly nodded to by his dean, whom the chairman has alerted. Either the home university must pay the competitive price to retain its own man or must let him go elsewhere and start developing his successor out of the raw material at hand. Whatever one may think of the effect of early eminence on young scholars, the effect on the university is to diminish greatly the sense of hierarchy and to increase in like amounts preoccupation with staffing and administrative paper work.

This description is of course one-sided. The university is glad to further a career, develop a talent, and through his research possibly add to the sum of human knowledge. But the one-sided view has point in relation to the material welfare of the best universities, for it is clear that in the sequence just described they are using their resources, as often as not, for the benefit of four-year colleges and the lesser universities. The balance of trade has so far been in favor of these institutions. There can be no objection to this natural flow of the current since the nation as a whole benefits, but when we come to the question of costs we shall remember that here is a large unpaid claim.†

* At Yale the subsidy of summer research for assistant and associate professors is automatic—part of the bill of rights.

† See Chapter 6.

SUBSISTENCE, NOT LIFE

A second modifier of what I have called the one-sided view is the economic situation of the young scholar himself. At the leading universities an assistant professor is likely to command a beginning salary of $8,000 and to rise by yearly increments to $10,000 or $11,500. If he lives in a large city and has a wife and two children, he cannot subsist decently—let alone in comfort—without moonlighting.* This is to say that, although the salaries for the upper academic ranks have risen to acceptable levels, the lower ranks in the leading universities are still underpaid.† This fact is what gives certain provincial colleges and universities the opportunity to lure first-rate men by making them what looks like a generous offer—say, $10,000 when they are earning $8,500 at the big place. If in fairness to his family the young man accepts, he may find that his pay rises slowly along a scale that does not go very high: the highest paid full professor at the lesser place may stand at $15,000 till retirement. The alert young, aware of the dilemma, stay at the large university and take a second job, or even a third and fourth. They teach in night schools, give lectures to women's clubs, write book reviews, edit paperbacks, and collaborate with their fellows on premature textbooks.

It is a hellish life, in which some of the best talent gets exploited by intellectually submarginal schools. In certain municipal colleges that offer graduate instruction, it is often the young instructors of the superior institution nearby that run the Ph.D. seminars. Confusion and debasement are thus hidden in the bustle and smoke of "expanding educational opportunities." And it is not surprising that after five to eight years of this double life of late hours in

* If he lives in New York City his position is especially difficult. The cost of living there in 1966–67 proved after study to be $1,000 above the national average; housing was for the most part abject and costly; and private schooling was a necessity, both for safety and for good instruction.

† This is not a new phenomenon resulting from inflation. Forty years ago it was a commonplace in most private universities of the East that to enter academic life one should have an independent income, however small.

distant, crowded classrooms the survivor emerges nauseated with teaching.

Meanwhile the administration of his main college or university must take steps to see that it does not get too little of the young man's time and attention. The junior ranks are permitted to "receive extra compensation" for additional work at their own university, the obvious purpose being to secure the best talent for the evening session or some other classes, and at the same time save the energy of the young from dispersion off campus. The reasoning is that, since they will in any case do extra work, they might as well do it for the same employer. There may not be enough such work to go around, but those who perform it can at least be kept from overloading. The attitude of chairmen and seniors is almost invariably friendly and protective, and the intervention of a chairman when a junior officer seems neglectful is mainly out of affection for the man and scholar and in the interest of his future.

THE UPPER CRUST AND ITS PERQUISITES

Salary scales vary between wide extremes.* But by 1966–67 the full professor at a respectable university could command a salary just as respectable. A strict dollar comparison with the lawyer, the doctor, the civil servant, or the business executive is misleading. So is a weighted comparison with the professorial salaries of earlier years. In the first place, the academic salary is earned in eight or eight and a half months of physical presence. During the other four months opportunities for full-time work—teaching, writing, or consulting—are open to most scholars, those in certain fields being of course at a premium. And these same opportunities, which are a new fact of professorial life, are abundant during the eight months of academic "full-time."

* To speak of a "starting salary" or a "professor's salary" without specifying the year or the place means very little—no more certainly than it would mean in discussing law or medicine. College and university compensation (that is, salary plus fringe benefits) ranges from what is a subsistence wage for the family to the comparative affluence of the scholar-consultant or scholar-administrator who earns $40,000 to $50,000 a year.

The conventions governing these outside activities are more or less explicit. Thus in the sciences it is understood by the government agencies which give grants or contracts that a scholar may receive under the agreement 2/9 (or in some cases 3/9) of his regular salary for summer work. During the year he is eligible for consulting fees not in excess of 1/5 of his regular salary. These norms came out of pre-existing university customs. Everyone agrees that contact with the world of practice can benefit the pure researcher. On the faculties of medicine, law, and engineering, the case does not need to be argued. In other subjects, to apply the maxim requires judgment; but in postwar culture, where nearly everything is consciously provided for, hardly any kind of knowledge escapes public and private demand, expressed in remunerative projects. What the government still ignores, the foundations cultivate and the patron promotes. Besides which, education now covers man and his life like a cosmic blanket, and it needs experts ad infinitum.

The temptations thus created are sometimes very great. Not long ago a specialist in an under-supplied field was found to be holding down one full-time appointment in a university and another in a busy state bureau—and thinking that he was serving the world even more than himself. The faculty needed no prodding to vacate his academic post, but in less glaring cases there is in most universities no machinery to enforce single-mindedness. Faculty members are very jealous of their freedom of action, and when a few years ago a questionnaire was circulated at Columbia requesting information on outside activities there was protest and boycott. Though it was made clear that no estimate of time spent or money earned was called for—only a mere list of activities, not even to be marked temporary or permanent—the outcry of a respectable minority proved that academic men no longer believe they owe their full attention to the university. In justice to them it must be added that on seeing that no action was to follow the survey, almost all the recalcitrants of the first year filled out the questionnaire on the second and third rounds.

When tabulated, these reports showed to what extent the university was furnishing help to the city, the nation, and the world, and this in no general or indirect sense. Whether it was advice on taxation to a South American government or help to the city in medicine, archival work or architectural problems, service at the White House or as assistant secretary to a large department of the executive, participation in state education and science or advice to businesses ranging from publishing to manufacture, it was apparent that the faculties of the university were supplying knowledge and bodily attendance at much of the world's work which thirty years ago was done without them.*

TRADITION OR CORRUPTION?

Before going on to notice some of the untoward results for men and institutions, one must be reminded that taking down the gate and walls is not contrary to the original spirit of the American university; rather it is the carrying out of its clear intentions. From one side, the land-grant colleges and state universities purposed to bring science to bear on dairy farming, forestry, and the extraction industries, in addition to health, education, and the general welfare. From another side, the raising into high-theoretical professions of the practice of law, journalism, business, and architecture—all formerly learned by apprenticeship—multiplied the contacts between the university and the world.

* I vividly remember, in the mid-twenties, one of the earliest examples of this now nationwide relationship. A professor of public law and government at Columbia, Lindsay Rogers, had been named by the Governor of New York to be "czar of the cloak-and-suit industry." The exaggeration implied by the word "czar" is a measure of the astonishment that was felt. Dr. Rogers would surely resign his professorship. Despite his brawn, strong mind, and loud voice, he would surely be outwitted by the traders and politicians. When none of this happened, a prophet might have foretold the present mingling of cloak-and-suit with academic gown, the transition having occurred in two steps—first, the help scholars gave Franklin D. Roosevelt in his first campaign, which led to the brain trust; and second, the high concentration of academics in the conduct of the ensuing war. The cloak-and-suit connection turned cloak-and-dagger for hundreds in the OWI, OSS, and other agencies. By President Kennedy's time the new order of things was a commonplace.

What is decisive on the point is that the founders of graduate study in science and scholarship in the 1880's also stated their desire to train servants of the public and the state.* John W. Burgess is typical: as a soldier of nineteen in the Civil War he resolved to find and help eradicate the cause of such senseless conflicts. Fifteen years later, after study abroad and wide consultation, he established at Columbia a graduate school of political science that should form the enlightened leaders of the next generation. His model was the French Ecole Libre des Sciences Politiques, with certain features of the German university added. Here and in Daniel Coit Gilman's all-graduate Johns Hopkins is to be found the first idea of the American university.

But what was meant to take effect through the somewhat indirect route of enlightenment, and what was compatible with other purposes when graduate study was the choice of a small minority, came to present difficulties when the purpose suddenly turned systematic, direct, and commonplace for college graduates. Universities in urban centers were naturally the first to respond to that "vital demand" already talked about in the eighties. Just before Franklin Roosevelt's first term it seemed clear to such an observer as the French diplomat and novelist Paul Morand that Columbia University was "a utilitarian center for making not scholars but men of action . . . men not isolated from the world but plunged in the mainstream of common life. . . . If Oxford is the home of lost causes, Columbia University is the home of those that are won."[2]

Then came the Second World War and with it an accelerated

* This ambition was linked with two others: the urge to break loose from dependence on the German universities, to which Americans who hoped to become scientists and scholars then repaired; and the growing impatience with the classical curriculum. As a New York magazine of the eighties put it: "If the old undergraduate course must be retained (and it is, in our opinion, in need of essential modifications), then there should be provided opportunities for advanced post-graduate study. That there is a vital demand in a city like New York for something more than elementary instruction in geology, chemistry . . . and a dozen other sciences that might be named can scarcely be questioned."—*The Century Illustrated Monthly Magazine,* vol. 25, no. 6, April 1883, 952.

social evolution such that even the European universities faced the "vital demand": by 1960, England had doubled the number of her universities and the Sorbonne, for example, was building new quarters for its department of Hispanic, because the number of students seeking the master's degree had risen from 15 to 2,000. These recruits to learning looked not so much to the scholarship of Cervantes as to positions in South American banks and jobs as air hostesses on South Atlantic planes.

The removal of the campus to the market place, the quickly formed habits of teachers in transit, the presence within the university of what are in fact outside employers with urgent claims on attention—all this has necessarily affected the teaching function of the university, and not alone the direction of its research.

To begin with, the teacher-scholar is hampered by the shortness of the twenty-four-hour day and his inability to be in two places at once. He can rarely be at leisure and pensive. He is harassed and "fitting in" the repeated calls on his help. Even if he is not a multi-project director, not a Nimrod or grant-hunter before the Lord, nor a consultant being squeezed dry of expertise, he is caught up in the general movement. If pure scholar still, he is busy declining offers of additional work; he is serving on committees of his professional association; editing learned journals and newsletters—in-house and out; promoting the interests of his subject in local schools or citizen groups; giving special seminars to bring up to date the nonacademic practitioners in his field; arranging exchanges of colleagues with foreign universities or overseas branches of his own, answering questionnaires from "new centers of excellence"; attending conclaves of counterparts on both sides of the iron curtain; joining study groups to "cut across disciplines"; and lecturing here and there, from the student societies on campus to the insatiable audiences throughout the land.

Moreover, since research has become competitive instead of spontaneous, the modern scholar must keep up till death not only study but production. To the extent that he is good he is at work, in the laboratory or the study, reading sources or typescript or proofs. On top of which, as everybody knows, every detail of the day's work has become, thanks to increased numbers and improved communication, more laborious and uncertain: it is a gamble or a feat to obtain a library book or receive letters on time.

Such is the setting in which the scholar faces the demands of his department, his students, and the university. The departmental demands consist of committee work: the executive committee, which settles curriculum and promotions; the search committee, already described, which recruits outside and assesses the merits of the juniors inside; examination committees, which tax the endurance of the stoutest, for each senior man examines in at least one language for the Ph.D., sits on a string of orals in subjects throughout the year, and during April and May reads ten or twelve dissertations, each followed by a two-hour scrutiny in committee. There are, moreover, masters' essays to correct and grade, fellowship applications to judge, letters of recommendation to write, book catalogues to mark for library acquisitions—and students.

Students come last, not by selfish choice, not on any theory, but simply because everything else is a group activity having a rhythm of its own. The group commands and the individual is neglected. This is a reason, not an excuse. And the further truth that on the whole academic men still cherish their students does not contradict what I shall have to say later about the students' legitimate complaints against their teachers. In other words, the flight from teaching is a fact but, apart from the singular laziness or escapism of a few, it is a cultural fact. To put it in still another way, the new university is the product of the new society and the flight from teaching is the by-product.

LOAD OR OVERLOAD?

The teacher's frequent distaste for teaching is, once again, the effect of numbers, not of students but of stimuli. Teaching, as I tried to point out years ago, is extremely hard work; it is the original and literal brain-drain, being the continual readjustment of one's thought to another's, not to placate or even to persuade, but to strengthen and enlarge and make more complex.* Now, in conditions of general calm and in a mood of mutual receptivity, the performance of teaching can be kept up for four or five hours during one day, including the tutorial or advising hours in one's office. The alternating off day is for preparation and administrative chores.

In keeping with this norm, the teaching load of thirty years ago was three or four courses of three hours a week each. Some of those hours were devoted to lecturing, which may be less taxing than discussion in small groups, depending on the small group. At any rate, the teacher of that time rarely felt that the student was a leech after his life's blood, even though the teacher then was responsible for more students than now.

Now the teaching load is an issue in every large university, and in raiding (as we saw before) the offers invariably guarantee no teaching or a reduced load. The reason is that today the teacher, before and after his teaching, is a driven wheel. It need not be *work* that unfits him for the full teaching load; the telephone is enough to account for it, and the mail, the committee minutes, the telegram from Washington, and that luncheon with the foundation executive, which must be prepared as carefully as a lecture.

At most universities the standard load varies between nine hours a week for junior officers and four or six for the senior, not including office hours. These last are left to the discretion of the men themselves, and some are so discreet as never to be seen. In consequence, certain institutions have formalized (for the sake of informal instruction) the hours when the instructor is expected to receive the solitary student. As "tutorials" or "preceptorials" or "regular office hours," they constitute an obligation like the scheduled lecture or seminar. But nowhere has it proved possible to

* See *Teacher in America,* Chapter 2.

define "the load" with exactitude. Some institutions that count courses by the semester rather than the full year promise their faculties a maximum of five courses a year, i.e., three in one term and only two in the next, top brass being favored with a total of three—two in one term and one the next.

But hearing this the panting candidate must ascertain several other facts: how much committee work is expected, how frequent are the faculty meetings, how closely supervised by the chairman is the keeping of office hours, and how large are the classes. In one typical instance, a distinguished scholar exchanged a five-course schedule (three one term and two the next) for one of two courses (one each term), but he found that instead of having 100 to 120 students each semester, he now had 600 and they kept him in office hours every afternoon of the week.

In addition to his students' demands, his department's and his outside employers', the teacher is subject to those of the university. He is liable to the sort of jury duty called for on ad hoc committees to judge his future colleagues. He may be also asked to serve on committees to coordinate the work of certain departments and schools, to study the merits of new proposals, to advise on research policies or housing practices, to adjudicate occasional disputes (the "President's Committee of Conference"), to award fellowships or prizes, to organize an anniversary celebration—or to further any purpose, old or new, that concerns the faculty.

There is, besides, an ascending series of governing bodies—e.g., committees on admissions, on curriculum, on honors—culminating in a council or senate that represents and legislates for the entire teaching body, passing upon the contents of programs and the requirements for degrees. All these committees use up man-hours and tend to take those hours from the same men. A wise administration always tries to reduce the number of special committees and to shorten their labors, so that scholars and scientists may be free for their proper task, which is to study and to teach. This wisdom and kindness is sometimes misunderstood as denying "participation."

THE HUNGRY GENERATIONS

The variety of these duties and the way they are discharged combine with the scholar's talent and temperament to shape his career: so much is a truism. Yet in the new university common pressures tend to give the crises of the academic career a few recognizable patterns. We have seen the crisis of the Man With an Offer. There is also the crisis of The Man of 57. He sees 60 looming—his last, broken-off decade, for he must retire between 65 and 68—and he suddenly feels that he has been learning the names of new students since the founding of the university a couple of centuries before. He wants to be free—from students not only, but also from committees, from voting "aye" at rubber-stamp councils, from reading fellowship applications and term papers, from seeing his colleagues and lunching at the faculty club. It is curious that this syndrome should occur in men who have enjoyed many opportunities to travel and to work at diverse tasks. But perhaps it is this taste of another life that creates the desire to jump out of the academic groove.*

At any rate, the most active minds at that age want a new deal. Some accept offers from industry and government—or from another university which they think will be utterly different. The "university professorship" (or "roving" or "distinguished" professorship) is designed to satisfy this longing for total independence. Some such deserters from the campus do return from business or the Civil Service as from exile, and a few roving professors have been known to beg for a scheduled class; yet the imperative need of change remains, which tells us that *being a scholar* is no longer the vocation it once was.

Farther down the ladder there is the crisis of the Young Men in a Hurry. They have achieved early eminence. At 32 they were being

* The same urge to break jail also occurs among businessmen and advertising executives. It has led to the setting up of university programs for "retooling" the restless mind.

cajoled by presidents to come or to stay, so important was their decision to the future of this or that famous university. The cult of personality is bred into their emotions, and it is natural that when three or four of them come together in one department they should form a junta of Young Turks. While a few of the older men are saying, "I'm nearly sixty and tired of teaching and committees —besides, they've invited me to do nothing at twice the salary," others are saying, "Those old codgers simply must go and let us run things. Why, they haven't even heard of —— (a young genius) or —— (a new piece of nomenclature)."

The trouble is that the old men ready to go are not the same old men being revolted against. Not everyone who nears sixty is wanted elsewhere, and there are many able, faithful teacher-scholars who mean to see their tenure out on the spot where they got it. Their lot can be bitter: the young care little for past achievement, especially in science, where subjects subdivide faster than amoebas and the latest is the best. In any subject, the fashion that counterfeits knowledge and is not destined to last is nevertheless not to be withstood at the moment.

Thus the struggle of old and young spares none, and it squeezes the young of a recent day who are now middle-aged. On which side shall they fall? Their quandary helps to produce the third type of crisis, that of Crossing Lines. These middle ranks, because of Early Eminence, begin to feel Old Man's Fatigue sooner than their predecessors did. They are in closer touch with young ideas and are made restless about their chosen line—why, it's ten years old. The key number of their decade has been left behind: 5 has yielded to 6, which will soon go to 7. The seventies—unbelievable!

Hence the desirability of breaking loose without actually moving. Departments are confining, run by rule and supervised by the central administration, whereas an interdepartmental group, an interdisciplinary program, a center for XYZ studies, or—blessed hope!—an institute would surely rejuvenate body and soul, open out vistas, jostle frontiers, and (while eliminating competition with youth and age) slip out from under administration. Besides, interdepartmental work brings together friends and colleagues of long standing; it is a pleasure in itself to build with them something new.

I do not for a moment suggest that all these self-regarding feelings are conscious, except in occasional flashes. The conscious intentions are scholarly, scientific, intellectually rationalized, and responsible. The point is not so much their nature as the environment from which they spring, itself seldom consciously judged by its inhabitants. Monetary advantage, for example, does not figure largely as a motive, because academic men (I am convinced) are still for the most part disinterested in their wish to innovate.* This is true, even though, once subsidized, they accept affluence like anybody else. To be sure, innovation that "cuts across departmental lines," e.g., institutes and centers, is likely to enjoy special ease and perquisites. But it is chiefly as liberation that these are sought. And this wish to escape, to forget about rules and handle a bit of money, is emotionally bound up with two fundamental rights of university faculties—their tenure and their academic freedom.

FREEDOM ON TWO LEGS

The practice of giving tenure to university professors is justified on the same grounds as the tenure of judges in federal courts: to make them independent of thought control. A guarantee of academic freedom—the right to speak freely in the classroom on the subject of the class—would not be worth much if it were subject to

* Exceptions are sometimes worth noting, because they mark the range and outer limits of the possible. At one university, an able scientist was needed to revigorate a department; vacancies were to be filled and new laboratories to be built. The right man was found but not appointed, because his demands included: a salary at the top of the scale, supplemented by the amount the government would have added for summer work on a project, *plus* $6,000 for serving as chairman, *plus* a $6,000 consulting fee for supervising the building plans, *plus* a $15,000 salary for his wife, also a scientist, *plus* a $10,000 a year travel allowance for the period of recruitment for the department.

anybody's challenge and the holder had to defend it, even before a fair tribunal. The scholar's role, it is felt, does not go well with litigation or worry. What generates the true scholarly atmosphere is a property right in the post itself, voided only by mental incapacity or moral turpitude. Therefore uncensored speech and tenure. On these unusual and inseparable supports academic man walks in freedom.

But the new circumstances of the university have changed the interpretation that some give to these terms, as well as the attitude of others toward their validity. There is a body of opinion for abolishing tenure as obsolete, and there is a widespread assumption that academic freedom is not one right but a charter of liberties giving the professor full autonomy—to choose what he shall do and when, to withhold any service he pleases, and to have a voice in all university policies.

Both views spring from the new worldliness. The opposition to tenure assumes that academic freedom is now so well established that no administration or board of trustees would risk violating it. This is probably true in the great universities and well-known colleges, which would at once be pilloried on campus and in the press. Faculties elsewhere would rally fearlessly to the victim's aid, and the AAUP would act punitively. But public outcry might not occur or be effective if the violation took place in an inconspicuous college. There, without tenure written into the statutes, a wrongful dismissal can always be passed off as having nothing to do with academic freedom. Like accreditation among colleges and universities, tenure benefits the small, weak, and uncertain.

Why then attack it? One reason advanced is that in these days, when tenure is obtained early in the career, the institution takes an excessive risk. The young genius may ripen into a dull old man, who has to be supported for years even when insupportable. Besides, knowledge moves on. There may no longer be need for a man in botanical taxonomy or historical sociology: ditch him! Finally—and this argument takes a slightly different tack—with the high demand for talent a good man need never fear unemployment. If he worries about it, it is because he is not "salable"; and besides, the scholar's life has been proved compatible with worry after all—see the practical messes they get into and out of. Competition as in business would soon weed out the dead wood and produce departments—if not universities—entirely composed of geniuses.

So far it seems clear that the majority of faculties still favor tenure. The AAUP helps to maintain it and is effective in policing its corollary, the "presumptive tenure" earlier described. That device prevents the exploitation of the young as cheap labor for introductory courses, and with it the creation of a body of journeymen who would never find permanent places in the system. Opinions may differ about the maintenance of academic freedom as originally understood if tenure should go. But it is obvious that without tenure the new interpretation of that freedom as a *liberum veto* could not last. In the present seller's market, therefore, university professors are most likely to cling, through tenure, to their freedom and their freedoms.*

It remains to say something about those who do not take part in outside activities, because they can't or won't. Some complain of being forgotten men and demand indemnity for the others' evident luck. This compensation they receive, at least in token amounts. Salaries, certainly, have risen because of the outside and inside bidding for services. Again, the government's support of science, and the foundations' of social science, have stirred the public conscience lest the humanities turn into a Cinderella. Efforts have been made to "find the money" and give Cinderella her traditional one-night fling. The trouble is that she works by herself, is not project-minded, does not *fit in*. But on strictly university income all departments, including the humanities, have proportional claims, and some disparities can thus be righted.

Even so, sympathy and equity are not enough. One cannot in justice call the general mood disaffection, but the feeling of incom-

* The pros and cons of tenure and its legal aspects are discussed in the AAUP *Bulletin* for June 1964, vol. 50, no. 2, 112 ff.

plete allegiance is catching; the search for "visibility" is endemic; every able scholar wants a show of his own. If the subject—language or literature, music or art history—does not lend itself to project-making, he wants his institute or an institute, as in the German universities before 1914. There are, of course, other outlets for humanistic talent—Fulbright professorships abroad, exchanges with South America and the Far East, or fellowships at the Ford Center in Stanford, the Institute for Advanced Study at Princeton, the American Academy at Rome, the School for Classical Studies at Athens, as well as the anthropological regions of Brazil or a set of "American" caves in Iran. The point is to change one's locus, to be away just like the practitioners in prosperous fields, to enjoy the world and postpone the encounter with students and dissertations. Who, on the campus or outside, would cavil at such ambitions when it is society that has encouraged them, largely for its own benefit?

Some effort, it is true, is made to recognize the stay-at-homes who do the most consecutive teaching and thereby ballast the balloon. Money and honor are bestowed on such men in the form of Distinguished Teacher Awards. The students feel strongly and turn out in force to applaud. The trustees are sincere in their congratulations. But the aroma of the consolation prize clings to these distinctions. Even on his own campus the "great teacher" can be explained away as a lovable man of average competence—"not enough for a great university." His counterpart, the average man of research, lovable or unlovable, is still felt to be worth more. The difference tells us what society, in its loving dependence on the new university, instinctively seeks and willingly pays for.

3 Students or Victims?

> What a blessed place this would be if there were no undergraduates! . . . No waste of good brains in cramming bad ones.
>
> —LESLIE STEPHEN

> Ah, Sir, I was mad and violent [at the university]. It was bitterness which they mistook for frolick. I was miserably poor, and I thought to fight my way by my literature and my wit; so I disregarded all power and all authority.
>
> —DR. JOHNSON

THE STUDENT AS AGITATOR

Any discussion of the students who rebel against the university as it is today can easily wind up as a post-mortem on Western civilization. There may be merit in the attempt; fortunately, one can take for granted in readers at least a newspaper knowledge of what the agitators complain about and seem to want from the institution. What is harder to do is to relate the feelings of both protesting and quiescent students to a common experience and pass some judgment on it and their respective responses.

They share, to begin with, the common experience of being young men. This fact implies that turbulence is to be expected, heightened nowadays by the presence of girls who share their views and their lives: the girl of today is the man of tomorrow. Students at universities have always been violent. When it is not politics that rouses their latent anger, it is the people of the town, whom they fight in ranged battles, or simply things as they are. The impression one gets of medieval students is of an army of tramps, spongers, and hoodlums. These traits are compatible with genius, as Villon proves, and the impression of disorder probably conceals, as it does today, the behavior of the majority.

Still, students will fight on slight or nonexistent pretexts. For example, in the halls and stairways of nineteenth-century American universities, groups would fight each other from mere contact during the interval between classes. And hostility to those who teach has been persistent. At Jefferson's new University of Virginia in 1825 the faculty petitioned the board for a police force to protect them from "personal danger."[1] Down through the nineties, American professors had recurrent, ugly problems of discipline in the old sense of the word. They were shouted down, insulted, pelted with refuse. The era of relative peace between student and university begins only with our own century, as a joint effect of younger admissions and the free elective system.[2]* Being in a course of one's own choice protected it from one's own disruptive acts; professorial safety was a by-product.

To describe this tradition of violence is not to condone it but to encourage the search for causes. Perhaps our lack of proper ceremonies for initiation into the tribe leaves the young to devise their own proof of manhood. That notion might account for the underlying and permanent impulse. But there are always local and temporary ones, and it is these that matter to the new university. What puzzles the public and many college administrators is that the young do not present a single front to the institutions they attend and attack. Some riot, a few object, the great majority pass by. No classification is even plausible: "beatnik" and "hippie" are useless terms, quickly outworn and not indicative of opinion and behavior. Some want peace, others drugs; some grow long hair, others spout obscenity. Still others would destroy everything in

* I remember President Nicholas Murray Butler's expressing surprise to me as a senior in 1927 that modern students no longer trooped out to overturn streetcars on the avenue, as he had done.

sight if they dared. Sober conservatives join the ardent petitioners for the open dormitory akin to the open town. The Vietnam war adds its chaos of emotions to the confusion of social and individual resentments, and all that emerges is an unrest which its most articulate creators declare to be without a program.

In these conditions is it possible at all to talk about "the students of today"? On the face of it the difficulty should be no greater than in talking about any large group in which circumstances and character differ. What is wanted is not a poll of attitudes but an insight into the common situation. Having noted the common situation of being young, let us go on to consider what is the common situation of being students.

The first striking fact is that modern society has turned itself over to education and created, without knowing it, a *mandarin system.* I mean by this that in order to achieve any goal, however modest, one must *qualify*. Qualifying means: having been trained, passed a course, obtained a certificate. "Show me your credentials. Where was this work done? What was your score on the S.A.T., the X.Y.Z., the F.O.B.? Any letters of recommendation? Good, but who wrote it? I mean, was he the man in charge?"

The young in college were born into this system which in this country is not much older than they, and they feel, quite rightly, intense claustrophobia. They have been in the groove since the sandbox. "Everybody to college" has been accompanied by so many organized, scientific attentions to growth and development, so much testing and guiding, that when "life" finally appears at the end of the tunnel and looks no different, the healthiest instincts revolt.

THE STUDENT AS STUDENT

The present difficulty of getting into the college of one's choice strengthens resentment; it induces apathy whether one wins or loses, for the outcome depends, once again, on the grinding of mysterious machinery. Many boys today actually do not want to be in college, regardless of their ability, background, or luck in admissions. Often they revenge themselves on the anxious, pushing parents by getting in and then flunking out. Formerly, the indifferent took studying in stride, and the college took them the same way, applying softer standards than now.* And in the past those who were eager for education found college a dazzling discovery, a new world to their Columbus; every aspect of it was the enlargement of their own wish. Today the freshman year is just another year.

The loss of intellectual revelation is partly due to the improvement of the high school and its adoption of much of the contents of general education. Many colleges today give the freshman the sense of repeating what he has learned. But that is not the only source of disillusionment. The curriculum seems to many students outmoded. They call it "irrelevant," which is a mistake, because relevance is a relationship in the mind and not a property of things. But their instinct is sound. In a number of colleges usually thought of as advanced and where the curriculum has been attacked by students, the reason seems to be that courses still promote the liberal, well-rounded mind, or assume the wish to go on and qualify, by specializing early in good scholarly fashion. These two complaints look as if they should cancel each other: what is there besides liberalizing and specializing? Most colleges offer a blend of both.

The truth is that behind each there can be very different outlooks and energies. Today, the liberalizing program that conveys the philosophy of old-time liberals is bound to strike the young as frivolously unaware of tragedy; and the specializing program suggests a faith in the eternity of conventional arrangements—jobs, professions, institutions—that the young are impatient with. They know their own uncertainties and they ask themselves: "Why should we, a class of fifty sophomores, be addressed as if we were all going to become anthropologists?—or editors of scholarly

* College admissions standards have been estimated as 15 percent higher than twenty years ago. Once in college this higher level is not only maintained but is made more taxing by the trend toward specialization (see below).

texts?" Add the decay of the teaching art to the contempt of the specialist teacher for all but recruits to his own line, and you build up a mass of discontent ready-made for agitators.

This last reference to teaching needs amplifying. The doctrines of progressive education triumphant forty years ago established in most schools the practice of teaching by doing and by discussion. These coincided with the introduction of free-and-easy manners and the maniacal insistence of the entire culture on Informality at all times. Colleges and universities followed suit by setting up as many small discussion groups (colloquia, seminars, preceptorials) as possible and by simultaneously letting the traditions of lecturing decline.* They did not give up large lectures—on the contrary, their size increased culpably with increasing enrollments—but they let lapse the *formality* of lecturing—its form—which was its principal merit. The casual style came in, unendurable to all but the lecturer. True, the old-time lecture might permit attention to wander and prevent individual confusion from being corrected by a timely question; but the structure given to a subject by formal presentation, the direct conveyance of order and connection among parts, the very staginess and rhetorical effects that a great lecturer might employ—all were instructive and are now rarely to be had. What goes on in the so-called lecture room is not recorded or supervised, but one gets a fair idea of it from the performances given at the meetings of learned societies.† And these remind us that formal lecturing had one more virtue: the unavoidable task of preparation and delivery imparted a didactic energy which is totally absent from the utterance of the man who wanders into

* The originator of the college discussion group, under the name of preceptorial, was Woodrow Wilson at Princeton in 1905. Like many another innovator, Wilson presupposed elements to work with which his own innovation helped to destroy. But *his* idea is as good as it ever was. (See the admirable little book by Hardin Craig, *Woodrow Wilson at Princeton,* Norman, Okla., 1960.)

† Even the guest lecturer who receives a good fee often gives an incoherent, improvised account of his subject, whether he speaks from notes or from a written text. The gratitude of audiences for a bit of form would be ludicrous if it were not pathetic and touching.

class and speaks from the top of his head, master of his subject though he may be in the abstract.

Nor should we conclude that because lecturing is poor the teaching art is at its height in discussion groups. Too many of them are but meandering exchanges of ill-expressed opinions. The technique of conducting such groups is nowhere taught or written down, and many professors would be astonished to hear that a discussion should be prepared in form as well as in contents. The special difficulty is to adhere to the form without rigidity, that is, without appearing to do so by stopping or diverting the conversational stream. Yet is is clear that if discussions lack form and fullness, no progress is possible from one to the next, and the idea of "a course" vanishes in what is actually a string of bull sessions.

THE STUDENT AS CRITIC

Students may enjoy these at the time; in the long run they resent the poor return in solid knowledge from their investment of time and effort. And what they may never realize is the damage caused by a loose and "tolerant" direction of the sequence of ideas. Never challenged about his own performance, except in matters of fact, the student has no chance to practice saying his say briefly and clearly, let alone learning what speaking to the point means. For these deficiencies we must blame a pseudo-democratic theory of free expression, carried out from nursery school onward and reproducing that first pleasant babble at every stage.

What the teacher does not ask of himself he can scarcely ask of his students; his self-indulgence begets theirs—the lecture, the discussion group is attended listlessly; it is an interval between the *real* pressures—term papers, examinations, volunteer and paid work, artistic and political activities, and the multiplied contacts of modern life, which cannot be avoided though they drain energy and time. Sensing this reversal of the idea of college, the best students begin to complain. They speak of the *impersonality* of the institution, when they mean the looseness of its grip upon them; they ask for still more informal arrangements, for chances to talk with their instructors at home, or at least alone and at leisure. They are not satisfied by the discussion group—it's now *conventional*—nor by the *regular* office hour, especially if it is held by the distrait "section man."*

To sum up, the student feels that he suffers from neglect. He is conscious of a greater maturity than his teachers credit him with or they would not subject him to cavalier treatment as they so often do—unpunctual, slipshod in marking papers, ill-prepared in lecture, careless about assignments—results, all of them, of the academic rout previously described. To put it another way, the student sees and resents the fact that teaching is no longer the central concern of the university or of its members.† His own maturity is of the feelings rather than of the mind, but he seeks what he lacks, and in his own view he does not get it.

After making all due exceptions (for there are still thousands of devoted teachers and vigilant college heads), the students' complaint is justified. The great shift to research after 1945 would alone modify the university atmosphere sufficiently to warrant the impression of neglect, supported as it is by the reality of "publish or perish" as the slogan of the profession. Since for the scholar the subjects of college work assigned to him differ widely from his individual research—his raison d'être—nothing unites him to his class; his link is with his few "recruits." The normal self-absorption of every able mind does the rest. That this spirit of *sauve qui peut* is not confined to large urban centers is shown by the survey made a while ago of Ohio University;[3] it is verified by every visit one makes to the state institutions in the West, especially those which have had to expand or multiply with great rapidity.‡

* The success of the freshman seminars at Harvard is said to be due not merely to their academic intimacy but also to the opportunities for going outside college walls with instructors and classmates to pursue research.

† That concern persists in the small colleges, though the best are being seduced by the idea of offering graduate work.

‡ E.g., Arkansas, from 7,000 to 18,000 students in ten years; Michigan crowded and sprouting on all sides; California proliferating campuses where all is new and unsettled, or else suddenly swamped—as at Los Angeles, where lately 2,000 more students turned up than were expected. The mood of the disaster area is neither surprising nor avoidable, and it is contagious.

Stopping for a moment to consider the institution rather than its clients, one might say that in the university old-style the split between its two functions of imparting and creating knowledge was bridged by the duty of all to teach undergraduates. Now that the world wants not just college graduates but "qualified men," trained in this or that specialty (which is always "in short supply"), the university has seeped into the college looking for early converts and counts on the students' interest in a profession to make up for deficiencies in teaching.

THE STUDENT LIFE

From this transformation come the grievances and also the changes in the student life. There are no longer campus heroes, either on the faculty or among classmates, which is to say no living models. Self-government is in desuetude. Literary and debating societies have been put away as childish things. The student newspaper has but one function, which is to denounce the administration, satanic limb of a corrupt world. Welfare work and broadcasting are the extracurricular activities most in favor, side by side with fugitive clubs devoted to the politics of protest, which brings outsiders to stir up "the establishment."

With these means students try to supply the interest lacking in their qualifying studies and to make their lives "exciting" and "stimulating." One would have thought that the present-day world was chaotic enough to provide all desirable shocks and that the university would be sought out for respite and meditation. But one must remember the sort of brainwashing students have undergone. Again from infancy they have been told that ideas and books are meant to be provocative, that speakers must be stimulating, that the best teachers are exciting; they have come to believe all this and are restless when not in the presence or pursuit of some detonating mixture. Unfortunately, most of the excitement is false and fails to satisfy; the students seek farther and, often as not, fare worse.

The fallacy of excitement is so generally misknown that it is worth a few more words. "Exciting" is not in fact synonymous with "interesting," it is usually its opposite. In excitement, time goes fast and thought is blurred. In a stretch marked by interest, time goes slowly, every minute is savored and its passing regretted. No doubt interest can rise to excitement, but these very words indicate a climax that draws its power from previous calm. Composers whose pieces bang away with kettledrums and cymbals from start to finish are not exciting, but boring; those who develop an idea from quiet beginnings to the highest tension and clearest resolution produce the greatest satisfaction. Students will readily think of other parallels from life.

So true is this that even modern, sophisticated excitement-seeking students will respond to a genuine academic use of calm, will learn the pleasures of drudgery, and enjoy the application of discipline. For discipline (which includes drudgery) does not simply prevent or restrain: it *demands;* and demand—contrary to excitement—arouses and directs action. The student is put on his mettle to *do,* whereby he disciplines himself, instead of merely subjecting his apathy to an electrode. The net result of this quieter but sterner pursuit is the *possession* of knowledge and the delight of possession, which differs radically from the sense of having lived from riot to riot or gone through a ritual to "qualify."

Nor is this all: what has been acquired with a will is always "relevant." It has become part of the structure of the mind and thus acts in every subsequent situation. That is how Latin or Greek may be useful to the statesman (if only in the way he will read a treaty or dispatch) and geology to the housewife—as an unconscious aid to perspective in workaday troubles.

The belief that a curriculum can be devised and kept relevant to the present is an illusion: whose present, in the first place, and relevant for how long? Students differ in tastes, knowledge, and emotional orientation. What concerns (or "excites") one four-year generation will bore the next, as anyone can verify by reference to popular music. And so it is with literature, politics, and the current view of creeds and crises.

If a university is not to become an educational weather vane, a sort of weekly journal published orally by aging Ph.D.'s, it must avoid all "relevance" of the obvious sort. The spirit of its teaching will be relevant if its members are good scholars and really teach. Nearly everywhere there is enough free choice among courses so that no student is imprisoned for long in anything he cannot make relevant, if he will only forget the fantasy of instant utility. That fantasy is in fact what rules the world of credentials and qualifications which he so rightly kicks against.

The same disclaimer must be made against the demand sometimes heard from earnest students that the university teach them "values."* The wish is not so laudable as it sounds, being only the wish to have one's perplexities removed by someone else. Even if this were feasible and good, the practical question of what brand of values (i.e., what philosophy, religion, or politics) should prevail would be insoluble. It is a sufficient miracle if a college education, made up of many parts and many contacts with divergent minds, removes a little ignorance. Values (so called) are not taught; they are breathed in or imitated.

And here is the pity of the sophistication that no longer allows the undergraduate to admire some of his elders and fellows: he deprives himself of models and is left with a task beyond the powers of most men, that of fashioning a self unaided. When the student accounts for his waywardness by saying that he needs "an identity," wants "to find himself," he ought rather to say that, although he has the materials with which to *make* (not *find*) a self, he is at a loss for a model and a discipline. A model, it is to be understood, is not a paragon for slavish copying; it is one image among several showing possible ways to be; it is an embodiment of "values."

That the absence of models inside or outside the university does not spur independence is shown by the increasing amounts of guidance and psychiatric help that students require. Dependence marks much of their life. In their truculent moods they reject the principle that Alma Mater stands *in loco parentis,* but they incon-

* On one notorious occasion Columbia University was sued by an ex-student for having failed to "give him a philosophy of life."

sistently ask her for more and more bounty and protection. Their extracurricular ventures must be subsidized: earning or raising the money would take time away from the work; their encounters with the police must be condoned, as in the past, on the ground of studentship—*in statu pupillari* being the counterpart of *in loco parentis;* their sociable desires must be served through a diversity of expensive arrangements; any initiative—an art show, a welfare scheme—must at once be received hospitably and made possible; and, passing over the insurance, employment, and health services that everyone now takes for granted, students assume that the university owes them the rest of the full life, expressed in a growing list of necessities, such as: free contraceptives, free legal aid in disputes with their landlords for those who live off campus, free theater tickets, free secretarial staff and *research funds* for self-appointed groups that want to investigate the mismanagement of the place. With the institutional masochism typical of our time, these requests are sooner or later complied with. One may argue whether the compliance is wise or unwise, but no one can argue that it betokens student independence.

WHO IS THE VILLAIN?

Before going on to observe the student as a graduate (and still a student), we must ask whether what has been seen so far supports the contention that he is a victim of the college he attends; after which we must glance at the riots and remedies he favors for the improvement of the university.

A victim, according to one simple definition, is one who has something inflicted upon him without choice and that he must endure. It would be too simple a rejoinder to student grievances to say that they do not *have* to endure their woes: they can stay away. They *do* undergo compulsion without choice and it comes from society, which makes a bachelor's degree indispensable for business and the professions, these being at the same time the recognized means of making one's way. College students are caught in the mandarin system. Therefore they do have to endure bad teaching, a petrified curriculum, and other marks of neglect where these obtain. To that extent they are victims entitled to redress.

Part of the situation, then, is clear cut. The other part, which confronts us with—among other things—cheating, civil disobedience, sex and drugs ad lib, the campus as soapbox, the cry for a voice in university administration, and the declaration of war against the institution as such, belongs not to academic theory and practice but to the tortured conscience of man; and although the conflict breaks out again and again at the universities, it is not to be finally judged or cured there.

To make this distinction is not to deny the responsibility of the university, merely to define it correctly. The foreign university has always been a political arena. It was professors and students who led the liberal-democratic movements of Europe during the nineteenth century. Today students still demonstrate politically, from Spain to Turkey and from Berlin to Japan.* They win concessions or are stood up against a wall and shot. But the American university has never been considered an agency of the state, much less a tool of the regime. Our state universities represent no party, and the politics of professors have been considered their own affair as citizens. What then is being fought against on our campuses? The answer, apart from the explicit opposition to the war in Vietnam, is: the whole of modern life. Not all agitators are against all of life, but some are and the rest single out detested parts. That is why they are rebels without a cause. The cause is simply to ruin the going scheme.

* The situation in Japan gives a foretaste of what a thorough domination brings about. There, students are in full control, physical and political. When they declare a strike, nobody dares to attend. The majority of the professors side with the students against the administration. Other scholars give their lectures and leave. No contact with students is possible. Moreover, specialism has gone so far, in imitation of the old German system, that even to mention a subject outside one's own is an offense. A course deals with one topic, one classical work, with the result that students in an American college that offers Oriental studies will know more of the Japanese (or Chinese) heritage than his counterparts in the native university.

If such is the students' purpose, the university is the best place to exhibit it, for many reasons. First, the university is where the students are, and where others may follow. Next, the university in its new form has taken the world into its lap and thus seems the willing representative of society. Again, the university, being an establishment, acts like that great bugbear The Establishment—wealthy, friends here, friends there, pull with government, secret links and secret funds. Since the great trusts of the nineties have receded into the mists of diversification, the university is the only corporation that spells power.

As for the animus itself, much of it comes straight out of the work of dissection that the university has been performing these many years. The analysis, the debunking, the "studies," the proposals for fixing everything and engineering every wished-for end have been largely academic products. At one time, on this very account, the university was an object of suspicion—"a hotbed of radicalism" was the cliché. But for twenty years the practical world has prodded the university to devote itself with even more passion to analyzing and debunking and planning. Little wonder that youth has learned how wicked and artificial society is, how far from reason and true science.

And this lesson has been reinforced by events seen in a certain light. "Youth is what youth has always been, eager for fine interpretations of life, capable of splendid resolves, but it comes up out of its childhood today into a world of ruthless exposures and cynical pretensions. The past ten years have seen the shy and powerful idealism of youth at a loss and dismayed as perhaps it has never been before."[4] Are these words from a defender of our students, justifying their disillusionment during the past decade? Not at all: they are the utterance of a young English graduate writing in 1928. That the words still apply suggests a continuity and a recurrence. The First World War shattered civilization, which is built on pretenses, and debunking began in earnest. In consequence the young—to follow our author of forty years ago—"think of their decisions . . . as of no essential importance . . .

feel born to set nothing right. . . . You can never get at their minds . . . [their] mentality is defensive . . . [and] the modern sceptic has no will to live."

The diagnosis is still good, not because the Second World War reproduced the cycle of cynicism and exposure of the First—students today ignore both wars impartially—but because the same light has been cast upon the sufficiently dire events of each succeeding day. That light comes principally from modern art. Novelists, playwrights, painters, and musicians preceded the academic analysts (no cause for surprise) in showing up society; and what the cultivated man and even the philistine have gradually perceived through art the young absorb instantaneously and make their creed. The coincidence that since 1945 the universities have taken up modern art as a subject and modern artists as a responsibility has only fed the fires of hatred against bourgeois society.

The upshot of this retrospect is that students who lash out at the institution within their reach are but acting out in life what their parents pay good money to see acted on the stage. The difference is that the parents probably became adults at a time when the idea of a career for themselves and a future for the world still had a steadying force. Now more than in 1945 when Gertrude Stein made the observation, it is true to say: "One of the things that is most striking about the young generation is that they never talk about their own future, there are no futures for this generation, not any of them, and so naturally they never think of them. It is very striking, they do not live in the present, they just live, as well as they can, and they do not plan."[5]

THE NEW CHRISTIANITY

In this apocalyptic feeling that the end is near, students are abetted by many of their religious counselors: apocalypses are their specialty. Hatred of the world, certainly, is an emotion the religious prophet thrills to find, and it is but a step from hating to destroying, still in the name of Revelation. This cluster of feelings (and hardly of ideas) serves to explain the mixture in many students of sincere and practical loving-kindness toward all men with hostility in word and deed toward particular men: these last in some way represent "the world." Other familiar sides of this spontaneous movement akin to early Christian behavior are: the abandonment of ego (façade, manners) in contacts with others, an indifference to clothes and cleanliness, a distrust and neglect of reasoning (drugs help here), a freedom in sexuality, which is really a lowering of its intensity and value (for the diminished ego makes all things mild), and—most symptomatic—a free field given to the growth of hair.

Parents and school principals see in this sudden capillary crop only a silly fashion, which they endure or try to curb. They realize no more than the growers themselves the historic influence of religion and politics on the hair and beard.* If it were not for the hair, an observer who had seen the campus repercussions of both the Great Depression and the Great Affluence would conclude that students responded to both exactly alike. But the beardless thirties were out to create a new world of which they had the blueprint. The hirsute sixties are out to re-create themselves without a plan. The former wanted to do, the latter to be—a free existence being symbolized by uncut hair. In the ones, the sense of history was strong; in the others, it is nonexistent or suspect. The letter of application of one extremely able student gives the tone: "I went to ——— with a scholarship in history, but gave it up because I thought it a form of narcissism suited largely to a few civilizations and an overwhelming deterrent to a finer understanding of mankind."

Here, of course, one may see again the effect of specialist teaching, which assumes that the branches of learning were created on the first day, like the animals, and in their present form. The

* See the interesting chapter with that title in Charles Mackay's *Extraordinary Popular Delusions and the Madness of Crowds* (London, 1852, vol. I, 296 ff.). For a good sampling of the passions involved, see Thomas Hall's treatise of 1654, *The Loathsomenesse of Long Hair.* And long before, the passing of the wild and hairy Rufus, son of William the Conqueror, was marked by a return to short hair, St. Anselm and a committee ordaining that "at least the eyes and ears of men be not screened from view."

student who deserted history had never been made to see how both history and the learning of history had fashioned his character, even to putting into his head the desire to study anthropology.

Still, it is good that students have begun to ask themselves what a subject does for the soul as against the professional journals. The most thoughtful put a troublesome question to the teacher who is willing to listen: since it is the university mind that has dissected the modern world, since the university is now in close alliance with the hypercritical modern art, since the university is no longer a cloister but is entrusted by society with great wealth and power, what is the university doing to reform the world—let alone its own too worldly curriculum, promotions, and public relations? At such a question a dean or president who overhears the last words may well wish that the university were once again a cloister. The "self-centered world" had its points.

But regrets, by definition, come too late, and university heads might as easily hope to accomplish the first part of the summons—to deprofessionalize and detechnify Western civilization by deliberate steps. The two difficulties are but one, and so is the students' feeling of entrapment. Nothing has been done to them that they have not also done to themselves and to others. For although it is important to understand the conditions that occasion the violence or apathy of youth—the conditions briefly sketched just now—it is equally important to remember that students have as much free will as anybody else. The environment is many things, from which some are "taken," chosen, by each living being in its growth and insensibly molded into character.

Thus the docile students who accept the mandarin system and set out to qualify are so eager for information and guidance that merely looking at them for an hour will fatigue the strongest teacher. And it is likewise evident that among others the rebellious motives are rarely pure. The idealism of youth is but one factor in a mixed economy, and what often goes with hatred of institutions is the fright and fury that Dr. Johnson confessed to Boswell in the words I have quoted at the head of this chapter. That fever and frenzy is one of the bonds between the students and the youngest faculty members. These two groups spur each other to march in protest and sign manifestoes against "the system" inside and outside the university. They undoubtedly uncover academic errors and abuses—the first-year course is badly taught, one seminar is out of touch with the field, the offering as a whole is lopsided. It is the business of a department to forestall such criticisms from junior officers backed by students. Failing this, the department must get busy with repairs and revisions after the fact.

But to believe—as the clean-up squads in their indignation do—that the evils were intended, or that the improvements will remain such, or that reform does not cause anybody unmerited pain—to think these things is to know nothing about men and institutions; it is also to lack candor about oneself.

This last point is one in which the university student's previous education has been grossly deficient. He has never been shown what an institution is and why it necessarily reflects (and often magnifies) the natural faults of individuals—not merely the individuals that run it but also and equally those for whom it is run.* The university is a good place to test this great lack, for as an institution it is uncommonly benign, indeed forbearing, and by and large it does not meet with a matching integrity in students.

WHERE ARE THE DISCIPLES?

The prevalence of cheating is but the most obvious example of what a jargoneer would call the "morality gap." Students expect honesty and truthfulness from teachers and administration but not from themselves. To cheat or not to cheat is an open question openly discussed in college newspapers throughout the country. Plagiarism in term papers, senior theses, and Ph.D. dissertations has naturally grown with the growth of the cheaters. Not all of

* A great dean and philosopher of forty years ago, F. J. E. Woodbridge, said in his valedictory that what he had learned as dean was "the difference between a university conceived and a university demanded." He was right to think it "a case of what life generally is like."—*A History of the Faculty of Philosophy* (Columbia University), New York, 1957, 57.

them go so far as to obtain their pocket money by stealing books from the college bookstore, but that practice too has become at least an available way of life. The idea of responsibility is, in fact, ill-understood by students, and I stress the word "understood." Cheating is a moral fault, to be sure, and the temptations of theft and sloth relate to the emotions, of course. But what is striking about many of the young is their emotional maturity coupled with intellectual adolescence, and I find in this a clue to some of their antisocial attitudes and demoralized behavior.

Many of them are, to begin with, very bright and quite inarticulate—the responsibility to words, logic, and an interlocutor seems not to exist for them.* In the second place, their mind is monopolized by their inner life, as in early adolescence, and consequently they do not readily picture a chain of likely events leading to a predictable conclusion. Technically, they are solipsists, and this helps to explain their attitude toward such things as library books and fines and student loans. The book they need they will keep as long as they like, either ignoring other users or coolly depriving them of a competitive advantage. The fine for keeping or losing books stays unpaid—but the withholding of the degree for debts to the university is an outrage, cruel treatment of innocence and youthful worth.

Similarly with loans: a survey at one university showed that some 75 percent of the undergraduate body took out loans in the form of deferred tuition payments. The schedule of partial repayments was absolutely clear, read and signed by the student at the time of application. Of those 75 percent, 80 percent defaulted at the first payment. Requested politely to appear and discuss finances, all but a few ignored as many as three notices. No threat had been issued; only the wish to facilitate an ongoing education inspired the administrative mind—coupled, to be sure, with the wish to maintain the loan-fund balance as high as possible for the sake of other students. Not a few of the defaulters, when finally

* As one of them said to a well-known teacher who was praising the student's intuitions and objecting to his incoherent words: "But I don't recognize the rhetoric of Aristotle you're trying to impose; I have one of my own."

produced, turned out to have cars. Some were angry at being disturbed; others cynically confessed that they were accustomed to seeing how far they could "push" any institution.

It is only fair to add that teachers will generally side with the student against the bursar, regardless of the facts. Education is more important than anything, particularly superior to money. In this vengeful belief, some instructors allow unregistered students to attend classes until such time as money turns up, when a retroactive registration may perhaps be finagled with the aid of a mendacious letter. The notion that money is not the sole issue here, but truth and probity (to say nothing of common courtesy in return for help) is a difficult one to instill into minds that have never conceived the institution which they "push" as representing the needs of other persons fully as interesting and worthy as themselves.

The same blindness of the fallow mind is found in the various modes of disturbance and destruction that student leaders devise to annoy the university and one another. From sullenness and a kind of bodily expression of contempt in class to the defacing of pictures, uprooting of telephones, wrecking of vending machines, and jamming of elevators, the idea seems to be that sabotage is a medium of communication and free from boomerang effects. If the damage occurred as the outcome of high spirits, it would at least be the price of pleasure, and its impulsiveness would save it from being a symptom of the arrested imagination. But the resolve to see nothing in front of one's face is a clear sign of the imbalance between strong feeling and fancy starved of thought.*

So true is this that the same know-nothingism obtains in situations that chiefly affect the students themselves: roommates will deny one another the slightest considerateness, it being now the mark of a sociable nature to accept everything that others do, however rude or inconvenient. Part of this new ethos is the pig-style of living, not limited to boys, and often dangerous enough to

* This malnutrition begins in high school, where certain pupils—often of favored backgrounds—join what is called "the grease," a group of refusers and resenters dedicated to failing, vandalism, and hatred of academic success in others.

bring the board of health into the dormitories of the well-to-do girls' college on the hilltop, or the fire inspector into the urban fraternity house which, though lived in, looks like an abandoned tenement.

Pondering these facts one begins to wonder whether presence at college has any purpose other than a ritual one. Nothing of thought, order, civility, or probity seems to rub off from teacher, book, surroundings, or tradition—not even the rudimentary hunch that there is a reciprocity in things, that if you step on the teeth of a rake the handle will smite you. Rather, the place prompts the best to all conceivable negations and the worst to a cheerless grind.

But that first wonder is lost in another, when it appears that the maquis and the secessionists want to take over the management of the institution. True, only a small number want a coup d'état. But from coast to coast groups of "sensible" students have called on provosts and presidents to request participation in such things as making the curriculum, promoting instructors, setting tuition fees, running the bookstore and cafeteria, choosing all outside speakers and candidates for honorary degrees—all this besides sitting on policy-making groups, from the admissions committees to the board of trustees, taking along the way the committees for allocating space, for authorizing research projects, and for making the budget.

On the freehanded West Coast, students at a private university virtually stopped classes over a scheme to permit any matriculated student to attend any university at any time: we are back in the Middle Ages with the wandering scholars, whose restlessness has points in common with our own. For the cry of participation obscures the secret will of the petitioners, which is not so much to run the university more efficiently as to toss things around, make holes to let in air, and change everything every few years. That inclination is visible in programs where students are asked for their suggestions after taking the course: they propose changes which, if adopted, are invariably reversed by the next participants, all unaware that they are advocating the reactionary *status quo ante.*

THE DEGRADATION OF THE DEMOCRATIC DOGMA

Through all these vicissitudes the observer must keep not an open mind, which is one degree worse than a sieve, but a mind in equipoise. He must not forget all experience and reflection in order to "stay young"—or why is he not a freshman?—yet he must recall his own kinds of impatience when young. He must, in short, *think*. The student's earlier schooling and the present unachieving world are much to blame; so is "the institution." But the institution has rights too—as the only bulwark of the timid, the sober, and the quietly talented. For this observer, then, the duty to teach is now linked with the duty to rescue the bright heedless ones. When they come and ask, more or less insolently, for "participation," their argument is that "we live in a democracy; we have a right to vote about anything that affects us." Then the enormities are named: dormitory rules, the cost of tuition, the outdated curriculum, winding up with: "we know who the good teachers are who should be promoted."

The conversation need not, and usually cannot, follow a logical pattern, but the topics it covers go something like this: Democracy is a political and social order. Its method and influence are well defined and for the most part written down. It is not true that there is a "right to vote about anything that affects you." For example, the contents of newspapers, books, and broadcasts—or the cost of living. You want a voice in the fixing of tuition fees for this university—have you a voice in the price of pot? Do you participate in the design of cars or the treatment of disease?

But these are theoretical considerations. What about the practical ones? You are going to remain here for one or two years, four at most. Do you really think that a large establishment (ugly word!) can or should change its ways at the wish of every college class? Indeed, out of some 3,000 of you those who want power or participation number perhaps 300. The "democratic process" you appeal to would therefore be likely to go against your present and future interests. And in the work of writing platforms and campaigning, what would happen to the work for which you and the silent majority are presumably here? The truth is that to speak of democracy in an institution set up to give technical services, such as a school or a hospital, is to misuse language and think like a child. Not even in the agencies of a democratic government is there direct democracy: the citizen in the post office does not participate in fixing the price of stamps or promoting the clerks.

There are other pertinent questions. Have students the knowledge and the time to give to administration? Once or twice, when an embattled delegation has inclined to pooh-pooh that difficulty, I have found it a clinching argument to bring out the university budget—800 pages of figures spread over ten columns each, a volume the size and shape of a cylinder block. With it, the thick memorandum file that supports each section proves without a word that ascertaining income and expense so as to set fees rationally is a yearlong occupation that cannot be mastered in a year.

Students who study cannot learn bookstore finances and dining-hall marketing, even if they are gifted from the outset with business instincts and a talent for catering. The same is true of admissions work and curriculum-making. Presumably the curriculum is made by scholars collectively familiar with what is done in dozens of centers of learning—else they should not be certified as teachers. Finally, there is the question of responsibility in its double aspect: first, to whom would student co-administrators be accountable for their acts? If to the student body, then the university is split between two authorities, the trustees' and the students'. And if the students in administration are answerable to the trustees, there seems no way either to make that responsibility effective or to save them from the imputation of being "company stooges."

As to the second or individual aspect of responsibility, the difficulty is as great. By the casual standards of the day and the permissiveness of past education, student reliability is at a low ebb. To be responsible nowadays means to have good intentions, carried out or not. Deadlines mean little and trespasses are self-forgiven as "human." Even the most earnest students do not take their own plans strenuously enough to see them through.*

Moreover, in administrative work, keeping things distinct is essential to survival, and the modern student's inclination is to mingle purposes and obliterate distinctions: study goes with eating and necking; dormitory life with sexual freedom; the Ph.D. with marriage. And the university means at once the establishment and the barricades. It is not likely that as policy-makers students would concentrate on dispatch, or regard as binding the seal of confidence in matters touching rank, salary, or susceptibilities. They would honestly not see why anybody should care.

BLACKMAIL NO CRITIQUE

It is a different thing for these same youths to claim the right of criticism. One need not be a cook to say the food is bad or a Ph.D. to say the course is pointless. Students are excellent negative judges of teaching and curriculum. In many universities they have been publishing comments on the course offering for decades, often with good results. On many occasions over many years their opinion has influenced or reversed departmental decisions on the future of young instructors. But to formalize this influence is difficult.† The students cannot know all that goes into the choice

* The following example is typical, recurrent, not just striking: at a famous women's college, a solemn delegation to the president begged for the privilege of expounding a list of student grievances direct to the trustees. This was agreed to and the time set for a 45-minute session with two student representatives. The hour came, but no students. The pair had to be searched for and brought, quite unprepared for their task. Nor did they fully understand why so much fuss was being made about fifteen minutes either way, about one trustee meeting or another.

† The spontaneous and annually varied ways of publishing comments about courses in student newspapers seem to me best. Where questionnaires have been drawn up by a Student Council for yearly distribution and the answers privately sent to the teachers concerned, the operation has tended to sink into the jargon of market research. And far from being more kindly, the private delivery of complaints to the culpable has a touch of the anonymous letter that goes ill with academic freedom.

of a man for a tenure post—his teaching if good is an asset; but there is his depth of mind to consider, his research, his age, his specialty, his compatibility—all these taken in comparison with older men on the staff and younger men elsewhere, and in conjunction with budget allocations and the strategy of retirements and replacements. To make all this clear to a student committee would require a two-term seminar, and when it was over the impression left might be that older men lack the pure heart and candid mind.

The impression may well be right, but if so the wickedness is but the hardening of the same traits already seen in some of the young cheaters, plagiarists, and fine-dodgers. I am uttering no mere *tu quoque*. It is not required of the young to show a stronger moral sense than the old, and it is not morality that is at issue, but the arrogant pretensions and airs of holier-than-thou put forward by the institution goaders. They can seize the privilege of irresponsibility if they will take the consequences. But they cannot turn it into a right to run the budget and lecture the trustees. Criticism is the students' prerogative under free speech, and they have it—though it seems at times a bit of effrontery also to claim sizable subsidies from the administration in order to print daily insults about it.* But let that pass. The "student question" for the university comes down to two points: is he primarily a student? and if, being a student, he elects to be secondarily something more, is he willing to take the risks and burdens of his ulterior purpose?

Students abroad who threaten violence to the government are occasionally shot. This is deplorable but it cannot come as a surprise to rebels who were themselves ready to shoot for their cause. Fortunately, the American tradition is milder; yet students at Berkeley who violated the rules of the university and were

* Most universities not only accord campus publications full freedom to be raucous, libelous, and obscene, but they generally set up liberal rules for picketing and demonstrating, forming clubs and inviting speakers. Taking the Columbia practice as representative, it may be said that the only restriction on these points has regard to acts that would disturb teaching, administration, or the freedom of other groups to enjoy a like opportunity.

suspended, then fought with the police and were arraigned, complained loudly of "double jeopardy." This amounts to crying in the same breath "Down with Alma Mater!" and "Sanctuary!" What good is a revolutionist who does not know what he is in for? Rebels who demand autonomy and coddling from the same public hands seem ill-equipped to take the reins of any enterprise, least of all the university they so badly need.*

There are goals nonetheless that students in their secondary capacity can and should pursue—say, an honor system for examinations. Experience shows that if such a system is not an old tradition (as at Princeton), it will not be adopted or will not succeed. The obstacle is the students' unwillingness to accept the means that go with the end, in this case a pledge to report cheating as well as to abstain oneself. From the same failure of resolve a good many plans of independent study have foundered after trial; the cost in will power was too high.† Yet the desire for "freedom" remains, as we see in the widespread demand for abolishing examinations and grades. But here again the mental confusion persists: is it the mandarin system that makes grades offensive? Then why not denounce it? To attack grades as "tyranny," and to think anything achieved by changing A, B, C, F to "Distinguished," "Good," "Passing," and "Failure" is to ape the advertiser's soapy mind.

* Apropos of revolutions, it is interesting to compare with the current outcry the words of a college graduate of 1795, also addressing his Alma Mater on the subject of discipline. "Our own interest and [that] of society have taught us that government must be executed with firmness and decision as well as with tenderness and care. Had this been otherwise, you might have possessed our love, but not our respect. We might have considered you good men but not as good teachers—we might have regarded you in your private but not in your public capacity." Daniel D. Tompkins (later Governor of New York and Vice-President of the United States), in *A Columbia College Student in the Eighteenth Century,* ed. R. W. Irwin and E. L. Jacobsen, New York, 1940, 59.

† In a large midwestern university a class of 300 in the philosophy of education was asked, after complaints on their part, whether they did in fact want to take the responsibility for their own work—reading, research, and preparation for a final "exit" examination. Ten hands went up.

About examinations students would have a good case if they analyzed the absurdity of the so-called objective, multiple-choice type. But proper examinations teach and train and belong permanently to the instructional art. To associate hostility to examining and grading with democracy and the dignity of man is absurd—unless these words merely cover up the love of ease. And this last motive is certainly not always the one at work, for at times students undertake self-policing to gain a point such as extended visiting hours for the opposite sex, and they then conduct tribunals and impose sentences that would make Torquemada squirm. Here the end has blotted out all care for the means, which have become a heady game. At neither extreme is constructive responsibility to be found, for lack of an *intellectual* component among the youthful emotions—hope, wrath, fear, and love of freedom.

One concludes that the "democratic process" and "participation" are not really at stake. One does so reluctantly, because the parallel between events on the campuses of the country and in the streets of cities and suburbs suggests that though political democracy is being flouted in both places, student unrest has only followed the pattern of the moment; and its adoption of protest "at large" expresses the malaise of futility rather than a passion for reform.* Believing that, as things are, change is impossible and the individual powerless, the recourse is to the blackmail implicit in a strike. Now, a strike presupposes, and in a sense confirms, the status of nonparticipant in policy; one does not strike against a body of which one is a member. And a strike has goals that can be stated.† But in their sit-ins, blocking doors, vilifying persons, and broadcasting obscenity, the campus agitators are only enlarging the tactics of the enfant terrible, whose chief trait is that he does not

* Student reply overheard as the campus canvasser was starting to explain what the petition to be signed was about: "Never mind. If it's a protest, I'll sign it."

† The student strike has a long tradition, ratified by high authority, as when Pope Gregory IX in 1231 permitted a *cessatio* if any injury to a student or his unfair imprisonment were not indemnified upon due representation.

quite know what he wants, though his desire to "see how far he can push" is shrewd and strong.

The condoning of blackmail tactics within the university has obviously grave dangers, for blackmail thrives on impunity and is free to go after any gain it desires. Certain students protest against campus recruiters from firms that make war supplies; others want the university to break its contract with a paper mill, because the manufacturer's labor policies are objectionable; still others threaten disturbances if government-sponsored research entails temporarily secret reports; and others again denounce members of the university who belong to certain private boards or public advisory bodies. A delegation visits the president and says: "these are our terms—look out!" There can be no end to such menaces, and if they are in fact enforced by "trouble," there can soon be no university. Or, rather, there can develop a university of the Japanese sort, a little totalitarian state under the dictatorship of the students, abetted by those faculty members whose politics jibe with theirs.

THE VERITABLE STUDENT

Remains Point One of the "student question": is he or she at the university primarily to study? The evidence put before beleaguered deans faced with disciplinary cases after riots is that most often the rebels and propagandists have given up all pretense of attending or passing their courses. Sometimes, as everybody knows, the leaders are ex-students—or outsiders in symbiotic relation to the student body. With these persons the problem becomes a legal one, felt as awkward by the new and all-hospitable university. But contrary to campus rumor, the treatment of nearly all genuine students has been extremely mild. Probation and suspension rather than expulsion have been the penalties for even quite outrageous acts, and generally no withdrawal of scholarship awards has been used as a disciplinary measure, on the sound principle that imposing hardship after the fault has been purged would be stupid and cruel.

But the principle that university heads have not been willing to adopt is the one by which in 1772 Samuel Johnson defended the expulsion of six Methodist students from Oxford. The merits of that case are not in point, only the statement: "What have they to do at an university who are not willing to be taught, but will presume to teach? . . . I believe they might be good beings; but they were not fit to be at the University of Oxford."[6]

There are three ideas here with which modern culture takes issue, and the divergence explains our plight. We believe in a teaching magic that does not require the student to be "willing to be taught"; with us, after failure, the burden of proof is on the teacher. Consequently, in riots the institution must lean over backwards to salvage the individual dish of education that was proffered and has been kicked aside. In other words—and this runs through the whole philosophy of permissive rearing—*reciprocity* is not called for, education is a right, and it is to be administered to the passive beneficiary like vaccination.

In the second place, we have dimmed our wits with the exactly opposite idea that there is no difference between teacher and taught: they are "both students, exploring together, each learning from the other." This metaphor-cliché about the teaching relationship has done immense harm to both parties. The teacher has relaxed his efforts while the student has unleashed his conceit. Whatever faint meaning is in the cliché tells us nothing about the hard work of teaching and the folly of "presuming to teach." Any example at random makes this clear: a professor of American history teaching a class the background of the American Revolution keeps removing their ignorance, correcting their mistakes, propping up their judgments. Only rarely does he hear from a student a fact he does not know or a thought that is original and true. That instructor and instructed are both still learning does not mean that they do so hand in hand and from the same starting point. A good teacher will tolerate a certain overconfidence in undergraduates—that is part of pedagogy—but to make believe that their knowledge and his are equal is an abdication and a lie.

Finally, Johnson's dictum makes a distinction between "a good being" and the fitness of that being for a place at Oxford. Distinctions are hard for us, especially where education is concerned.* If everyone has a right to it, surely a good being deserves it more than most. To every good being, a B.A. But what if he does not want it, or wants but cannot meet its demands? We then deceive ourselves and him, at the cost of truth and fairness to others, and in the name of kindness. Laxity is not kindness, but cowardice, and it causes pain and humiliation long drawn out to the very persons being "helped."† The rest are victimized, disgruntled, and not one sinner is saved. To put it in a generality: with human beings total facilitation has never facilitated anything. Much of our collective misery and most of our educational discomfiture come from a false premise, coupled with the national vice of charitable cheating.

GRADUATES IN PERPETUITY

In spite of every mishap and stumbling block, a great many students who have or have not rioted, who are or are not made by nature for academic pursuits, pass their last examinations, receive the B.A., and continue their studies. In the best colleges, from 75 to 90 percent of the graduates go on to further academic work, for full- or part-time. The professional schools take up a good number and all are full-time. The others branch out into pure science and scholarship, international affairs, and the arts. Not all these students are as yet sure of their intentions. "A year of graduate work" has become in the United States a social form, like a shower for

* Excepting always in athletics, where all parties are really serious about what they do.

† Any experienced examiner for the Ph.D. will agree that the most heartrending cases are those of dissertation writers who should have been denied candidacy five, six, or seven years earlier, instead of getting "the benefit of the doubt" at each hurdle.

the bride. The association of ideas is not fortuitous: during that year many of the women graduate students get married and start working as secretaries to support the husband graduate student. Or both go into welfare work, schoolteaching, or some business, preferably cultural, at parental expense. This extra year beyond the B.A. encourages four-year colleges to offer graduate programs, but it occasions disquiet in universities, because of the great expense that may lead only to an advanced dropout.

The strong universities can protect themselves by accepting only declared Ph.D. candidates and trying to estimate the strength of the declaration. At Columbia, a succession of administrative devices initiated in 1955 led, by 1966, to a graduate-student body working entirely full-time and strongly motivated to finish, at least with an M.A.* Given the demand for teachers, the M.A.T. (Master of Arts in Teaching) might have been expected to win greater favor than it has. But the Ph.D. is still king and allows no rival to the throne. Except for those ready to accept posts in secondary schools, the M.A. is either a station on the way or a badge of dishonor. This last indignity obtains in the natural sciences, where the degree is automatically awarded to those who after two years fail the qualifying examination for the Ph.D.

The graduate student may or may not rebel like his younger brother, but he feels no less hemmed in, no less alienated from "the system." For he finds it duplicated, caricatured in the maze he is treading as a graduate: Why this kind of work? Why more and more Ph.D.'s? Why Ph.D.'s at all?

That octopus—as William James called it—has not relaxed a single one of its tentacles; rather, it has grown additional ones. Universities by the dozen now offer the Ph.D., some genuine, some travesties, because the college market wants the label on its faculty members, even the junior colleges.† Even in the leading universi-

* The transformation was made complete and secure by a series of provisions due to the inventiveness and patient persuasion of the Dean of the Graduate Faculties, Ralph S. Halford. (See also below, Chapter 6.)

† In weak colleges the great title is Doctor. Anybody can be a professor; but a Ph.D., like a classical hero, is worshiped for having been through Hades and out again.

ties, which have somewhat rationalized and humanized the system, the obtention of the doctorate is still an ordeal. It is costly and time-consuming. The demands are still artificial: a contribution to knowledge of book length, and written to satisfy from three to five unknown judges; written and rewritten; "researched" abroad (except in American subjects or in science); buttressed by competence in two foreign tongues (what about English for one?); produced while adjusting to married life and baby-nursing on little or no money; and all this to get a teaching job without ever being taught how a faculty member should think and behave—the whole rigmarole is as wasteful and ineffectual as it was when James first deplored it.*

Many able students still find the last step, the dissertation, beyond their strength, not intellectually, but financially, socially, emotionally. Their talents as teachers are used here or there, but ultimately in a place lower than their original worth. So far, all attempts to rescue this mass of ability by creating a new "teaching degree" have met with only small success. As long as college catalogues are printed with degrees following names, and people believe that all Ph.D.'s are created equal, those letters will exercise on American higher education the baneful influence that Lawrence Lowell so often denounced, blaming Daniel Coit Gilman of Johns Hopkins for the needless invention.[7]

For the university that "turns them out," the Ph.D. is a great expense and a great labor. Each candidate needs a sponsor, for whom the supervising and examining of dissertations is all the more distasteful that most of them are exercises in fact-gathering rather than contributions to knowledge. And with time overspent and professorial research at a premium, the conflict between duties grows acute. In the sciences it is resolved by making the student an assistant in the teamwork for the grant and letting him use a part of the results for a thesis. But this option is not open in other fields; while at the same time, in all fields, postdoctoral students offer themselves as aides, all paid up by some bounteous agency.

* "The Ph.D. Octopus," *The Harvard Monthly,* March 1903; reprinted in *Memories and Studies,* New York, 1911, 329 ff.

The temptation becomes irresistible to bemean the graduate student to a level of quasi neglect close to the undergraduate's. The maxim has already been heard from the resigned graduate student that "life begins as a postdoctoral."

But that is a partial view, and to complete the unhappy cycle it must be said that the ablest postdoctoral students, in the sciences, often think they are being exploited by the senior scientist. He relies on their first-rate work for his project one year, two years, and then will not let them go.* To the subsidizing agency he certifies that the promising juniors would benefit from still another stretch in the same laboratory; there is really very little that the young serfs can do. Gratitude and fear of reprisals keep them where they are.

Meantime the institution that houses postdoctorals is uneasy at their multiplying number, for they take up room, consume materials, and in short, generate costs.† They are in fact students, yet they pay no tuition. Their stipends cover only their expenses—nothing for university overhead—and only occasionally are they permitted by the terms of their fellowship to assist in teaching or laboratory supervision. And thanks to the understandable possessiveness of their mentors, it is not even possible to find out centrally who and where they are. It is suspected that in most large universities, particularly those with medical schools, from three to eight hundred such troglodytes lend their presence to the great work, the last offspring of the old university—or the first of the new.

* The practice in science is for published reports to carry the names of all those who took part in the work, including that of the director of the project or laboratory. Although he undoubtedly "contributed," he may not have *worked.*

† Johns Hopkins took the lead a couple of years ago in attempting a census of postdoctorals. Other universities (notably Wisconsin and Columbia) did likewise, but no common mode of dealing with them has yet emerged.

4 Administrators Above and Below

The first qualification of the highest administrator is that he should think of something which he need not think of, which is not the pressing difficulty of the hour.

—WALTER BAGEHOT

Haven't you studied chemistry? Don't you know that the air we breathe is composed of oxygen, nitrogen, and odium?

—REX STOUT

THE RASCALS HAVE A USE

It sometimes seems to a university administration that their sole business is to keep the students calmed down, the faculty on campus, and the neighbors contented. But administration is not troubleshooting, and these feats, though incessant and grueling, are only incidental. Administering a university has but one object: to distribute its resources to the best advantage. Resources here is not a genteel word for money. The resources of a university are seven in number: men, space, time, books, equipment, repute, *and* money. All administrative acts serve this one purpose of stretching capital and dividing income fairly and fruitfully.

But those who carry out this purpose do not form a single,

detachable force. It is a congeries of persons and devices. What is known on campuses as "central administration" is but one part; and its ostensible power, derived from the trustees and based on a few statutes, is little more than a concentration of *influence*. Technically, the president can do whatever he wishes, and his aides—the academic vice-president or dean of faculties and provost, the head of business and finance, the director of projects and grants (or of scientific research)—are responsible only to him. Actually, their authority is hedged about on all sides by the strength of school deans, department chairmen, directors of institutes, senior faculty members, standing committees, and campus opinion. When one looks for "the administration" at a given university one must knock at almost every other door.

Since so many are involved and the greater number are the scholars themselves who are running departments and manning committees, the thought sometimes occurs to outsiders, Why do the faculties not suffice? They deal, after all, with the main job, which is education. Many academic men, who ought to know better by now, also believe in the desirability of an administration composed of themselves, plus a president and a secretary, as in the good old days. The actual administration is always "top-heavy" and the needlessness of deans is the subject of periodic articles demonstrating faculty self-sufficiency.

The simplest rebuttal is to ask the objector "Do you want to bring your own chalk to the classroom?" Administration is seeing to it that the chalk is there. The chalk is of course a symbol for everything that teachers and scholars want, from libraries and cyclotrons to retirement pensions, medical and life insurance, leaves and promotions, advances on salary, mortgages on house purchases, and the protection of academic and private rights.

The "main job," education, also requires that courses be scheduled and catalogues printed, students registered, classrooms and offices assigned, heated, and lighted, and so on down a long list of services, useless if not provided regularly and on time. Offhand, such management does not seem suited to the tastes and talents of part-time elected improvisers, which faculty members would necessarily be. Indeed, at some of the state universities where the faculty has tended to side with the students against the administration, one cause of hostility has been that the management of affairs was in the hands of part-time deans and cumbrous committees, who simply did not get through the necessary work.

Moreover, administering in the American university is no longer the intramural and academic business it once was. We have seen how the whole world intervenes and makes demands. Anyone is free to regret the passing of the word-of-mouth, spur-of-the-moment administration still conceivable twenty years ago; but even then it had ceased to suit the faculty. They had begun to fret at the uncertainty and irregularity of the decisions affecting their more and more complicated lives. It suited even less the outsiders who were becoming partners in university work, and who were accustomed to regular procedures. In short, organization and system came in none too soon to permit the university not only to discharge its multiplying obligations but also to defend the "main job" against the onslaughts of the new society. Simply to respond is now an effort requiring generalship, and if a university agrees with President Brewster of Yale that its duty is "to make the strongest possible effort to remain a cohesive community,"[1] it must at every instant be on the qui vive.

THE USES OF UNIFORMITY

Obvious as it is that the university is a power dealing with other powers and that in its complexity it resembles the government of a large town,* what follows is generally hard to accept. The age loves casualness and hates the visible forms of organization while expecting its benefits. It likewise hates power but seeks it in the shape of status. In the university, organization and status clash in

* Of 25,000 souls and up: for example, officers of instruction and research: 4,500; students: 18,000; clerical, technical, and janitorial employees: 1,800; administrators: 780.

and over the person of the new academic man. Scientist or other expert, he is an important public figure, not easily replaced, strong in his tenure, connections, and affluence. With his peers in the same university he forms a kind of Olympus—omnipotent gods who sometimes get in each other's way.* It is logical that the professor has grown more powerful with the university's new worldliness, but it is a problem that he is less tractable just when the institution needs a more uniform rule. And to say the institution needs this is to say that he needs it too, for comfort and common justice.

The two are closely linked. In a faculty of three or four thousand persons, someone is always doing or wanting to do something out of the ordinary that requires money, space, leave of absence, additional help, or marks of recognition. It is inevitable—and inevitable also the desire to have the matter settled promptly. These desires, moreover, raise technicalities not of the university's making. The tax laws, the government research agencies, the zoning laws, the politics of city hall, the metaphysics of foundations—all condition policy, which must be administered by persons as conversant with the technicalities as with the academic goal. Hence the need for a regularity which offends the petitioner (who would enjoy being an exception), but which speeds his request and gives him no less and no more than the next man. Evenhanded justice under the law is essential, for the grapevine is always vibrating with reports of what is or is not possible, and the slightest unjustified deviation from the norm brings indignant protests or cynical demands.

Good administrators are frequently accused of wanting to keep everything tidy. The charge is correct, and so are the administrators. That is what they are there for—to contain natural chaos. The drift of life, the fact that the living cannot be lined up like bales of hay, will supply plenty of disparities from fairness and efficiency without adding to them by favoritism or neglect; so that

* This is the reason why universities and hospitals are so likely to be ill-administered. See Appendix D, No. 94.

the sophisticated saying that "rules are made to be broken" is ill-conceived and it misleads otherwise intelligent people. If a rule is bad, it should be replaced by a good one. If a good rule, as will happen, encounters a situation so unusual that the rule itself turns absurd, naturally the competent administrator will break or bend it in that one instance and note the exception, which becomes part of the rule. The art of the administrator is to maintain a balance of contrary forces, like the pair of muscles that pull against each other when we lift our arm. Only by the tension is the limb under control. To administer is to reduce vagaries to a minimum, thus clearing the path for the useful and the agreeable.

These principles read well in the abstract; every reasonable person nods assent. The difficulty comes in the particular case to which a standard is applied. At a university the standard is by definition the educational result. Suppose our earlier case: an instructor finds that a student attending his class is not registered and that the reason is lack of money. "Educational result" suggests to him that he let the student attend without paying fees. At the end of the term the instructor will ask that retroactive academic credit be entered on the books. The registrar will refuse: there is a rule against it; the rule had to be made to stop that very abuse. Muttering denunciations of moneygrubbing, the instructor will appeal to the school dean, who ought to support the registrar but sometimes will side with the rule-breakers against The Administration, which "thinks only of money and rules."

It is at that point, actually, that education enters, for the parties have to be taught that (1) if some students pay fees, waiving the charge for others is monstrously unfair; (2) registrars must not falsify records, even in an alleged good cause; (3) money is a resource the university depends on for the very educating that is invoked. Though represented here as a contemptible hindrance, money will in fact be shortly asked for by that selfsame instructor when he wants additional library acquisitions or help in some project of his own. As for the student, there are loan funds and part-time jobs to be had without twisting the simple rules of good administration. It may be red tape to go through the formalities of getting a loan, but it is graft to take the short cut connived at by the instructor.

VARIATIONS ON ONE NOTE

The example just given illustrates the principle that to distribute resources is also to establish controls. In what follows, the subjects discussed will range far from the instructor and his needy student, but the principle remains the same. The elaborate machinery of modern university administration is but a set of devices for securing and controlling the use of the seven resources listed above. Not all institutions take the same means to perform the one task, but though officers' titles and the powers and channels of decision differ, the similarities are greater and deeper than the diversities. The pattern to be described is that of Columbia after its modernization during the past twelve years; but it is not put forward as superior, except where an occasional advantage appears in the course of comparison with a score of other institutions.

The term "central administration" as commonly used implies outlying parts with local administrations of their own. Those parts are the *schools* (professional), *departments* (arts and science), and *institutes, programs,* etc. (various). Each is referred to as a *division* of the university, regardless of size. Every such unit or division is responsible to one or another dean, but one of the deans, that of the graduate school of arts and science, stands in a peculiar relation to his charges. There are so many of these—forty-four departments—and they are so diverse in subject matter that no one man could supervise them. These forty-four departments are grouped (at Columbia) into three faculties.* Elsewhere they

* The Columbia arrangement is historic, not modern: the faculties of political science (1880), philosophy (1890), and pure science (1892) embrace the departments formed at various times to conduct work in subjects from Anatomy to Spanish and Portuguese.

Further to complicate understanding, the departments of arts and science form a single Graduate School. Almost everywhere the graduate dean is an important personage, but he is not the head in the same sense as a dean of law, because of the range of work under his care as well as the size of some of the units: the English department of a university may be as large as a small college.

The heads (chairmen) of the departments are accordingly responsible for their programs, just as each dean is in his professional school. The institutes, centers, and special committees report, like the departments, to an appropriate dean. But, again, the director of a large institute is on the same footing as a department head, and the dean over that director—let us say the dean of the Faculty of International Affairs—holds a place akin to that of the dean of the graduate faculties over his chairmen: he serves as mentor, coordinator, and budget supervisor, rather than as operating head.*

The running of all these divisions alike is the combined effort of the administrative head (chairman or director) and his committees. The head of a department or institute is a teaching member of the unit to which he belongs—he is thought of as "one of us" in the great nationalistic war of We and They. The head of a school, a dean, is thought of as an administrator, and since he usually is a former member of a department, his deanship has evidently unfrocked him. The reason for this change of attitude is not so much his exercise of power as his control of money.

---

are each vertically of a piece, so that their roots reach down into the two undergraduate divisions, Columbia College and General Studies, each with its dean. Moreover, some departments, such as Anatomy, belong to the Faculty of Medicine as well as to Pure Science; similarly, most of the divisions of Engineering have membership in Pure Science. There are practical reasons (here unimportant) for these overlappings, and they do not interfere with good order.

* Attention must be drawn to one last piece of terminology that may cause confusion: *arts and science* mean English, French, History, and so on, coupled with Chemistry, Biology, and the other natural sciences. A *School of the Arts,* however, embraces Painting and Sculpture, Dramatic Arts, Film and Broadcasting, etc., and it doubtless has links with older *departments* in arts and science, such as art history, music (theory and history), and with *schools* as well, notably Architecture.

For his power is in fact very limited. He can work only with a series of committees—on instruction (curriculum), admissions, appointments (recruitment), placement, etc.—and those committees are entirely manned by members of his faculty. The dean is usually chairman of the committee on instruction and sometimes of the others, but he does not dominate them, even when he is a "strong dean." Whether or not peace in the house matters to him, he depends on his faculty colleagues for producing the only kind of success that can redound to his credit. Besides, their demands upon him are so continuous that he is probably too busy to care about power for its own sake. Finally, he has to run an administrative staff that may number as many as one hundred people,* and he owes part of his time and thought to an indefinite mass of alumni and donors. At most institutions deans are appointed by the president "at the pleasure of the trustees," that is, for an indefinite term. Deans have no tenure as administrators; experience shows that one virtue they have in common is resignation.

Chairmen of departments also work with committees, but they maintain their daily relationships with other scholars as pure colleagues, and in fact represent these colleagues' needs to central administration very much like delegates. Accordingly they may be as busy but not as suspect as deans. Chairmen are nominally—and in a few places actually—appointed by the president; most often they are chosen by a departmental vote for a fixed term of three to five years. In most medical schools, chairmen are by tradition permanent, and appointed by administrative fiat. The practice also obtains for the departments at some universities, with varying results. A head who is a fixture can become a bar to change and a source of injustice, and it is likely that he will not remain much of a scholar. In addition, a permanent chairman tends to become an administration man, which has some advantage in efficient communication, but greater disadvantage in its incitement to departmental growl-

* E.g., in an undergraduate college with a well-developed system of admissions, student aid, and extracurricular activities, seconded by advisers, psychologists, and dormitory counselors.

ing, which becomes just as permanent as the chairman.* Finally, there is the hybrid system by which chairmen are appointed for a term of years by the president, ostensibly at his own free will, but actually as the result of an informal caucus in the department which amounts to a democratic nomination.

A chairmanship is usually accepted with genuine reluctance; it is the epitome of a thankless task; no emoluments and no glory go with it; the only reward is the thought of service, and sometimes the possibility of developing or rebuilding a department along a chosen line. Chairmen continue to teach, but even if on a reduced schedule, the total burden almost always precludes research. Lately, when scarce faculty replacements have had to be wooed in person, one knee down in alien soil, the chairman has had to enlist the aid of an associate chairman, to stay at home and deal with daily problems. A chairman and his associate may be re-elected indefinitely, but they soon cry mercy and are let off.

A change of head as frequent as every three years need cause the department no trouble, but it does put on the dean or dean of faculties a never-ending duty of quiet coaching in administrative techniques. Within the department, continuity is best assured by the administrative assistant, usually a woman, who is—or ought to be—the strong connecting rod and link-motion between central administration and the particular division. She is the one who after a couple of years knows the routines and can guide a chairman, prepare the regular reports, forestall and fulfill requests for information, save time by acting as intermediary between the department and the many services of the university, and do all this not only for "her" chairman but for the department members and students as well. Unfortunately, chairmen do not always know how to choose and use this all-important aide.

Unfortunately also, this same point of contact between We and They is generally the most uncertain. Ability, devotion, and initia-

* A notable case of success under such a system is that of Princeton University, which combines permanent chairmen with good departmental morale.

tive are well-distributed among administrative assistants, but what might be called the ambidextrous nature of the position makes it a difficult one to hold and to fill, the more especially as it is not at present a steppingstone to anything higher than itself. The result is that the young women who undertake it are likely to interpret their role either as that of "girl Friday" to the successive chairmen or as that of skirmisher for departmental interests against the rest of the university.

There is no denying that cause is often given for this embattled attitude, but even after the removal of causes the problem remains how to bind the departments to the center—given a changing group of chairmen—without imposing a deplorable tyranny. Since the departments and institutes make up from two thirds to three fourths of the whole university, the close or loose linking of these divisions with the center affects budget-making, communication, speed of change, expenditure and waste, student relations, and faculty loyalty—in short, morale and efficiency combined.

A CABINET VERSUS A HIERARCHY

The connection between central administration and the school is more direct than the connection with the departments. It is also more intelligible to the teaching body, because the dean interprets. Though he may strongly oppose a central policy, he at least understands why a rule or a change is called for, and he is not, like the chairmen, temperamentally averse to forms and statistical reports.* The peculiar position of the graduate dean, which has been previously explained, makes it necessary for him to persuade "his" chairmen one by one as if they were so many deans. He is naturally more successful with those whom he knows well. If the matter is of great importance (e.g., moving a department to other

* When budget forms were first issued to the chairmen of the Columbia departments, I had an ironic phone call from a great scholar and humanist who said: "Apropos of these columns for showing the distribution of a salary according to the divisions served by the instructor, what makes you think I can divide 10,000 by 3?"

quarters, or achieving a reduction in course offering, or denying a strongly worded demand for new budget "lines," i.e., positions, it may be better for someone else to undertake the diplomatic task, perhaps even the president himself.*

This fact exemplifies the general truth, which cannot be too often repeated, that a university administration has only influence, and only so much as its few leading members can muster through their own character, background, or skill as individuals. Statements of policy can be issued, faculty committees themselves pass resolutions, and the state of fact not be changed an iota. What the university is and does is defined only through action set going by personal suasion, often against the power of faculty resistance, which is great: a young instructor can defeat the registrar and two full professors can rout a dean. It is not that nothing *may* be done without consent; it is that without consent nothing *can* be done: what is urgent, and perhaps sensible as well, will none the less fail to occur. That is why I have called this chapter "Administration Above and Below": administration is everywhere in the university, though I decline to say whether "above" refers to the faculty or to those officially labeled administrators.†

Let us assume that the faculty supplies the ultimate directives, from above; below toils the administration hired for daily execution. Any central administrator who knows his job takes it for granted that his function is to serve the purposes of the faculty—supplying the chalk at the needed instant. What compels him to go further, disturb faculty ways, or use his influence as it seems *against* faculty wishes is that he has a synoptic view over a group of perhaps one hundred and fifty divisions (counting the administra-

* Close and sustained contact helps to develop influence. A graduate dean who can meet and, even better, dine with his departments develops in them the sort of trust he needs on countless occasions. But these dinner meetings take much time and great concentration, as I know from experience.

† The solemn reminder "Sir, you may not be aware of it, but *we* are the university" was uttered by a Nobel Prize winner at the head of a faculty group when an able military organizer who had undertaken a university presidency expressed surprise that "the employees" did not fall in with an order that seemed appropriate.

tive units).* He sees how they form one another's environment and how they are affected by society and its members outside. He is thereby brought to think that he also sees where their well-being lies. He accordingly makes decisions, rules, and plans, and tries to put them to work. He is legislator, judge of the particular case, and diplomat when the rule and the case cause friction.

That he cannot "pull rank" and order things done is a phenomenon not limited to universities; pure hierarchy has broken down everywhere, even in the army. The point is not to regret its passing but to make the substitutes work. Clearly, among intelligent people who value individual qualities, the substitutes are: facts and reasons properly presented and reinforced by the intangibles of personality and the equivalent of patronage. These determine the actualities of government in an educational institution. The chief dean or provost makes policy acceptable to the deans, who do likewise to their colleagues and subordinates. The president, vice-president, and head of business affairs assist in this work according to circumstance and subject matter.

Good policy presupposes a knowledge of things as they are, and this need gives rise to the related functions of a "cabinet" and a group of offices or "civil service." The cabinet consists naturally of the president and his associates—the vice-president of the university, dean of faculties and provost, vice-president for business and finance, vice-provost for projects and grants, coordinator of university plans, and director of university relations. They meet twice a week for whole-morning sessions to which they bring all new problems of some size. Though each except the president is a "specialist" with a domain which it would be foolish for another to encroach on, they all know the university as a whole and have different sets of friends and sources of information. The object of the meetings is to bring this reservoir of knowledge to bear on each question: a scheme for opening a new scientific station abroad, a department that wishes to split into two (because ology and applied ology are incompatible), a protest from inside or outside,

* See Appendixes B and C.

a new ruling about overhead by the government auditors, and so on ad infinitum. The free debate about what will work, who will object or be victimized, and how to insert the proposed practice into the network of existing ones is never time wasted. One man alone, however competent, could neither think fast enough to hit on the best devices nor foresee all side effects.

The same group, with or without the president, meets again with other "specialist" officers as a committee on space allocation, as a committee on real estate and physical development, as a committee on university relations, and as a budget committee. These are main functions that keep the cabinet's information up to date and give unity to policy as it crosses the lines of mutual implication: a new activity costs money (budget); it must be properly explained (university relations); it requires space (space allocation, real estate, maintenance). After each step, the coordinator or vice-president for business or dean of faculties has to inform his branch of the civil service about the new rule or function and its place in the whole.

The civil service is an expanding group of offices.* At the risk of repetition, one more list of recurrent matters must be given here. It is not complete; it could not be. Its purpose is not to show again the range of topics that must be promptly handled, but rather to make the reader imagine for himself the variety of facts that enter into policy and thus understand why in the new university there have to be so many offices with specialized, unmergeable functions:

alumni affairs; street policing; architectural plans; contracts for new construction; proposed gifts; government grants; fund-raising drives; dormitory rules; prospect or sequel of riots; extension of insurance and other fringe benefits; status of lawsuits, setting

* See Appendix C for a list of posts created and new functions served at Columbia since 1955. At that time the university had no director of personnel or of financial aid and no one in the sole charge of government projects and grants. The Budget Office consisted of one man and two women, and the graduate faculties were administered—as one scholar put it—"by Miss Lucia Neare, with the able assistance of successive deans."

tuition fees; supervising standards of admission; studying effects of proposed federal and state legislation; appointing committees; issuing or revising guides and manuals; salary scale; income and budget estimates; announcements to the press; participation in conferences; proposed institutes; adding or phasing out divisions of instruction and research; allocating space and permitting alterations; planning major renovations; ensuring radiation safety, renewing labor contracts; relocating neighbors dispossessed by new buildings; holding scholars against raiding; mechanizing routine by computer; replacing and promoting administrators; preparing council- faculty- and trustee meetings; revising current budget and preparing the next; meeting demands of government auditors; responding to proposals for exchanges and affiliations; awarding honorary degrees; organizing anniversaries, ceremonials, lectureships, and other public functions.

THE UNSHAKABLE CURSE OF MEETINGS AND DATA

These and similar matters fall into five kinds, which are precisely the ones brought together in the cabinet: (1) instruction and educational administration; (2) business and finance; (3) scientific affairs and sponsored research; (4) university relations (with its own constituency and with the outside); (5) development of new undertakings and coordination over-all.

Since these categories cut across all the divisions of the university, some way must be found to bring the divisional heads into the circle of counsel. With the school deans, this is easy. A monthly meeting with the president and cabinet, immediately after the trustees' meeting, disseminates a large amount of information; fortnightly meetings of this same group with the dean of faculties, and individual conversations between a cabinet member and the officer concerned take care of more particular things.

With the department and institute heads the situation is more complex. The University Council brings together four times a year the body of deans, the cabinet, and a group of civil service heads, together with an elected faculty group that also meets separately as the President's Advisory Committee of the Faculties. This committee, like the council, may discuss any matter and send recommendations to the president. At the council meetings the president and his aides report on important issues as fully as time permits. Yet the faculty contingent has the feeling that much of the agenda is "boilerplate" requiring only a perfunctory vote, and that there is no time for the "real issues." The mood persists and leads to the demand for "participation" that I take up below. Here it must be said again that the difficulty is not one for universities alone—all large organizations experience it.

What about the civil service itself—how does it keep itself abreast of policies and contribute its share of wisdom to the whole? The fifty or more offices fall into two groups—those supporting chiefly the educational side and those supporting the business side and physical plant. The heads in each group (or of any subgroup) meet with one or another top officer. The educational group meets with the provost.* Business and finance officers meet with the business vice-president, or the controller, or the director of buildings and grounds. All told, the sum of meetings is great, and critics say that they waste time. But busy people, as these administrators are, do not long tolerate useless meetings. What must be reckoned up is not the hours spent in meetings but the ratio between those hours and the time that would be needed to disentangle snarls if everyone went ahead as a solo player.† Obviously, the frequency of meetings must find an upper limit, which is related not so much to the size of the institution as to the number of *aspects* that each individual presents: e.g., professor,

* The title of provost means different things in different colleges and universities. Often he is simply the dean of faculties, that is, the president's aide for academic affairs. At Columbia the title recognizes the need for that educational officer to be also in charge of the practical means supporting education. The provost is therefore chairman of the budget committee and supervisor of all the offices that serve the departments and schools—registrar, admissions, bursar, etc. See the organization chart in force from 1958 to 1967, Appendix A.

† One example of the value of meetings was the improvement in cooperation between administrative assistants and other university offices from the moment an assistant provost was assigned to meet with these assistants regularly and listen to their excellent suggestions.

taxpayer, government grantee, state resident, insured for medical and other risks, and so on. Each aspect determines wants, which translate themselves into administrative decisions, classifications changed, actions carried out, and records stored and retrieved.

Surveys of fact are not easy in an enterprise which does not buy and sell and where the main product has no weight or size. "What is what" cannot even be ascertained by asking the person involved, either because it would offend or because he cannot be expected to give away his friend or his group. For such facts administration must once more rely on the wide acquaintance and observant judgment of its deans.

Still, many facts are plain enough and can be counted. The old university was in no way equipped to collect and keep up to date masses of names, figures, and averages. Nowhere was it in greater need of modernizing than in the sector pretentiously known as "institutional research" and more simply as Facts and Figures. The advent of the computer brought new hope, although installing it is a cataclysm. First, the current information must be reduced to system, in order that the several aspects of, let us say, each student may be captured, glued together, and sent from office to office via one computer card. This one achievement takes several years of toil, beset by error, complaints, and high costs.

Then, as soon as current figures are available, the desire is for norms, which means obtaining comparable data for past years. Now, things shift from year to year and nothing turns out comparable. That is virtually a definition of life, and it is brought out by the computer's unbending principles. Judging from noncomparability, life at a university is uncommonly lifelike. Add to this travail of computerizing the traps created by natural ambiguities (e.g., is a prize fellowship to a graduating student to be included in student-aid funds?),* and you may gauge the impediments in the

* This example is among the simplest. But to take the variety of grants and gifts: with and without strings, or required reports, or obligation to return balances, or fixed or flexible uses, and then frame distinctions among them so as to add like to like is a puzzle for philosophers.

way of finding out with reasonable exactitude what goes on. The gross effects are clear enough; but if policies are to fit a changing reality, each type of situation must be defined by some features that are characteristic and computable.*

PRESIDENT AND TRUSTEES

Easy access to the mountain of facts becomes more and more needful as universities discover that they are unable to settle down to a certain size and shape. Growth keeps on, whether or not maturity is reached, and the notion of optimum proportions flickers ahead like a will-o'-the-wisp. Facts and figures are thus needed in hopes of planning the stages toward the remoter unknown.

Doing so is imperative, because the unchecked momentum of one part can easily bring it into collision with another and topple it over. To take a simple example: if undergraduate enrollments are to be increased, the laboratory work in science calls for an increased enrollment of graduate students to serve as laboratory assistants. Therefore laboratory space must be enlarged to accommodate not one but two groups of students. Nor is this all. The graduate students will draw on the teaching of additional senior professors, who will need office space for themselves and an increased clerical staff, to say nothing of lurking postdoctorals and extra equipment for research. Hence, quite apart from dormitories and meals, fifty more freshmen a year spells multiplied rather than added persons, square feet, dollars, recruitment, government research, and incremental administering time and costs.

For this sort of planning, a university coordinator, an office of planning, and outside consultants do not quite suffice, because every division is affected not merely in physical and financial ways

* Beginning in 1960 with the conversion at Columbia of the registrar's records to punched cards, the progress of computerizing and "administrative data processing" (systems analysis and programing) had gone far enough by the spring of 1967 to permit the installation the following autumn of a so-called "System 360," which should gradually assume all the tasks of storing and organizing numerable facts.

but also in educational and emotional ways. Where are the new freshmen, the new instructors coming from and going to? What inducements will be offered them and what changes in the relative weight of existing divisions will this augmentation occasion? These are "political" questions, and nothing less than a committee of deans, sitting with central administration and speaking for their faculties, can settle them.

Ultimately, of course, all responsibility rests with the president. He makes up his mind on the strength of what is told him by his cabinet and planning committee, on the basis of computer figures, on the arguments and memoranda that come to him from every authorized or self-appointed adviser. Decisions involving large sums, building plans, and new units go to the trustees for approval; but only he decides what he can and cannot take to the trustees. Almost always their consideration of the proposal follows and rewards his thorough study of its merits.

The president has himself been an object of study since the new university began to show its spots. He has been termed "demoted" from educational leadership to various roles deemed odious: a public relations man, a fund-raiser, a bureaucratic troubleshooter. He has been declared obsolete, called absentee landlord and traveling salesman. The truth is that as in every institution the tone and style of the university always depends upon the head. He does not have to hold Napoleonic reviews and shake the private's hand in order to communicate his presence and control. The president's grasp of what goes on and his guess at the future filter down through his inescapable contacts and conversations with senior men in both administration and faculty. The cabinet and the council know his mind and, being heads of large sectors, his half dozen aides rely for effectiveness on his backing, even when there is no time to ask for it or he is not there to give it. The relationship is not indeed mystical, but it is emotional. One president who, before his elevation, had suffered from vacillation above him told the simple truth when he said: "There's no frustration like being a provost without a president."

Whether or not this knitting together of influence among six or seven men is what the critics of universities would recognize as educational leadership is another question to which I will return. At the moment I am concentrating on forms of government, well aware that for an exacting spirit mere operation is not enough, but also aware that when a juggernaut like our modern university is in full career its running and steering is not a trifle to be left to chance or taken for granted.* True, a top administrator should not forget the difference between the golden and the leaden functions he is supposed to perform, but he had better not neglect one set at the expense of the other or he will soon have no university to administer: specifically, his scholars will desert. And in these days when Alma Mater is always pregnant and produces not one new birth but a litter, all the golden aims of university "responsibility to the nation, the community, the whole world" are mere hot air unless defined *in action* from day to day.

ADMINISTRATORS: CAPTIVE AND UNTRAINED

It is the presence of golden aims—education itself and the ideal of public service—that makes it necessary for the administrator of higher rank to be a university man. He must, in fact, come "out of the classroom," and it is an advantage to him if he is also a respected scholar. The first requirement has reason behind it: the emotions and standards of academic life still differ enough from those of business and the other professions to call for the ability to read the academic mind. Able executives from business or government find it hard to make out what will be congenial or tolerable or insulting to "the professors." And since faculty attitudes defy quick description, a dean from the ranks cannot easily instruct a business vice-president from outside in the ways of addressing his

* It is noteworthy that the first periodical devoted to such questions was started only a short time ago: *College Management,* New York, vol. I, no. 1, May 1966.

new colleagues. But young men not long out of college and not hardened in business ways can learn those of an institution where authority is diffuse and a direct order unknown.

The second expectation, that a dean or a president shall be a distinguished scholar, is not sensible, but it is strong in the academic soul. A faculty or school is always hungry for prestige and thinks it will get it from serving "under" a great man—the greatness being measured by a professional, not public, yardstick. The same faculty will bemoan the fact that in turning administrator their great man is lost to science or scholarship; they will resent him if he is a bad administrator, but they want him none the less. No amount of ability, charm, or deference to academic worth atones in their eyes for being less than distinguished. One woman college president who by the strictest criteria was excellent, who let the faculty alone, raised much money, and provided all services efficiently was belittled to the last day of a fifteen-year term for lacking the decorative virtues of past scholarship. This is hard to believe but it is true; it is proved every time a vacant deanship is to be filled and faculty advice is sought. The hope is that some notable scientist or engineer or humanist will interrupt his work in order to "lead" the faculty—a faculty that will thwart him as often as the whim takes it while relishing the incense of his reputation.

Naturally, this happy marriage can seldom be arranged, and schools have to make do with hard-working men of modest pretensions. What is not to be thought of, from any point of view, is the professional administrator. There have been attempts to raise up a generation of such men, but so far they have failed.* One might indeed predict that if preparation succeeded, action would fail; because the very thought of deliberate *management,* aimed at and trained for, would concentrate the spirit of resistance in faculties and bring about the defeat of the certified administrator even before he had framed his diploma.

* The training of hospital administrators is also difficult, but the greater amount of technical knowledge required provides at least a curriculum for the aspirants, whereas the essence of university administration defies analysis; it is a branch of the black art.

In truth, the best administrators for a university—I mean presidents, provosts, vice-presidents, and deans, not the various heads of supporting services—are likely to be those who are reluctant to serve. Certainly, they must not find in administration a chance to enjoy the exercise of power. Without thinking at all meanly of what they have to do, they must know (and need no reminders) that what they do is mere facilitation.

DEANS DISARMED AND DISAPPEARING

Twenty-five years ago, in discussing the academic scene of 1944, I contrasted the loosely self-governing European university with the American, which is run by a complex gearbox assembly of deans within deans,* each of whom had even then become "an overworked, harassed arbitrator, housekeeper, public orator, and employer of men."[2] Today the duties are what they were, multiplied in height and breadth by deficit budgets, proliferating topics of teaching, and faculty and student unrest. Clinching faculty appointments was described earlier; that effort, clearly the most important, is now continuous.† Yet it is but a part of the dean's responsibility to "feed" his school—money, prestige, concessions from central administration—and to keep the alumni happy and free-handed with gifts.

At the same time the dean must see to it that the course offering is adequate, up-to-date, and well taught; that the students are reasonably satisfied; that scholarship funds keep up with inflation and student needs; that the quality of applicants to the school remains high and his admissions office chooses the best; that his graduates obtain good posts and ripen into generous alumni. Finally, the dean must persuade the central budget committee that

* *Teacher in America,* Chapter 13.

† Offers of appointment have begun to be made for two, three, and more years ahead, the appointee wishing to fulfill intermediate engagements abroad or to take a year of "decompression" between professorships. A dean, weary of the hunt, said: "It should be possible to put their names down at birth, like boys you hope to get into prep school."

his needs are tremendous, fully justified, and not to be postponed without disaster.

In part because running a university is close to government by supplication, in part because the rewards of other academic work have become very great, at the present time deans and all other high administrators are hard to come by. The dean of a college has to bear, beyond the normal load, the added burdens of close, often oppressive, alumni relations and of student excitability. Throughout, there is ever more of the difficulty characteristic of government administration: serving the needs of invisible people—people who expect for their own benefit the exertion of a quick, sure power which they refuse to grant. In this century an administrative job is less a post than a predicament, which is why few are the administrators who work a nine-to-five day or can notice a break between one week and the next. Rather, it is a continuous scrimmage that nominally begins at 8:30 in the morning. A dean who has resigned, who is "out of the kitchen," *functus officio,* feels like a convict released for good behavior.

No wonder that entering this Alcatraz seems less and less inviting. The young scholar on the make does not want to jeopardize his professional chances by interrupting "production"; the man in mid-career has all the plums he wants and a far freer schedule;* the older man is weary precisely of the routine detail he would have to swallow by the cartful. It is a tribute to the academic world that able persons still recognize the importance of "deaning" and make their long or short sacrifice to it.

Even scarcer than deans are the candidates fit to head the business side. In the commercial world, the able ones can command three times the salary that the university can offer; in the university, those less than able are a menace. A lucky chance will sometimes bring to such a post a man with the requisite qualities

* One inducement to this group has lost much of its strength: formerly the difference between a professor's salary and a top administrator's was as 1 is to 1.5, the higher entailing eleven months' work and no leaves. Now that the professorial scale has gone up and that research money is to be had for summer work, it often happens that professors earn more than administrators.

who is early-retired from his own business and public-spirited enough to wrestle with university finances. The effort calls for a willingness to learn intricacies quite different from those of the most complex business,* and to deal with a bewildering number of persons who are not at their best in money matters. It takes a good man at least two years to learn his university.

At other times it is possible to raise a younger man from a subordinate office—bursar, projects-and-grants, registrar, budget director—to the post of vice-president for finance, of business manager, or of controller. Such a person has rather little to learn. But the occurrence is rare, and what the market offers is a succession of men whom industry has consigned to the second or third rank and who hope for the dignity of a headship in what they think is a less exacting place. That hope is a delusion. Such men tend to be far less businesslike than the deans, provosts, and department chairmen; they learn little or nothing, and soon the main functions from payroll to budget to government contracts develop occlusions that the educational administrators must help clear up.

The remedies for this shortage of men are few. The only source of adequate talent is the one that was tapped for the first time not long ago by an astute university president: he offered five-year terms to a group of quite young men who had proved themselves first-rate in the middle management of small or medium-sized firms. Their shift to the university was a promotion in salary and responsibility, and they cleaned up in a few years the encrusted routines of their predecessors. They can shortly leave the academic world with titles and records worth the attention of important businesses—particularly if the trustees of the university help with emphatic recommendations.

THE SECOND LAYER

Critics of university management have sometimes said that it is too thin at the top, to which some institutions have responded by

* See Chapter 6.

appointing vice-presidents freely, as in a bank. Public relations, alumni affairs, development (i.e., fund-raising), arts, science, professional schools, affiliates, and what not other divisions, natural and artificial, have been set up as bailiwicks for those new chiefs to run. Under this system each man obviously has less of a load—except the president or provost who must coordinate these satraps. If no attempt is made to knock their heads together for unity, the jurisdictional snarls soon threaten to compromise the entire administration in the eyes of the faculty, ever ready to damn the whole for the failure of any of its parts.

What is in fact needed is not more policy-makers and treasury-raiders, but a more numerous and knowledgeable group of aides to the members of the cabinet, each of whom needs to have facts gathered, requests digested, replies drafted, and an eye kept on the maturing of pending matters. Such assistants could subdivide (without partitioning) their principal's domain, and could in his absence act with increasing responsibility on the many questions that recur and are subject to rules.

Faculty members, it is true, tend to go to the top for every request and on every impulse. It is important that they should continue to feel they have access to the president. But if he is known to be a great traveler, or if for good reasons he is being protected from visitors, then the vice-president, provost, or dean of faculties is the target, and the consequence is only slightly less detrimental. After a while all things, including a request for a new desk lamp, will come to the provost.

It is not hard, however, to persuade most persons on a campus, that there are other channels than the one they have dug for themselves. For regular matters they can get regular service from someone other than the head of the line, from a junior who sees a career in university administration, who is intelligent, diplomatic, and well-paid, who will accept training right down to the kind of phraseology he should use in drafting agendas, and who thrives on a steady enlargement of his responsibilities, without wanting to exert a power that his principal himself has not got.

If caught young, such men can become top civil-servants and be accepted as professionals without being scholars; they can enjoy a prestige of their own and share fully in the amenities that are widely believed to adorn campus life; and they can do more than any other agency, human or electronic, to render efficient the workings of the great machine. The only hazard is making them acceptable to the faculty. The best way is to let them emerge gradually, Cheshire cats in reverse, from behind the figure whom their work is to support. One phone call routed to them because old X is absent and deftly handled by young Y will create a happy precedent: the assistant is not only affable, he seems to know, he suggested a course of action, he offered to get it approved and to call back, he *did* call back!—the whole thing settled within an hour and without the scholar's stirring from his office, instead of having to wait for an appointment and spend forty-five minutes in preliminary chitchat and three iterations of the little problem.

Moreover, if vice-president X suddenly has the stroke he is entitled to and is out for six weeks, young Y can carry on and keep the paper work moving.

The value of the "second layer" would be enhanced if on its side the faculty would yield to fate and learn to make use of its own nearby helpers. I mean the typists, clerks, and others who form the departmental and school secretariats. The faculties, which are afraid that the Managerial Revolution will usurp their role in the university, would do better to lead a Clerical Revolution of their own, by delegating much of the nuisance work they resent yet persist in doing. All their smaller wants could be transmitted by a clerk instead of pursued by the scholar himself champing at the telephone. That scholar, these days, refuses to read mailed notices, even when they offer him free parking: let them be read by the administrative assistant and the facts relayed by her at an opportune moment—and so on. In time, too, the prejudice against dictating equipment and a secretarial pool could be overcome, and the chore of writing dozens of letters of recommendation thereby lightened. Until now it is only departments of science which, under the burden of government-sponsored work, have accepted the clerical revolution. That might be an argument for spreading government contracts to all units, for education's sake.

MERITS OF THE WRITTEN WORD

The organization of a civil service presupposes the existence of set procedures, and "set procedure" means "rules written down." Much as faculty sentiment favors informality, it will no longer work. A codification of practices and a shelf-ful of handbooks are indispensable. The questions they answer are multitudinous: Is a faculty member insured for air travel while on university service? How is service in this case defined? How soon after a sabbatical leave can he take an unpaid one? What secretarial help is he entitled to, in the regular term and in the summer? Whom should he call, other than the president, if he loses his office key?*

Those who contrast printed rules with the simplicity of an unwritten "British constitution" commit the fallacy of assuming in their scheme something that is not to be had. Reliance on custom works admirably when everyone remembers what the custom enjoins and never dreams of breaking it. In the catch-as-catch-can mobility of the present day neither condition holds. There are too many newcomers and the oldest living inhabitant has just left. False impressions and strong desires pulverize precedent and produce instead inequity and indignation. Chaos is near when cases are numerous, endlessly varied, and dealt with by persons acting only under general instructions.†

Nor is this all. When no rules are on record, the time spent in explaining, weighing, giving decisions, over and over again by word of mouth is pure waste. The *Faculty Handbook* takes three pages to

* See Appendix C under Documentation for a partial list of the written materials that Columbia University, starting from scratch, found it necessary to produce in the twelve years of its modernization.

† The advent of government regulations in campus activities, from student loans to faculty travel allowances, has begun to familiarize the community with the inevitability of system.

describe the three kinds of leaves, their allowable frequency and postponement, and the salary, tax, and fringe-benefit consequences attached to every option. Since in an average year there is a total of 145 leaves, some for one term, some for two, some with salary, others without, and still others of a special kind known as Exemption From Teaching Duties; and since moreover the plans of a good half of the leave-takers change—some more than once—as to the time and length of these leaves,* it is obvious that the clear choices offered by the code help rather than hinder decision, while also guaranteeing fairness at any time and from year to year.

To be sure, fairness does not always seem important to an applicant who claims dispensation. He argues that giving him a special privilege takes nothing away from anybody else, and that the administrator is only standing on a technicality for the pleasure of saying No. The answer is that all arrangements in social life are technicalities; the right of property is but a legal fiction. Hence what must be looked at is intention and results. The rule against two-year leaves protects graduate students against being stranded for two years by their sponsors, or new students being drawn to a department by the name of a scholar who will not be there. So the "technicality" amounts to a safeguard against educational fraud. Rules and institutional integrity are complementary.†

Two other advantages follow from the existence, not merely of written rules but of guides to services and policies. The ability to

* The late announcement of faculty fellowships and grants—Fulbright, Guggenheim, etc.—contributes to the apparent shilly-shallying. Shifts in departmental plans also lead a man to postpone or anticipate his leave. Now that the terms are stated and known, the attempts to break the rules for purely self-seeking reasons are very few.

† This obvious principle is illustrated by another frequent summons to overlook "technicalities." A distinguished scientist who values the services of a research assistant hired on government grant will request for him a professorial title: he is said to have equivalent qualifications, though he does not want to teach—perhaps cannot—and has not been chosen by any department. The title is denied and expostulation begins: "What's a title, after all?" Obviously it's something important enough to be asked for; and if it is given indiscriminately to nonteachers, who will be the first to complain? Those whose own professorial titles will have been debased by the common report: "at X university anybody and everybody is a professor."

turn at once to the right spot where the desired good is being administered fosters the sense of institutional cohesion, brings the university as an active presence into the individual consciousness. The printed list of benefits reminds the beneficiary of the reason for administration and suggests the continuity of the relationship between him and it. Likewise, when he adheres to Faculty Rules and Departmental By-laws, he is not only spared repetitious decisions about voting rights and committee structure, but he is given a sense of an organism with a life and traditions not dependent on whim, his own or anybody else's. Such rules prevent factionalism and usurpation and they help maintain a modicum of uniformity.

But the rules must be good, that is, they must fit the actualities and be readily revised to do so; they must be as few as possible; and they must be couched in the language of declarative sense, not of intricate compulsion. When of this sort they help the administration too by showing where gaps in policy still exist. The persons milling around a modern university are of many kinds—they are "populations" with distinct wants.* Until the kinds are recognized, defined, and assigned different obligations and privileges there are always people who risk being *heimatlos*. They may find themselves overcharged in tuition, denied library or other privileges, or caught in contradictory and unexpected demands for the degree sought. Only a systematic survey of the registrar's rules and a continual filling in of the lacunas created by new programs will avert embarrassment or hardship. The same is true of employees: they must at each grade receive uniform benefits and know that the rule is strictly kept. Personnel policy, which is an old story in business, is relatively recent in university administration.

It is in the keeping of rules by exact reference to the facts of the individual case that the computer comes into its own. It unites the

* To give a few examples at random: students on the GI Bill of Rights; Naval ROTC students; undergraduates and others who follow a partial program by agreement with an affiliated institution granting the degree; "visiting scholars"; summer "auditors" with library privileges and no credit in audited courses, etc., etc.

aspects of the person which in the past kept straying on innumerable forms.* Its only danger (and it is a very great one) is that the ability to correlate many kinds of information tempts to the production of computer reports so voluminous and detailed that the official who thinks he needs them is buried rather than informed.

THE BLISS OF IRREGULARITY

Rules and forms unquestionably confine the free spirit, and the very mention of them is odious to the cultivated mind. That is why in the university there is an ever-present tendency to flee the center and take refuge in some irregular grouping and share the joys of nonorganization. It is hard not to feel instinctive sympathy with this desire. It is the longing for a college in which the porter at the gate, who knows everybody by sight, is the central administration. But the simple life does not go with large aspirations in the midst of an industrial state. The professor was really free when his sole links with the university were his students and his pension: but then he did not ask for anything else; he did everything for himself.

What rules cannot do is to make alike what is radically unlike. In most universities it is difficult to set norms that will apply as well to the laboratory sciences as to the "reading departments." It is also difficult to put into words the institutional behavior of doctors: the medical school is unassimilable, and so to a lesser degree are the Schools of Social Work, Journalism, and the Arts. Exceptions have to be made: exceptions are made.

For different reasons, institutes, centers for regional (area) studies, and other programs cutting across departments tend to develop a unity that resists the idea of a wider common law. And at times all the divisions would like to be self-governing and mutter

* It can also make successive actions continuous and rapid. Thus on a "360" system, an authorized person can type out a purchase order on a machine connected with the central and thereby have the check drawn, the account debited, and a "tickler" provided for verification when the merchandise is delivered.

about secession. This is the nationalism that has spawned in the world 130 sovereign states and would split off from the old Western nations one small province after another. Many, perhaps all, groups nowadays are haunted by the dream of being able to act exactly as they want. The dream is a trap, because the desired freedom smuggles out with it all the former benefits of dependency. Just as the small state expects to be defended by the bigger powers while defying them with impunity, so the small group in the university wants the corporate prestige and services while running its own affairs unsupervised. No scheme will make such an anti-reciprocal relationship anything but unworkable in the adult world. It is sometimes tolerated in adolescents within the family.

Restlessness is, naturally, not stopped by arguments. Sometimes a high efficiency in central administration abates it. But nearly everywhere the outlet demanded and discussed is Participation. We have seen how far university administration is even now diffused among the schools and departments and their members. The work they do is no make-believe. Through the men they appoint, the students they admit, and the programs they approve, the faculties make the university or the college what it is. No one tells them what it should be. In addition, as we shall see in Chapter 6, they press in utter freedom for the money they think they need, and make their case before a committee that shares their professional outlook and studies the facts with scholarly care. All this is surely policy-making; it is unmistakably administration from on high.

Yet many members of faculties want also to have a hand in the work of the nether regions. Something occurs that affects a department or an important member of it, and the cry is raised that the faculty has been dispossessed of its ancient rights. Suddenly, the good old prewar times (1941? 1917?—or 1898?) are appealed to, because "without faculty consent" a parking lot will be built upon, a fund-raising campaign instituted, or the academic calendar modified. Sometimes the questioned move has been submitted to a faculty or council meeting that the protesting member did not attend—or did not attend *to*. But often there has been no formal consultation, and the issue is whether the faculty should not hear and discuss everything that affects it.

THE LIMITS OF DEMOCRACY

The case for student participation in university government was taken up in the previous chapter. Is the faculty differently situated and qualified? As to that, certain distinctions must be made. There is a kind of canvass already well established in university practice: where new faculty housing should be built, whether a second nursery school would serve the needs of faculty children, how much more parking space must be found—all such questions are submitted to referendum as a matter of course. But there are many less personal matters that administration takes to the constituency too: whether an affiliated institution should become part of the corporation; whether a program of foreign exchange should be started, or the expansion of a professional school allowed, or the offer of an endowed chair accepted. All these possibilities are discussed at length with the appropriate dean or chairman, who invariably consults the persons affected. No institute or program is either set up or "phased out" without long consultation, in which the interested faculty groups are often supplemented by wise men from neighboring divisions. What is not done is to bring in the entire faculty of a school, or some vast senate representing the whole university, to pass upon each such step.*

To be sure, there are many matters—more each day—in which the central administration feels it necessary to restrict discussion to the cabinet. The budget directives, the buying of land and buildings, the dickering with city, state, and federal governments, the progress of talks with a donor or foundation, the award of prizes, the strategy of labor disputes and legislative lobbying—these and

* In some universities, most often state universities, a string of committees and a senate receive notice of such proposed actions, and when the campus is not agitated by some public issue tangential to the actions, a rubber-stamp approval is given.

other matters are kept confidential until near the end. If this is not done, within twenty-four hours of the first tentative idea headlines appear in the local press, and approval mixed with protests is voiced even before the outline of the project is firm in the minds of the proponents. One absolute in university administration is that otherwise honorable faculty members cannot be trusted with certainty to keep a secret, even after pledging to do so.*

When allowance has been made for confidential negotiations and for subjects that faculties regularly discuss, there remains a range of topics that they periodically feel an urge to claim jurisdiction over: tuition rates, salary scale, fringe benefits, acceptance or rejection of gifts, corporate and other affiliations—anything that can even remotely be thought of as modifying the life of the individual or the institution. This cry of "participation" often goes up when a faculty member receives an offer from another university and is made privy to its plans. Why has he never heard of the plans at home? He goes to his dean or to the dean of faculties and asks for a blueprint of his future and the university's. He may add that all his colleagues should know too, as they necessarily would if all decisions were put back in their hands. "Why, the first time I heard about the new way of charging graduate tuitions was when a student brought me the notice!"

He is right on both scores, and he deserves an explanation of why things happen as they do. It is logical that the university which invites him should have plans, for it is rebuilding a depleted department and getting him is part of those plans. His present department does know that retirements will occur in two, three, or five years, at which times promotions or replacements will be called for; but right now there *are* no plans, there being nothing to plan about. The university planning committee concentrates on those parts of the whole that need attention, and for the very sake

* This incontinence is especially deplorable in the conduct of ad hoc committees on tenure, when the candidate gets to learn who has said what about his merits. Often, too, students hear the opinions of their examiners in Ph.D. orals. The academic stuffiness of an earlier day had some merit.

of planning, i.e., controlled change, it seeks stability in parts that need not change: the goal is optimum enrollments and staffing, not expansion for the fun of it. Plans must not simply reflect an endemic restlessness; they must turn it into energy by containment.*

Still, shouldn't the whole faculty participate in all broad policy matters as they arise? Then the faculty as a vested interest would not cry out when tuition goes up or is differently assessed, when a school is permitted to expand or is added to the galaxy. To entertain this suggestion is to lack the concrete imagination of what has to be done and what a faculty can do. At bottom the faculty does not want to administer; it thinks it does, by fits and starts, when conditions are such as I have illustrated. The faculty quite rightly keeps repeating that its proper task is teaching and research, and that it must not be loaded down with paper work, committee work, and other forms of bureaucratic tedium. But administration is nothing else than these. To do any part of it would require professors to spend hour upon hour away from their books, their experiments, their students. With all that able academics do outside the university as consultants, authors, and lecturers, they would have to be relieved of all their university work, their main role, in order to act as part-time administrators. That is in fact what is done in the short run when their knowledge proves essential to guidance: the members of the Macmahon Committee on the Educational Future of Columbia University† were exempted from all academic duties for a year. How uneconomic, what downright folly, it would be to make a habit of impounding scholars and scientists in order to use them as miscellaneous help in administration! It consumes enough of their time when they serve on councils and committees more or less directly related to their daily work.

* Otherwise the outcome is the one portrayed in the cartoon of the applicant at the employment agency: "I devised many a long-range plan for my last employer before he went bankrupt."

† See Appendix C.

If participation does not mean hammering out policy from the details up, but only passing on matured proposals as a member of some large representative senate, then the objection is of a different sort but no less conclusive. Large bodies cannot readily keep abreast of changing situations. They discuss points at large, forgetting background and ignoring minutiae. They are subject to the misconceptions that take root when many people are gathered together and attention is easily distracted. What centers their ideas is an appeal to familiar principle, moral or professional, which encourages factionalism rather than gets business done. The meetings of school faculties, usually less than a hundred strong, display these characteristics whenever a consequential issue comes up. A university legislature of a thousand or more does not in fact "represent" anything or anybody. No one can say to whom it is responsible, yet it can slow down or halt administration and may permanently split the institution into irreconcilable factions. Group prestige then becomes involved and votes turn into trials of strength, useless for administering and weakening to education. The faculty groupings themselves are not free, whether they fall into the hands of manipulators or waste their time in the politics preparatory to each drama.* The only clear result is that "participation" by such means is self-defeated.

THE ADMINISTRATIVE TEMPER

All things considered, the mixing of scholarly pursuits and administrative responsibility is not to be desired by the practitioners on either side. Scholars as committeemen are likely to become impatient with the niggling routines, as well as impatient with their colleagues; while on the larger questions both the committee and the large council are hampered by the very virtues of scholarly men. A scholar wants all the evidence before he reaches

* Detached observers have noted how harmful have been the actions of large senates in universities where quarrels with students or regents or presidents have taken place.

a conclusion; he is not to be hurried into a snap judgment.* But running an institution calls again and again for intelligent guesses and a sense of timing. One reason why administrators keep long hours and deal in bad prose is that the report has to be done overnight for a meeting hastily called to fend off trouble or seize a good opportunity. The resulting state of mind is the antithesis of respectable scholarship and science; an able faculty group will want a semester to decide what has to be done next Thursday.†

What is even more disqualifying is the tendency of many scholars to trust to what Hazlitt called "naked generalities" which can apply to every emergency.[3] The great staple of faculty meetings, for example, is to debate "breadth" versus "depth" in curriculum. On this issue good men can disagree to the end of time.‡ Such differences of opinion reinforce the fear of finality which is natural to persons who are always revising knowledge. William James vividly describes a friend and colleague in just this situation: § "He hates clearness—clear formulas, clear statements, clear understandings. . . . He shrinks with an instinctive terror from any explanation that is definitive and irrevocable, and hence comes to say and do things that leave an avenue to retreat—at bottom it is connected with timidity in him—as a *dreamer* he is bold; when it comes to acting, he-wills-and-wills-not. . . . He has too complicated a mind!"[4] Complicated minds are just what a faculty must

* A distinguished scientist who was a member of the original Atomic Energy Commission told an audience of his colleagues on rejoining their ranks that what he had learned in Washington was the art of deciding on incomplete evidence, coupled with the truth that *not* to decide by a certain time was only another form of making a decision. These elementary truths came as a surprise to some of the scholarly listeners.

† Nothing is more embarrassing to an administrator than to hustle his faculty advisory group, unless it be the need to go ahead without their advice. Thus a president once seized the opportunity at a trustees' meeting to get enacted an increase in the university contribution to pension payments, knowing that a faculty group was studying fringe benefits and would not report its preferences for three months, preferences that the trustees might reject. The faculty reproved the president, but accepted the benefit.

‡ As someone aptly said about the We and They conflict: "at some point every faculty would certainly lynch its dean—if it could agree on a date."

§ The psychologist G. Stanley Hall.

consist of, and it is no discredit to them to acknowledge that they are handicapped for transacting business.*

As for the academic men who have proved themselves as consultants to industry and government, they tend in their outside dealings to make allowances which they deny to their university. They let business people carry the burden of compromise which they refuse to take on at home. Mistaking rigidity for principle, they look into campus problems not simply with the care of a researcher but with the moralism of an inquisitor. Now, in any institution, competing groups cannot all be satisfied at once. Knowing this, the moralist reaches an impasse at every turn and agonizes over his inability to mete out perfect justice. This distress helps to explain why successful university leaders are so often drawn from departments of history, political science, and public law. The reason is not that these men are weak in scholarship or low on moral sense, but that their original choice of studies indicates a taste for dealing with human confusion in the light not of certainties but of probabilities.

Administrators of equal merit can of course differ widely in temperament and in training, but whether they come from the historical or the natural sciences, the humanities or the fine arts, they cannot long survive without certain capacities. Some of these are implicit in what has just been said. Judgment, decisiveness, and speed are indispensable. If the first criterion of administrative law is equity, then the first for the executive is sensitivity to differences between cases. He plays no favorites but he need not act like a guillotine.†

At the same time he must always make clear that the interest of the institution is as real as that of the person. We hear much these days of the dignity of the individual, but there is a dignity of the institution which sustains that of the individual. An administrator

* An English scientist put it rather cruelly to me as we were leaving a meeting of the Senate at Cambridge: "We're all terribly clever—but silly!"

† He recognizes, for example, that certain discrepancies are not removable short of a long siege: department X refuses to hold tutorials; department Y dislikes the grade of preceptor, etc. Let them!

who continually yields to pity or camaraderie, or who promises a favorable ruling to each party in a dispute sustains nobody and earns not simply contempt but hatred. He also makes it certain that the work of his office will bog down in "problem cases." His visitors come with the slogan "Go in and see what you can get." All sense is lost that the university is a creation older and greater than its members and stronger than its parts; and at that point it is indeed no more than an ill-run soup kitchen, with policy degraded to an accidental resultant of forces.

SOME ADMINISTRATIVE DEVICES

Just as the dean must act as if he were an upright judge, so he must act as if he had the efficiency of a tycoon. There are few if any golden rules in life, but there is one in the life of a dean: answer all letters within a week. A dean must be able to switch his mind quickly and fully from one situation to another. If he delays answers to requests or suggestions, he will double or triple the number of times he switches his mind to each, uselessly. To be sure, the contents of most messages are not weighty. Intramural administration is a mass of trifles, but every item matters greatly to the petitioner, whose sense of "the place" depends greatly on the way trifles are handled. And some of them matter after all: to be in a class teaching or in Africa observing; to be away this year and not next; to grant a passing grade and ultimately the degree, or the opposite; to have the benefit of a visiting lecturer's thought or to have missed him—these are the decisive acts of the university's collective existence. If they look small it is only because their effects are remote. Yet careers, characters, discoveries, and disasters are the result. The significant sum of incidents makes the educational enterprise at least as imposing as the output of a million cars, half of them defective.

If this is true, the counterpart of those incidents which are the substance of administration is equally significant. That is why faculty criticism of the administration should be encouraged. It should be precise, and it should bring into play a second imperative of deanship: full disclosure. When anything has been done wrong, or something unusual is to be done for the first time, the only hope of aid from the faculty is to take the expected doers into one's confidence. This principle does not go against the caution that withholds private or secret news from a large meeting. The smaller group has an interest in the reform or innovation, and given that stake the risk must be taken. Full disclosure carries with it the further imperative of candor as to past error or present perplexity. Don't be so foolish, either, as to give an air of premeditation to what has been improvised. Again, full disclosure means talking and writing like a man, not an official. With this philosophy and the merest restraining of others' energies great things can be accomplished, free from the taint of We and They: after full disclosure I have never in twelve years of administration found a single faculty group anything but eminently reasonable, in desire or suggestion.

Besides making headway, the administrator's constant aim must be: *simplification*—for the same reason that the householder mows his lawn and prunes his trees. It is a harder task in a university because every twig resists cutting, and even inanimate *forms* find defenders. These limiting conditions require that the dean be conversant with every detail of the structure and working of each unit. And this too is hard unless he has an encyclopedic memory and well-ordered files. To these he is continually adding his notes on meetings and interviews. It is often impolitic or paralyzing to make jottings during the encounter; he must learn to Boswellize. But he must use those notes for the next meeting, saving time by starting where the other left off.

Finally, meetings, interviews, and cooperative efforts of longer span must be *run*. There is no such thing as a self-propelled committee, any more than a report that writes itself. Coaxing and coaching are the most delicate parts of administration. Too much input from the chair will retard the metabolism of the committee. Too little turns it into a party of lotus-eaters drifting downstream. A committee has been known to take nine years to come out with recommendations for a new program and a new building that all professed to want from the outset. Such delays do not occur in universities only, but they have a better chance to occur there, because of the habitual courtesy among equals and the unwillingness of deans to risk their influence through unpopularity. This calculation only confirms the truth that university administration is a game for gifted amateurs, who succeed only if they will gamble on being misliked. It is in fact a safe gamble, because faculties have candor too: they gladly acknowledge results and readily thank the coachman for having cracked the whip.

THE TRUSTEES—WHO ARE THEY?

It seems a paradox that a regime on the whole so diffident should have to enforce an ever-growing list of inside rules and outside restrictions, should have to manage and distribute more and more services, privileges, and money. But a moment's thought shows that it is only these that preserve in the hands of modern university administrators the little free choice they have. Swept along the welfare stream, faculty and students expect from their institution all the advantages of feudal protection; the administrator responds, and governs by stating opportunities and limits: he will do all he can, but—given the number of requests, given the rules of Internal Revenue, given the resolutions of the AAUP, he cannot act as he would like. His pain is genuine, because he is still a faculty member and loves freedom. He sees that in a company of scholars the bureaucracy he stands for arouses two unhappy feelings—"why am I being treated differently from X?" and "why am I *not* being treated differently from X?" Bewildered, the wanton scholar is torn between the sense of his uniqueness, which the modern world exalts, and the lust for equal rights, which the modern world inflames.

The resulting sense of oppression leads to the illusion that in other institutions life is much freer. The administration is more enlightened there, the teaching load far lighter, changes are frictionless and the trustees a benign influence. This vision of paradise is evenly distributed among universities, sustained for each visionary by some actual feature that he makes symptomatic of the whole. Such a mood may be steady or may come and go; it is a mark of the self-absorption that has overtaken most sensitive people who are also successful. It turns them into enemies of administration, believers in the conspiracy theory of history, which they see borne out in front of their eyes, on the campus.

The conspirators are often thought to be the trustees, to whom central administration kowtows from fear and stupidity. Who the trustees are, what they do and why, is not quite clear to their denouncers.* Trustees (or regents) are by definition men of business, bankers and lawyers, with a sprinkling of alumni, all reactionary—just look at Berkeley! Yet if only ours were like the businessmen and bankers on the board at O, they would give us leadership and prosperity. This desired leadership does not mean directing academic programs, curtailing academic freedom; it means adding to our prestige by letting us engage all the great men we want for bigger and better departments, which in turn means raising the necessary money.

In this fantasy the one solid thought is that it is best for the trustees to have no part in administration. Interference in matters that the president is responsible for has more than once disrupted a sound institution; it argues in any event a lack of grip on his part.† But the trustees have a great role none the less, and though a university can be worse, it can hardly be better than its board.‡

* On any large campus, few among the students and faculty could name as many as a quarter of the men on the board of trustees. An exception might be made for institutions like Harvard, where the top governing body is under ten, rather than the twenty or fifty usual elsewhere.

† About ten years ago, the board of a liberal-arts college revolutionized itself in the light of this principle. The board cut its numbers in half, set retirement at 70, and put the president back in the saddle. The good results were immediately apparent.

‡ An excellent description, *The Role of the Trustees,* will be found under that title in a published report by a committee of Columbia trustees headed by William S. Paley (Columbia University Press, New York, 1957).

What gives strength is not only their power to attract endowments and gifts (or alternatively to create the confidence that makes the legislature willing to pass the ever-mounting budgets), it is also the firmness of gait that they impart by taking their duties seriously and serving as a final court of review. Trustees generally exercise strict control over financial operations; they are good accountants. But they often fail to inquire into the balance among the activities undertaken. Not that they should alter it against the demands of the faculty, approved by the president; but intelligent doubt is desirable, being enough to make everyone down the ladder scrutinize and make rational what is put before the board the next time.

Again, trustees have at times rejoiced over budgets that showed a surplus over the year's expenses. They should on the contrary have been alarmed. The money is there to be spent, for education, and of course for value received. A budget corseted too tight often means that some purpose or some group of young teachers has been starved, merely to show off the president's businesslike mind. As for balances left over in gift funds, they tend to dry up the flow of further gifts and to create the worst possible reputation: "They're so rich they don't need any more."

For both these purposes—review of activities and inquiry into the meaning of the budget—it might be useful to have on each board at least one notable (or retired) representative from the academic world; not indeed from the same university as the board directs, but from another of kindred type. He might serve for a set term, and be a ubiquitous member of committees. The alternative is for the trustees to develop closer personal relations than they normally do with members of the faculty and administration other than the president.

LEADERS ON REQUEST

Where in the system leadership comes from is the one remaining question. Or rather, it is a question that is asked, impatiently, by those who think that the new university should show "capacity for change, "innovation," and "bold answers to the challenge of our times." This demand apparently discounts everything that has happened in universities during the past fifteen years, and takes for granted two manifest impossibilities: one, that a huge confederation staffed by highly independent individuals can move like an army at the command of a chief; two, that a modern university can depart from practices common to its kind without loss in the competition for faculty and students.

Chimerical suggestions aside, there is a place for leadership within the university: the history of recent reorganization at Columbia and elsewhere shows it in action. Its source is at the head, and its success hinges on the definiteness and practicality of the goal. Yes, but what of *educational* leadership? Can a dean nowadays not be such a leader? What is an educational force if not a dean?

I am tempted to answer that educational leadership is for the most part an empty cry, and like "innovation" it means nothing. At the first genuine "boldness" now being called for nearly everybody would protest. And there can easily be leadership down the drain, innovation into folly.* To lead a change in education presupposes a new idea: how many new ideas are there in a century? One must not dignify by the name of idea the restless change-over of petty arrangements that prevails in American schooling generally. After each tremendous battle over the curriculum these shifts leave it much the same in effect, and the participants too weary to do their job.

In science and scholarship new ideas obviously come from the workers in the field. A university supports innovation when it supports them. It would be comical if a dean or other administrator took credit for leadership when he provided only intelligent facilitation. And it would be sad if in echo of a past era he surrounded his practical efforts with ringing declarations of progress, fit to arouse only a shrugging distrust.

* Or more often into nonsense—nonsense filling hours of meeting, reams of paper, and taking the time of people who might conceivably teach.

To be sure, a dean promotes change by his questions and his reports about what goes on in the world of learning at large. He can be a good gadfly, but he should not try remaking his school or university according to a plan in his head. Indeed, leadership by an administrator is best when it concerns administration, when it aims at greater simplicity, efficiency, and coherence—above all, coherence. It is then he serves education, not when he entertains a scheme that forces him to become a partisan. For his impartiality is his chief strength: he backs with equal sincerity quantitative sociology and electronic music, the sciences and the humanities. It is his business to serve *them,* not his likes and dislikes, though he is free as an individual to propound in print his ideas about music or sociology—or even administration.

5 Friends, Donors, Enemies

The good Lord gave me my money, how could I withhold it from the University of Chicago?

—JOHN D. ROCKEFELLER

They know not, neither will they understand; they walk on in darkness: all the foundations of the earth are out of course.

—PSALM 82

THE INEXHAUSTIBLE AGENDA

The last chapter has kept our eyes trained on those parts of the university that serve its primary and internal concerns. But passing reference to external ones has reminded us of the composite nature of the institution. On a certain day a few years ago—it could have been any ordinary day for the six assembled around the table—a three-hour session with the president of the university had dispatched a good deal of business; it broke up after each of the seven men had taken his share of new matters to deal with or look into. These were the assignments:

(1) study the offer of an estate across the river; (2) find out whether a proffered art collection (noting terms and costs) would serve instruction in art history; (3) attend a foundation meeting to learn about a project being urged on the university; (4) ascertain what funds a certain Washington agency had just received for de-

fraying the costs of construction in a given field; (5) see this year's application for federal loan funds completed and sent off before the deadline; (6) finish and send off the annual report on research to a section of the Department of Defense; (7) confer with the ROTC inspector about the changes desired in the scheduling of naval science; (8) confer with the Mayor, who wants to keep professor X as a commissioner for one more year (first ask the dean what he thinks about it); (9) look into the argument between the Z foundation and the controller's office about the financial reports so far submitted; (10) draft a set of suggestions for the immigration rules being revised that apply to foreign students and scholars; (11) get a ruling from the Internal Revenue Service about the deductibility of research travel while on sabbatical leave; (12) send wires to the Congressional committee now amending educational legislation; (13) confer with the housing and welfare commissioners on the best way to rehabilitate the inmates of a tenement lately bought; (14) find out exactly what the state law means by requiring the name of every user of a hypodermic syringe; (15) discuss with Y Theological Seminary their proposal for joint degrees; (16) ascertain the facts in complaints by the dining-room employees so as to have a statement for the press if need be; (17) try to get agreement from affiliates about uniform handling of joint appointments and entitlement to benefits; (18) decline with diplomatic skill the two proposals to set up a fund for lecture series on limited topics; (19) tell local precinct captain that university picketing rules should in future take care of sidewalk congestion he had to deal with; (20) notify State Department of willingness to enter exchange of scholars and students with iron-curtain country; (21) inform Indian center for thought transference that no member of philosophy department is now available as receptor; (22) obtain cost estimate of participation in consortium for digging holes in ocean floor; (23) notify regional director of Selective Service of new procedure for certifying student status; (24) ask appropriate departments for nominees to refill government-sponsored lectureships abroad.

These two dozen topics suggest the character and variety of the clients that the university responds to in its ecumenical phase. I am using the word "client" in its original Roman sense, according to which the interests of the client and of the patron are deemed the same; the patron offers service and protection, and the client contributes to the patron's support on great occasions. These occasions are now of daily occurrence. Clients are friends and friends bring gifts. The university has never been so surrounded by eager petitioners with money in their hands. The foundations and the government are notoriously in the business of making grants and it is a very big business. Corporations have followed suit more modestly, and for the successful citizen or his wife, one ambition is to qualify as a donor.

Individual donors are a plentiful species; if it is being carefully preserved, it is from love of increase, not fear of extinction. In all these friends, warmth of feeling is sincere and full of respect. They show a deep concern for their favorite college or university, whether they are alumni or not. They resent slurs upon it, furnish it professional aid gratis, give its problems thought, remember it in their wills, and when called up in emergencies will respond with affable speed. It is a touching experience for an administration to be enfolded in this faithful attachment, to see the light of unselfishness replace calculation in so many countenances as soon as university interests are invoked.

The relationship, of course, does not end there: it has a paradoxical outcome that cannot be passed over in any report on the contemporary university. We shall soon come to it, but to understand its causes one must first see how the university's friends, individual and corporate, carry out their charitable purposes.

THE EL DORADO OF RESEARCH

The federal government began to make sheep's eyes at the university in the forties, when to subsidize research for defense (notably the investigation of atomic energy) began to seem a reasonable use of tax moneys. The influence of academic scientists soon established the principle that the best investment for national goals is aid to pure research; that is, inquiry into natural processes rather than the solution of problems that arise in applying physical laws and effects to practical use. By now, the National Science Foundation, the Department of Defense, the Atomic Energy Commission, and the National Institutes of Health are fountainheads of money for men, equipment, and buildings devoted to pure research. Work on applied research is supported at independent research institutes, some of them loosely linked with universities but differently staffed and run. Facilities for instruction have been added to the subvention list so as to keep up the supply of scientists, and some money (from these and other agencies) has begun to go toward the same purposes in the social sciences, the humanities and the professional schools.*

The university is thus to an increasing extent in partnership with the federal government. Some call the relation dependency, but the situation is not as clear-cut as that word would imply. The government gives grants to support approved work by scholars and scientists; it also contracts for specified team projects. On these the university is expected to show that it is contributing a share to the total cost: Alma M. is not wholly a kept woman.

The demonstration of cost-sharing is complex and need not detain us here. What matters more is the other aspect of purity. Contracts and grants are awarded only after a review of the project and its participants by a board of academic scientists. The expenditures and the indirect cost allowance (overhead) are authorized by the government agency and then minutely audited by government auditors. Presumably the government, acting for the nation, obtains from the best scientists in the country just what it wants. What does the university get?

It gets equipment that it could not otherwise buy. Electron

* A number of state governments also have aid programs, often restricted to the very needy colleges and not open to the church-sponsored, which are thus left entirely on their own.

microscopes cost tens of thousands, cyclotrons cost millions. Advanced research could not be carried on without this large capital investment in machines, and neither could up-to-date instruction. The universities could certainly not have begged from the public the amounts required. It follows that the taxpayer has helped keep science within the university. For in its need science would have followed money wherever it was—in government or industrial laboratories, where keeping itself pure might have been extremely difficult.

On its side the nation has benefited from a vastly increased output of academic science. By providing stipends for graduate students and money for salaries (including extra pay for summer work), the public treasury has made science boom on the campus. A department of physics, for example, can put all its senior men on half-time, can therefore engage a second set of distinguished researchers, also on half-time, and provide them with trained assistants, abundant clerical help, and the latest equipment—all for the same purposes that a physics department was originally expected to serve: teach undergraduates, train Ph.D.'s, and produce discoveries. In the medical sciences this increment in staff and output is particularly large, and indeed the federal contribution has become the mainstay of university medical schools.

Critics have seen in this transformation the danger of government control. If by this is meant political or personal interference with what a scientist or a private university chooses to study or to think, the fear is unfounded. Government officials are more afraid than anybody else of doing something construable as meddling. Yet interference of another kind is there, the by-product of two natural concomitants of subsidy—legitimate supervision of expenditure by the government and legitimate ambitions in the science community.

Here begin the grave troubles. The mere management of contracts and grants has been for the universities an ever more onerous duty, which brings the government in as co-manager. Computing and justifying the Indirect Cost Allowance (overhead), which varies with the volume of contracts and the shifting rules of the U.S. Bureau of the Budget, creates the first great uncertainty in university finances: are we really self-supporting? Are we even close to solvent? The ratio of government money to gifts and endowments is a critical index, for the removal or reduction of federal support would knock a prop from under a heavy structure. Wise administrations do their best to keep science departments from hiring more senior men (necessarily on tenure) than they could pay for by dismissing nontenure junior officers. But departments are sanguine and aggressive, and there are universities and technical institutes where it is obvious that a cutback in government research spending would create havoc.

Meantime the calculations go on within the labyrinth of government regulations, the composite theology of NDEA, NSF, NIH, ACE, and all other permutations of the alphabet governing "Title 4" or "Circular A-21 Revised." No religious order, no single enterprise ever worked under the rulings of so many masters. Still worse than this bondage is the campus illusion (or rather, the rooted error) about the largesse resulting from the government's Indirect Cost Allowance. Professors and departments persist in regarding it as "profit" which they "earn for the university." They demand that it be turned back for their own use—for more equipment, more assistants, more departmental scholarships. The truth is that by past and present cost-sharing rules the university has always paid out of its own income a portion of the expense of government research: the indirect cost allowance is not a profit; it is a partial reimbursement.

THE ALIENATED MEN

These are some of the ways the government has "interfered" with the relation between the university and its distinguished men: outside money has made them suspicious of the institution, sometimes antagonistic to it, as well as psychologically dependent on the government agency from which they get their contracts. Scientists go about the campus saying that it is they who support the "departments that don't pay"; the great investigator maintains: "I have to go to Washington again to raise (= find) my own salary"; they feel exploited.

Meanwhile the government repeatedly tries to make the university police the terms of the contract. This the university must refuse to do—how can it with decency, let alone effectiveness, become snooper and guard over its members, making sure that they do not engage in commercial consulting that would benefit from federally paid research, or certifying that they contribute to government work the portion of effort due by contract?

Ever since "cost-sharing" was written into the law by a misguided legislator sympathetic to universities, all controls have been tightened and agitation about effort-reporting has seethed everywhere. The animus has usually been aimed at the institution for not defending its people. Circular A-21 from the Budget Office was meant to make practices uniform and fair; it has only led to the throwing up of contracts, to resignations, mass meetings, and heated letters in the scientific press. What the government wants to ensure is that the scholar who claims half his salary from government funds (as agreed in the covenant with the university, not with him) does give the government half of—what? Not half his time, for the university, which pays the other half salary, has never required a specified amount of his time. Well, then, half the effort that he would give to university work if he were on duty full-time. But by common practice full-time for the university means a full *teaching* load, and even that measure does not help, for scientists teach fewer courses owing to laboratory supervision being taken into account. And—to say nothing of the puzzle facing the man who directs two or three contracts—there are quasi-administrative duties to be reckoned in.

That the load is well understood but variable across the campus, as well as indefinite for a given person in a given term, does not satisfy federal authorities accustomed to buying soap on the large scale. They return to Effort as something the researcher himself ought to be able to assess and certify weekly and monthly: they point out that incredible as it seems, they trust him! Unmoved, he replies that the very idea of self-justification is offensive; he works long hours or short, at night or while shaving. Science (especially mathematics) is not to be won by mere industry, and when he is in the vein it is no effort, no effort at all.*

It is only fair to add that the earlier and looser reporting to the government was occasionally taken advantage of by unscrupulous grantees—not many perhaps, but enough for disquiet. Putting together their representations as to work on campus and outside, it appeared that some were selling 140 percent of their time. During the summer months they would be found traveling abroad while receiving two ninths or three ninths of their salary for directing a contract on the campus. At present, a number of formulas are being worked on, each adapted to the temper and habits of the institution, to comply with the government's childlike curiosity about the metaphysics of effort. Perhaps the report should call for an estimate of the *genius* deployed for each contract within the month: there would then be full compliance.

The repercussions of government science in the academy cannot all be traced. One of the most regrettable, certainly, is the envy generated in departments other than science—envy not so much of the life of a project director as envy of administrative attention. All the space, new building, personal care, and publicity seem to be concentrated in the scientific corner. And when shrewd classicists and musicians began to learn about cost-sharing, it was their turn to say that *they* were helping to support the jamboree of science out of scarce endowment income. To which the reply came, Why not join the fun? The humanities and social sciences thereupon adopted what they deemed the scientific fashion, they

* See correspondence in *Science,* Dec. 8, 1967, and January, 1968, *passim.* In October 1966 the deans composing the Association of Graduate Schools declared in a fighting resolution that "the present requirement for reporting effort by individual members of the professorial staff . . . admits of no meaningful compliance."

went in for counting something and asking for a grant to pay computer time. So far, the amounts received have been negligible.

What possible ill-effects on science itself the golden flood has had is a question with many answers. Reputable scientists have deplored—others have denied—the bandwagon effect, the slewing of the impetus toward certain types of research which is thought to be "more readily supportable." If true, the evil lies at the door not of the government but of the boards of fellow professionals who review the projects. In any system that establishes common rules there is always a trimming down to common ideas, which exclude the eccentric and possibly inspired individual. Again, waste through duplication has been charged. Until recently no directory of government projects under way had even begun to be compiled; heaven only knew how many laboratories were poring over the liver fluke and the nucleic acids. Even with a directory, birth control for projects will be extremely difficult.

An unquestioned result of the subsidy is the interlocking of university prestige specifically with contract money: without contracts you cannot "buy" the best graduate students, because the best want to do only research and none of the teaching they did before. Nor can you attract the best scientists, because they want the best students and the most expensive equipment, *plus* the summer bonus of two ninths or three ninths chargeable to the contract.* Note in passing that this closed circuit takes away from teaching half the senior men and the best juniors. Lab assistantships and section teaching are now marks of intellectual inferiority. It was Senator Ribicoff who said: "If anyone has lured the teacher from the classroom, it is Uncle Sam."[1]

The vacated space has been filled, perhaps, but by nonteachers, the postdoctoral fellows mentioned earlier as a growing unofficial group within the university. Among them, moreover, is a new type—the grant hog, who subsists nearly into middle age upon a

* Some new state universities show in their proposals to NSF and other agencies how openly they regard the addition to the staff of "two $100,000 men" as a condition of academic prestige. The figure refers not to salaries but to the contract totals hoped for as a result of their presence.

succession of fellowships and grants at different places. He is undeniably a jolly good fellow, but unattached, and hence one more inorganic molecule on the campus. Finally, behind the project and its academic servants stands a corps of hired technicians who may be of high caliber as scientists, but whose work is also something that goes on outside the university structure. They have from the beginning pressed for professorial titles and generally been denied them. Recently they have been accorded academic fringe benefits at government expense. Less well treated at some universities, they have formed a trade union.

To sum up, government sponsorship of a large sector of university work has had the usual effect that money in quantity always has—it is unsettling. The good results are plain and not disputed: the money was indispensable in an age when science works with expensive machinery and scarce talent. The bad results are numerous and variously perceptible.* Envy, greed, and fraud have been stimulated;† teaching has suffered another blow; the university as such has been the worst victim: semidependent and dropsical, it has been diverted from its course and diminished in internal authority by the very means that were expected to strengthen it. Most lately, it has become the arena of political battles and the target of demonstrators who proclaim that by accepting government subsidies the university is abetting crimes against conscience and humanity. The charge is ignorant and not always sincere, but altercation brings down a little more into the bear pit an institution once capable of using detachment and dignity to good educational purpose.‡

* For a detailed description of the changes brought about in the workings of one institution, see the excellent volume by W. G. Bowen: *The Federal Government and Princeton University,* Princeton University Press, 1962.

† A world-famous scientist, himself in charge of a large research center, said in an interview: "Science is replacing rivers and harbors as a political pork-barrel. When people start talking about States' shares of research funds, it makes me sick to my stomach."—Maurice Ewing in *Newsweek,* May 22, 1965.

‡ Angry disputes in public between faculty and president, students and administration, trustees and president have become so frequent in the news as to seem the normal state of the institution.

SOCIAL CHANGE AT THIRTY DAYS

Not money but the love of money is the root of all evil, and it is a tossup whether the scrimmage for contracts exemplifies that love more deeply than the hunt for grants from the private foundations. The flow of funds from that source may not be so large, but it began earlier and its conditions have been even more deeply formative of the new university. The three largest foundations—Ford, Rockefeller, and Carnegie—carry on encyclopedic programs. The remainder, now numbered in the thousands, thanks to the tax laws, are more specialized. Almost all desire novelty and use the project system. These two facts are the two sides of one coin dangling before the projector's eyes: he must think of something which has not been done before (and which falls within the given foundation's province), and he must describe at length how his object will be achieved.

While he is so employed, the chiefs and assistant chiefs of the largest foundations are not idly waiting for the proposals. They are men of education and worldliness, great travelers and listeners, and their outside view of universities is tempered by their numerous friendships within. They consequently notice gaps, needs, talents, and opportunities. They act on this knowledge by proposing departures, new branches of study, and the reformation of old ones by injections of new men and new plans. Over the past forty years an impressive number of the activities we now take for granted, in science especially, could be traced to the timely priming given by a foundation. Outside the sciences, research and teaching in international affairs have been largely foundation-fostered, and so has work in the remoter languages, in the improvement of curriculum, and in social research. On top of this, foundations have distributed large sums in fellowships and training or travel grants, usually through intermediaries, such as the Woodrow Wilson Foundation and the American Council of Learned Societies.

But until lately, when the Ford Foundation made outright grants to colleges and universities for general support, the foundation bias has been single-minded in its pursuit of novelty. It is not unfair to say that foundations were the first to conceive of the university as an instrument. "A grant from us," said one leader of the profession, "is a piece of venture capital for social change." There may be in this idea a questionable confidence about the direction social change should take, but the granting officials are very modest beyond that point. They leave the details to the university researcher, for they believe in science—their faith in the university is a faith in the expert planning and directing of social change. In this belief the university as such is not so much supported as used for ends defined by others. Since these ends half originate in the minds of scholars or are accepted by them, one can say again that a new university partnership has come into being.

THE MAN WHO CAME TO DINNER

Its terms do not simply duplicate at private expense the linkage with the government, nor does the relation resemble it in its side effects. The main feature of foundation grants is that they are pump-priming. A sum is given for three, five, at most ten years of estimated cost for a specified purpose, usually research, teaching, or a combination of both. Every time the university accepts such a grant the university is expected to do two things: carry the overhead and find the money to continue the work after the end of the grant. In short, by taking a grant the university has incurred present and future expense of indefinite amount—an amount bound to increase, for overhead rises by inflation and all salaries go up with length of service.

To these outlays one must add hidden costs, such as money-raising and others, which help create the present well-to-do pauperism of the university. There are afloat in the world of academic administration copies of a famous letter written by the distinguished president of a private university to a foundation head, about the upshot of a $34,000 grant made by the foundation to start a subbranch of science research. In eight years (five since the expiration of the grant) the cost to the university was close to half a million dollars. That the host department had been split into angry factions on the issue to go on or not to go on is an incidental.

The obvious remedy "If this is known, why not resist?" will not work. Once started, the foundation tie with the university becomes a close (and proper) connection between heads of subject-matter divisions within the foundations and the talented, enterprising members of faculties. The quickest way to alienate a scholar or scientist from his university is for an administrator to look askance at a grant which is well on the way to acceptance in the foundation hierarchy. The man will pack up and go "where they believe in his work," which means: "where the cost of grants is swallowed without a murmur." All devices so far tried will not prevent an able man and an alert foundation prospector from lunching together; and at that lunch the university goes into debt just as surely as if the treasurer had signed a promissory note.

The foundations often express annoyance, quite reasonably, at being assailed simultaneously by a dozen projects from a single university. They ask why the submissions are not controlled, or at least put by the president in an order of preference. For very big requests the president does have to write a formal letter of application to go with the project statement and its budget. But by that time it is too late to balk. The president, moreover, cannot know which of the many requests submitted will succeed; he dare not stop this latest one, which may be the winner.

Again, he is responsible for a vast array of departments, of which a quarter or a third would welcome the spurt of prestige and activity resulting from grants: how is he going to determine priorities? Whatever he does, he will be accused of playing favorites—for or against science or the humanities or sociology—and his calendar for the next six weeks will be a mass of interviews with ruffled researchers and their friends. The foundation's difficulty in limiting the number of grants to a single institution is thus in part its own doing, and so is the university's impossible task of saying No to a golden-eyed projector.*

The salutary No sticks equally in the throat when the foundation comes to the university with a "great idea" and a grant of several millions to make it good. Under the definition of the new university it is "an instrument of the people," and expected to forge the means to any public-spirited end. Almost any undertaking that has the good in view and that can be dressed up to look like the experimental side of training or research is accepted as a university obligation. The hospitable attitude is not the administration's alone: faculty members are consulted and rejoice at the news of the prospective grant which, once awarded, attracts a frantic school of gudgeons around the fat bait.

It is thus that a dozen of the leading universities—not all metropolitan—are now found managing large programs of urban renewal and race relations, engaging in the improvement of housing and rehabilitation of moral derelicts, uplifting economically depressed areas, or supplying art to the community—all this without evidence that they are equipped with the talent, organization, or experience to succeed. No one can cavil at the motives of good will and courage behind such departures from central university work, but no one should deny that they are improvisations, fraught with the great danger of social projects, the "rathole phenomenon," by which money is spent, honorably but without result. Whatever the outcome, improvisation is hardly the article

* Gulliver and his host at Laputa were early in this perplexity when they encountered the man who was extracting sunshine from cucumbers: "In eight years more he should be able to supply the Governor's gardens with sunshine at a reasonable rate. . . . I made him a small present, for my lord had furnished me with money on purpose, because he knew their practice of begging from all who go to see them."—*Gulliver's Travels,* Part III, Chapter 5.

on which the university as a fount of knowledge has hitherto based its claims to trust and respect.

JOKERS AND PENALTIES

Some of the large grants whose goal is social betterment through the more appropriate means of research and training (e.g., about the problem of overpopulation) present another difficulty which is constant in the relation between foundations and universities, that which might be called "hidden matching," thus: x million dollars is given for a new institute—staff, building, laboratories, consultants, travel, everything of the best, no expense spared. BUT the university must find the land, which can easily cost a million if the new institute is to be desirably close to related activities; and the terms of the grant allow no reserve for meeting future costs out of grant income. The university which is richer by x million may have to divert as much as $\frac{x}{2}$ from endowment to help the foundation help the public.

On the small scale (but it mounts up), grants to individuals, notably for literature and the arts, are similarly a gun in the ribs: Mr. or Mrs. X, novelist, poet, or critic, wins the coveted award (ACLS or the government's National Foundation for the Arts and Humanities). Invariably Mr. and Mrs. X's regular salary is $3,500 more than the grant, besides which the contributions to retirement and other fringe benefits come to another 18 percent of the total sum. Unless the university is to prevent the faculty member from enjoying the honor and the free time by refusing the leave of absence, it must put up $5,000 to $6,000 every time one of its distinguished people is rewarded for merit. Affording the talent comes high.*

* And now the Woodrow Wilson Fellows for graduate study will receive only the honor—no money, which puts a further pressure on university funds, formerly enriched by a "cost of education" allowance from that foundation. For completeness' sake, another but much lesser drain on resources should be mentioned: large foundations sometimes make small awards to individuals, always through the local university, which is expected

To be sure, there is a case to be made for foundation practice. Great as these treasuries are, they are not bottomless, and their sense of public responsibility prompts them to spread their income as wide as possible. Hence their seeming parsimony in any single grant—no overhead, cadging administrative help, putting the burden on the institution for eking out, going on, writing reports, facing inflation, and never (under pain of displeasure) bettering its financial situation with the gift. As I said at the outset, the foundations could truthfully swear that they have done the best they could and that they have done great things. Yet it is just as true to say that their help has also brought hardship. Both truths belong to an understanding of the university situation.

Nor is the hardship purely monetary. Consider a few more circumstances, not indeed created by the foundations, but reinforced by their generosity. It is from the culture, from liberal opinion, from the New Deal, from the fidgets of the century that we take as an axiom: "Rapid change is inevitable" and follow it up with its contradiction: "Be an agent of change." The school system says this to little tots that cannot even change their diapers, so strong is the hope that everyone will "be creative." All are encouraged to write a project, go in for research or pseudo research. On the dizzy heights of the academy projects abound; few are sufficiently criticized. They are full of wind and water, much too overwritten to be seen through—a ten-line summary would destroy them. Meantime some part of the collective common sense has been destroyed instead, as a result of the mutual courtesy about verbal flatulence which is as strong in the university as in the U.S. Senate.

And, alas, when somebody or something *is* creative, what difficulties he or it encounters!—just the way it was before the invention of "support." Doing things, not just describing them, or

---

to administer the fellowship, without overhead of course—the foundation has given so much money already! In actuality this administering has a measurable cost, never reimbursed.

doing things unjudgeable because truly new, does not generate good projects blessed with cash. In fact, the moment success crowns such work done without aid it incurs *disreward,* and this by a logic in keeping with the assumptions mentioned above. For example (and it is no imaginary one), suppose that a small group of innovators—young, hard workers, single-minded—finally reach acknowledged professional success. They have had to beg their way, putting together a small-foundation grant with a matching fraction from the university. When their worth is manifest, the foundation, true to its laudable aim of spreading good things, will readily give good round sums to *other* universities, in order that they may start exactly similar work; with that money, the newcomers naturally begin bidding at high rates for the men who have proved themselves in the original group. Seeing that the new money is going elsewhere, and the men also, the home university very likely shuts down its own genuine creation as not worth carrying on—obviously superfluous.*

This modern definition of *encouragement* has its place in the larger mythology of "new centers of excellence." The ideal is, as usual, praiseworthy—there is room and loud cheers for all the excellence we can assemble, anywhere. The practice is something else. When money for the purchase of excellence is given to an institution of less than the top grade, the assumption is that a first-rate man or two on the campus will induce excellence in their colleagues like a current in a surrounding coil. The facts are against that assumption. If it were true, one could engineer a Renaissance at will. What one gets instead is high bidding for the man or two at some institution already excellent, and the possible destruction thereby of the department deserving that label. Excellence is rare, because it requires a concentration of congenial

* The dean of a professional school once submitted a project for advanced work to a large and sympathetic foundation. The project was admired, but he was told that his school was in such good shape that it could not qualify for help. That help was given to a less good school, whose dean on receiving the grant called up the originator of the project, saying: "Now, then, how do I go about this?"

abilities. If talent is to be transplanted, the raiding must be done by the carload, as President Harper did to Clark University seventy years ago in order to excellentize Chicago.* He did not add a great center to those then in being, he merely moved it fifteen degrees west. But at least he knew what he was about; he did not sterilize his stable of excellence by offering jobs free of teaching, which would mean no contacts and no influence, and which would have wrecked Clark without building up Chicago.

The strength of such a group is not to be had from a kind of project that often attracts foundations because it looks highly articulated and promises the productivity of a machine. In this second kind of collective effort, all but one or two persons are employees, capable no doubt, but not likely to give off sparks of genius when brought close together. The man of ideas who conceived the plan does need these helpers to carry it out, but in all probability he finds himself delegating its direction while he keeps up the money-raising. For the foundation and the government, the university and a few interested corporations and individuals will only subsidize that part of his purpose which coincides with theirs, and he becomes perforce the perpetual promoter in place of the scholar, or man thinking. Imponderable as may be the effect of this and other common experiences on the atmosphere of the university, it is not unreasonable to find in the prosperity of such projects a source of uncritical confidence in mere machinery, a strong and irrational belief that great things can be done without the direct exertion of mind.

WHITE ELEPHANT OR TROJAN HORSE?

A true pluralist society is plural in every corner, and universities may rejoice that the foundations all together have been able to

* The same principle holds for library purchases. It is desirable nowadays that colleges and universities should go in for Oriental Studies, but large gifts here and there for the purchase of obscure and expensive research materials in those fields only raises prices, scatters resources, and impedes research.

counterbalance the weight of government subsidies. In their turn, foundations have as foils the private donor and the corporation, both of them less bound down by rules, good and bad. The corporations tend to give modest amounts, but regularly and for general purposes. Blessings on both these characteristics! As soon as corporations were released by judicial decision from the obligation to spend money exclusively for business in strict quid pro quo, they seemed to relish the freedom and to *give gifts.** They may specify or sometimes merely indicate preferences—for the department of chemistry or of geology in a university, or such and such undergraduate colleges in the region; for the office of student aid or for faculty research; but these broad choices cause no discomfort to the receiving institution, because these divisions are already established and always thirsty for money. It is no trouble at all for them to spend more; and in the rare instances where the bucket is full, there is a tap at the bottom through which the general income of the university is drawn off for other uses and replaced by the gift.†

Occasionally, it is true, a corporation will offer a gift that is a contract payment in thin disguise. It must then be respectfully unveiled and the desired job of research or teaching accepted as a paid assignment, or the money refused. But this embarrassment is rare, and the only feature to be regretted about corporate giving is that it still comes in small packages.

The individual donor, alumnus or friend, is of course as unpredictable as mankind itself. As alumnus, he probably contributes to the so-called Annual Fund of his college or professional school, a

* In 1956 half a dozen presidents of private universities issued a Statement of Principles on corporate giving which by chance or design corresponds largely to present corporate practice. The Statement would at many points help other types of donors to understand the philanthropic act (*New York Times,* June 25, 1956).

† This operation shows why it is self-defeating to give scholarship money with any overt or secret idea of putting a particular geographical or other group at an advantage over the rest. If the university has a fair amount of money and has done a proper job of allotting it, "the rest" will benefit also by every addition specified for the group being favored. The only exception would occur if in some year no "native of Toasting Fork" should apply.

collection of modest amounts that none the less keep supplied with much-needed tens or hundreds of thousands the student aid office, the dean's discretionary account, and the reserve for unforeseen purposes. When well organized these annual funds become a regular part of the university income, and it is clear that during the past decade every private institution would have suffered great penury without them.*

The wealthy donor, alumnus or not, may choose to exercise his charitable impulse by giving a building, endowing a chair, setting up fellowships and scholarships, bequeathing part of his estate, turning over his art collection, or adopting a department or line of research as his particular protégé. It is when pursuing these ends on a large scale that the donor will earn the gratitude of the university if he can grasp its needs, and will appear as a difficult friend if he does not. As there is nothing to deplore in happy events, there is little to tell about the perceptive donor. When the elderly lady, without fuss, turns over a small fortune to the college, or the vigorous businessman consults a few friends among the trustees or administrators of the institution and draws up a will embodying his wishes in a form adapted to the academic realities, hallelujahs go up and his name is a cherished memory as well as a piece of engraving on brass or stone.

It is only those in whose power lies every gift but that of giving who cause anguish and, what is worse, who inflict hidden injuries. There is no pleasure in detailing faults, but there is need to make some inferences from them. First, the Romans had a great point when they said "He gives twice who gives quickly." The danglers of gifts are a menace to all the functions of the university—teaching, research, and administration—by soliciting the attention of

* Annual Funds prosper in proportion to the number of organized alumni and the length of time they have been organized; so that colleges of equal size may receive unequal amounts. The cost of organization and maintenance at fever pitch is high and bears a higher ratio to receipts when these are small. That is why only colleges and certain professional schools benefit greatly from annual funds. The graduate alumni in arts and science are an unprofitable lot, except for the occasional Croesus. Besides, graduate alumni tend to nurture their earlier, undergraduate attachments.

harassed people and wasting their time on a shopping tour of possibilities. Next among false friends come the self-appointed partners who, having made an impressive gift, try to continue managing it, and end by acting like part-time administrators or semitrustees. Unless seen and resisted promptly, the intrusion can become a cancer. Unfortunately—and knowing this may be an unconscious cause of the meddling—modern institutions are afraid of standing on their rights, much less their dignity: there is always the hope of a second gift, and that hope works like blackmail.

Less crude but equally dangerous are the donors with a purpose. Often they wield the sole authority in a family foundation. They have retired and hit upon a cause which they would bribe the university to take up as its own, though it is neither a current need nor a desirable extra. No matter how much money is offered in this guise,* it works as a harmful diversion of energy.

Sometimes such a donor can be persuaded to accept an alternative project that does fit into the program, but usually the moneyed man feels entitled to his whim; he has as much right to be creative as any foundation and he says so; he is, moreover, offended that his idea should not be taken up at sight, and so he is not in the best state to learn why it cannot be. When a president is in this fix with a donor, he has need of all his faculties: they can give him just cause to decline, especially if the donor expects that for his down payment the appropriate academics will turn to and raise the rest of the needed sum. Such a suggestion is frequently made by persons who would like to honor a public figure by naming a chair for him, but stop at heading the list of sympathizers—let the university solicit the rest.

In general, for reasons that lie deep in the democratic mind, the idea of giving has been clouded by other ideas, which range from managing and wanting account rendered to seeking submissiveness and making a good buy. Shakespeare thought that "There's none/

* Or house and land. Many an estate, here and abroad, is proffered as surely useful for university purposes, when actually the gift will only serve the donor and cost the university. Like foundations, most donors prefer to ignore overhead costs.

Can truly say he gives if he receives,"[2] but our mores tend rather to find the quid pro quo more natural and friendly, more equal. Donors expect not only the usual acknowledgment with heartfelt thanks; they look for their names on buildings and in brochures, sometimes classified by amounts given. They have come to think that for half the cost of a building their name should cover the whole of it. They do not blush to find their good deed bruited about, but lap up flattery; and most characteristic, they insist that whatever they give shall not in any way relieve the overstretched income of the college or university: it must be a new expense, *their* project, which must stand out separate, even on the budget sheet.

It must be said again that there are enough exceptions to this frame of mind—downright contradictions of it—to supply the makings of an opposite subgenerality. But there are not enough to swamp the rest, as is proved by every handbook on fund-raising. And the subtle danger remains, quite as if these ostensible friends were secret enemies. To be sure, if these are enemies at all, they are so without animus or awareness. The suggestion would shock them. But how else define persons whose deeds bring confusion into the aims and works of an institution and weaken its power to do what it should and must do?

In this sense—the sense in which we say a man can be his worst enemy—obviously the chief helpers of the new university are all equally compromised, not the self-willed donor alone, but the government, the foundations, and those industries that have made demands or held out temptations that disregard what a university is for. It is all very well to say that the university should not let itself be seduced, bribed, or blackmailed. I repeat, in a democratic welfare state resistance to demand of any kind is extremely difficult. Everybody is for public service; it has the force religion once had, from which it follows that to hold back from a proposed good is blasphemy. The very demand for a piece of welfare shows need and therefore establishes a rightful claim. The underlying conviction that the university is an instrument of the people is interpreted to mean that the people should wield the instrument, an idea reinforced by prevailing beliefs about tax exemption and the deductibility of charitable gifts.* The tax-supported state university is even more obviously the people's instrument, and there is every disposition in all universities to live up to this popular ideal.

TRUST-BUSTERS AND IMAGE-BREAKERS

The discovery of a flaw in the arrangement comes only when one takes a synoptic view such as is attempted here, or when by chance some scholar or university head points to one or another sign of damage attributable to the friends and supporters of universities. The public then makes a serious mistake if it thinks it is seeing a conflict between traditionalism and modern ideas, or a selfish, self-centered institution repulsing the people in its need. The issue is more important than slogans and names. On the one hand is the question whether the people want a university or something else; on the other is the evidence that the university cannot bend and twist for the sake of money and popularity and continue to perform as an educational institution. Certainly the spectacle of the public schools would lead one to suspect that as welfare functions increase the removal of ignorance declines.†

As to the first question, it does not seem on the face of it that the moneyed powers want the university. Their support is for

* Dinner-table conversation often assumes that tax exemption for educational and charitable uses keeps very large sums out of the public purse. Actually in New York State, which has a larger proportion of property used for these purposes than most states, what is exempt on this account is only 12.6 percent of all exempt property and only 3.75 percent of all property. The exemption has two advantages: it keeps the activities that are so supported out of local and state politics and it saves the taxpayers the difference between the large total of private contributions and what taxes on the exempted property would bring.

† American school superintendents are among the unsung heroes of the century, but their work in education is at its lowest ebb. Their grueling duties have to do with securing nurses and dentists, bargaining with bus drivers and caterers, dealing with the politics of school boards and churches, setting up defenses against crime, fire, and vandalism, and devising ways to squeeze into the school day courses designed to reduce motor accidents, premarital pregnancies, and social disorders.

everything other than the central business. If any donor of a building has ever given for its maintenance, he is the philanthropic equivalent of the unknown soldier. So much is clear. What do the less affluent and articulate see in the university? Some, a means of rising into the professions via the mandarin system. As students (and parents of students) they make no objection to the system, but they see the university as a passageway, a ramp which they would just as soon find shorter, cheaper, and less steep. They are not to blame if they have so little time, money, or meditative bent. Others, who may be students, ex-students, or bogus students are, as we know, cynical, hostile, violent. The latter group do *not* want a university. The former do not want *a university*.

This census leaves the alumni, whose love is often laced with anger, and the outsiders, the neighbors, townspeople, and newspaper readers observing from far or near. Among all these are some of the university's declared enemies, enemies in the full sense this time. In city or country, they may be tenants in houses owned by the university and threatened with eviction if it expands. Or, though safe themselves, they do not like to see the community overshadowed by "it"—that is, by the multiplying scientific laboratories, the dense army of technicians and other highbrows, the unkempt boys and unrecognizable girls acting as if no one else was alive. Town and gown have never taken to each other, but nowadays the antagonism is heightened by the sight of a hairy monster with tentacles.

The university is, moreover, the only target left for the muckraker since the trusts were busted; it is the only big corporation you can go out and see flaunting its greatness on the open street. And it is not only big but hard to get at, harder and harder to get into. It speaks of its admissions standards, which may well be a cloak for snobbish discrimination. When it encroaches on neighboring property it speaks of necessary expansion. Where is the necessity? Isn't it big enough, strong enough, proud enough as it is? Most of these university people no doubt are pleasant-spoken when you meet them at the grocer's, but collectively they are stuck up, keep their children out of public school, and object to the run-down state of the neighborhood. They complain of crime, vice, drug peddling, and assaults on their girls and their professors. They bring in extra police and join with the churches and hospitals roundabout to hire a night patrol. Who do they think they are, with their iron gates and gaudy costumes, and their names always in the papers? What is brains, after all? They *pretend* to feel democratic, but how far have they pushed integration?

It would be useless to answer that the very notions of racial, political, economic, and educational equality of opportunity have come out of the heads of those professors and their unreadable books. The liberal imagination, for what it has been worth, is an academic product. But argument is not to the point. The neighbors visit all manner of vague resentments on the place—it is "red" and reactionary; it is selfish when it takes and patronizing when it gives. We need them and we don't want them. In short, it cannot do right and therefore cannot be right.

WAYWARD SCRIBES AND MORALISTS

In this ambivalent mood the public is abetted by the newspapers and some of the local politicians, who find issues and publicity in safe protests. Universities have become daily news since the era of research and riots, and the newspaper coverage of campus doings is extensive without being enlightening. The university is the institution nobody knows.* It walks alone, has no party or press to stand up for it—and no news story of uproars or achievements

* I may cite as illustrative a conversation with an official of the State Department at the time when the exchange of students and scholars with the Soviet Union was being negotiated. We had previously disposed of the objectionable fingerprinting of our prospective visitors and all seemed well, when the telephone rang again: "They say now that they want exchanges only with the two universities of the first rank, Harvard and Columbia, because they will use only Moscow and Leningrad. What do we say to that?"—"Well, you tell them we have a dozen or more first-class universities; the ones on the list they're objecting to are the equals of the two they've heard of."—"We can say that? It's true?"

makes it more intelligible; the different places are different, no one knows how; and yet all are alike in appearing academic, that is, unlike familiar life, common motives, ordinary business.

There is in this picture a good dose of wishing it so: it perpetuates admiration and envy, mixed sometimes with local pride, sometimes with anti-intellectualism. Words like "prestigious," "top-ranking," "elite," coupled with "the professor said," convey the feeling of being outside, in the warm company of plain folks. It is but fair to add that this uneasy attitude is also common among educated people, who have been *through* a university; it is found even in university trustees.

Lately, the frequent reports that the universities are in trouble, with students, professors, and their own budgets, have encouraged the press to criticize. This is legitimate if the editorial critics acquire at least as much knowledge of the institution as they do when they reveal the inside workings of the White House or City Hall. But the number of reporters on education who possess or even suspect the need of this knowledge is extremely small.*

The journalistic stance, moreover, is a permanent barrier to understanding. For example, when a great eastern university (not Columbia) announced its latest increase in tuition fees, the local newspapers requested a press conference with president and deans. One of the early questions was "How much over the cost of education will the new fees bring you?" The answer: "Nothing over; it will provide enough to keep the students paying about half the cost." At this, the press conference sagged. But there was another important question: "How far beyond other colleges will this tuition rate take you?" The answer: "They've been ahead of us; we're only catching up." Here the reporters snapped their notebooks shut, feeling they had come out on false pretenses.

It was in the same town, later on, that a visiting political figure was the object of a hostile student demonstration, which after a

* Outstanding among newspapers that carry educational news are the Los Angeles *Times,* for fullness and good sense, and the *Wall Street Journal,* for thoroughness and exact detail.

time brought out the television crews on trucks. At that point the students were beginning to disperse under the suasion of proctors. But this would never do for the cameramen; they kept shouting "Don't quit now! Give us a little action!" A great lark, but such incidents suggest that newspaper interest in education is only an application of the professional outlook: the function of the press is not so much to represent events to the public as to represent the public to events, making the latter conform to the public's existing impressions.

The press thus parallels the jury system, in which able counsel do not try to make the jury understand the facts, but adapt the facts to the understanding of the jury. This may be useful and effective generally, but it is a poor preparation for the intelligent admonishing of universities. To scold a university head for mishandling student disturbances one must know more than journalists generally do about faculty prerogatives and student inflammability. The rules for picketing or inviting speakers, which can be administered by an assistant dean or proctor, do not take care of mass meetings with sound trucks or disruptions planned by outside professionals.

It is even brasher for a paper to monitor educational policy. When some time ago a university school for adult education changed the age of eligibility for admission, dailies and weeklies uttered indignant opinions showing no grasp either of the mild technicalities involved or of their important meaning. Explanations in writing and by word of mouth are of course discounted as being necessarily false, because *presswise* there is to everything an inside story that is discreditable. That assumption permits things to be made lively, it *personalizes* them.

The personal touch reached its high point, perhaps, in some of the headlines that "covered" the unhappy events at Berkeley. One was: "Clark Kerr *versus* Savio"—the prizefight of the week. Nobody with a particle of feeling for the university as an institution could fail to regard that headline as anything but infamous, the worst kind of editorializing, that which hides under the forms of impartiality. At other times, in a fit of Puritanism, the journalist will gravely comment on the appointment to scholarly chairs of persons too well known to the public: "Publicity as a measure of status is, of course, commonplace in the present-day world. But should such standards be those of the University?"[3] Them's my sentiments too, but they would come with greater force from the moral judge if shortly before that remonstrance he had not prodded academic persons to give him a juicy story of conflicting departmental feelings on that same appointment; the net effect being uncomplimentary to the appointee and to the institution.*

These details may be thought trivial in the chaos of the world, but their symptomatic meaning is not trivial. It is no accident that the editorial reproof referred to a post subsidized by public money. Now, the political, the personal, the debunking are inimical to an institution whose whole effort is to achieve detachment, fairness, and truth. This is not to say that universities are staffed by angels or that critics must keep hands off; it is to say that with each step taken toward the free-for-all of business and politics the university loses something of its virtue. And by virtue I mean strength, as in the origin of the word.

To generalize, in accepting the role of public service center and the moneys that go with it, the university has made itself answerable to eight publics, whose acts and words often turn them into foes, like the brethren of St. James blessing and cursing out of the same mouth. The eight publics are: parents, students, alumni, donors, foundations, neighbors, governments, and newspapers. There may be nine if there exists a general public not already distributed among the eight. For the institution, the penalty of not agreeing with the assumption that it is an undischarged debtor to

* Another curious summons frequently served on universities is that the buildings and statuary they erect shall please the newspaper critics. One such, on being told that a building was considered by its users very convenient and comfortable, replied: "That's nothing to me. I care only about exteriors." And another condemned the sculpture given by a donor as doing nothing to encourage the latest wave of creation in that art. The next step, surely, is screen tests for college presidents.

the public is abuse cast in ready-made phrases—ivory tower, lack of relevance, traditionalist views, indifference to consumers [*sic*],* ingratitude for public support, and (supreme insult) *elitism.*

Still, the university must sometimes put its own concerns first, and even be too busy to give a quelling explanation. For there is one ground that the university must take and hold inviolate if it is not to go down as a great goose killed for its golden eggs. That ground is that it must remain a *definable* institution. The clients whose purposes we have scanned assume that its interest and theirs are identical. But that which is hardly true of any two human beings or groups is not true in this case. What is true is that mutual benefit can accrue to two parties with different interests and a good understanding when each maintains its independent power to perform.

Today, the forces of money, criticism, and affection too, pull the other way. The desire to blur lines and blend activities overtakes the best minds. One proposes low-cost public housing with shops on the ground floor and college classrooms and offices just above: it will help reconcile the neighborhood to the presence of the university—as well as create the right environment for study, because life is life: students do go into shops and cohabit in apartment houses.

Another argues that keeping real artists out of the university by requiring academic work is brutal and stupid. They don't need mathematics and history if they are going to paint like Leonardo and compose like Mozart. But they need degrees, so let them take what they like and justify their presence by the good they will confer through mingling with the rest.

A third thinks it is stuffy to teach courses unrelated to events outside. When a big Impressionist exhibit comes to town, or Olivier in Shakespeare, or the Bolshoi Ballet, the appropriate departments should suspend their regular classes and work up seminars and lectures *relevant* to the current show and compulsory

* Louis B. Wright, who reports the remark, is quoted in the *Bulletin of the Council for Basic Education,* March 1965, 4.

for all the students in the department. In that way study could be kept *exciting*.

The love of the mishmash, the passion for dissolving unities, is only another label for dissolution, and it is important to recognize that scholars and teachers share the blame (or credit) for aiding the subversion by their bright thoughts or their easy compliance with external demands. The resisters are none the less agreed about the nature of the enemy: "The current philosophy of education," writes a young historian in a southwestern college, "is slowly undermining our position. We are becoming a 'community college,' our purpose is to solve social problems and feed trained technicians to the labor market. The urgent need to train minds to face the more abstract problems of the individual . . . is not only being ignored, it is not even recognized."[4]

THE BAILIFFS IN THE HOUSE

In this confusion the administrator is not best placed to gauge the effect of his quick decisions, each of which may make his university more popular and less whole. But the ark is in his keeping nevertheless, because nobody at the university sees or feels so much as he. His occupational disease is the bends, or caisson disease, which comes from violent changes of pressure. He may conceive of his institution as stable and unified, an establishment designed for a particular set of tasks, entrusted to a group qualified by talent and training. But what is continually thrust upon him is the grander vision of an open-ended supermarket of which the hired help will cheerfully take on any part of the world's work.*

Meanwhile, nothing stands still. In twelve months a fair exchange of students or medical service or library use, or a partnership in a South American astronomical station, ceases to be fair or to engage the interest of the participating scholars; or a community

* The first public defender of the university fabric, before President Brewster of Yale and Chancellor Heyns of California, was Robert M. Hutchins, then president of Chicago. See his latest essay in the publication cited in note 1 of Chapter 1.

project widely praised turns politically damnable and socially criminal. Everything must be revised, all structures recast. It is crisis government, permanently.

Because this instability is made worse by the drain of cost-sharing, grant-matching, and general placating, a search for strength must be made. The institution needs to be independent once again, and longs at the same time to join its well-wishers and prodders in some vast embrace characterized for a time by comradeship and contentment. The answer to these specifications is the fund-raising drive—a great deal of money. The goal is in the millions, not from dreams of avarice but because the minimum sating of present demands will cost—whatever the figure is. A hundred million, two hundred, is not extravagant: each sum is a careful paring down of the estimates for a program actually free of trimmings. The reasons why so much has to be got for so little will occupy us in the next chapter.

The spiritual importance of the fund campaign is that it is the final invader. Of course, it is cruel in order to be kind; it destroys in order to build up. And fortunately there are books and firms that assist universities to undergo the ordeal.* It is not hard to imagine that turning oneself inside out is the least of the feats required for raising money in large amounts. Every other ingenuity and adaptability is needed as well. When properly run with the aid of outside professionals, a campaign is just that: all energies are mobilized into coordinated aggression. The president now heads two distinct armies, inside and outside. Deans leave their schools to coast while they hunt down marked men; department heads are coaxed and coached to write descriptions, plans, prophecies; policy meetings and public events multiply, rivalries sharpen, the sense of emergency becomes permanent: it is a crisis mounted on a crisis and begetting heaven knows what offspring.

The gleam that hypnotizes the hundreds of workers, on and off campus, is that there is a case to be made for the university. The

* Perhaps the best, because clearest and shortest book on the subject is *Designs for Fund-Raising,* by Harold J. Seymour (McGraw-Hill, New York, 1966).

case (I quote an authority) "should aim high, provide perspective, arouse a sense of history and continuity, convey a feeling of importance, relevance, and urgency, and have whatever stuff is needed to warm the heart and stir the mind."[5] Warming the heart involves "the appropriate use of music, pertinent quotations, speeches or statements by the right people, dramatizations of function through colorful ceremonies based on youthful participation of one kind or another, and measures that evoke the best that has gone, pride for the present, and warm promise for the future."[6]

Allowing for the freezing effect that prescribing deliberate warmth is bound to have on the reader, the scheme of a campaign is easily seen to be propaganda on the large scale, making use—still according to our authority—of the most reliable weaknesses of men, including "fear of the stranger . . . which goes for the world of ideas as well as for the world of people."[7] The drive must "be conducted in an atmosphere of optimism and universality," by men who know that "most people incline toward glimpses rather than studious reading . . . [think] facts are just fine especially when they are accurate and easily grasped—but [know] . . . that you can't make good succotash out of nothing but lima beans."[8]

The great universities have gone in for this propaganda and come out again, richer—or at least with large sums in the bank. But no one knows as yet what they have sold to the Devil for the price. I raise the doubt not because there is anything degrading about money or about asking for it but because under modern conditions the tremendous effort of the campaign is propaganda without a doctrine: what is there to say? Talking about needs is expressly forbidden. The past must come in but lightly. All is promises. "The case" is doubtless no worse than any other piece of what Acton called "accredited mendacity": it represents each university, each department as "distinctive," it cites impressive figures, it photographs for the millionth time earnest young faces gazing at the light through test tubes. And there are plans of future buildings. But the true university remains hidden, through nobody's fault, and possibly to its own advantage.

For surely it and the campaign are antitheses. The university stands for the very opposite of what will make the campaign a success: the university does not fear strange ideas, it does not indulge its pride, it does not lather up optimism, it does not make facts into succotash. Or am I wrong? Ought I to have said: it *should* stand for these austere principles, but does no longer? If so, the cause lies in the peculiar character of modern giving and modern friendship toward institutions, in those impulses directed not at fulfilling the recipient's known purpose (as, say, in the old church) but rather at enhancing the giver's self-expression, his "creativity."* It would be useless and unjust to reproach individuals for what is a mark of the whole society, but the tendency is not in doubt. "You have to remember," says the head of the most successful charitable federation, "that we are basically a fund-raising organization, and we can't raise funds unless we are meeting the needs that most of the money-givers think need to be met."[9]

One more word is due the fund campaigns: they all surpass their goals. And virtually all of them do it the way emancipated students pass their examinations, not quite scrupulously. The campaign goal is declared to have been reached, but this is because whatever has been paid in or pledged during the time of the campaign goes toward the total. Among these windfalls which mask the actual program deficits are continuations of earlier gifts and unlooked-for grants for restricted purposes. Even parts of the campaign program receive support with unwelcome strings attached. But this side felony, no money is really resisted, and a candid survey might disclose how much, or how little net, unmortgaged, usable free funds the fund campaign had brought. It is that hypothetical net, from whatever source, that we must now see at work supporting the university.

* If this seems harsh, think of Christmas. There are, surely, two kinds of givers—those who give the tie, the scarf, the book that they would like to possess, and those who make the effort of thinking to give what will suit and please. Are we to say their love is equal?

6 Poverty in the Midst of Plenty

> There is nothing which can better deserve your patronage than the promotion of science and literature. . . . Whether this desirable object will be best promoted by affording aids to seminaries of learning already established . . . or by other expedients, will be well worthy of a place in the deliberations of the legislature.
>
> —GEORGE WASHINGTON

> Accountancy—that is government.
>
> —LOUIS D. BRANDEIS

THE PRINCE IS THE PAUPER

By the evidence of the preceding chapter it is clear that the financial situation of universities can only be ambiguous. It has many rich friends who pour money into it—and manage thereby to add to its costs. It raises great sums from powerful foundations and draws on the public purse at all three levels of government—and even this aid fails to fill the void. It charges high tuition fees that pay less and less of the cost of education—and thus the increased enrollments that all desire further impoverish the institution.

You will say that is only the lot of the private university and the facts doom it to become a ward of the state. Not so: the state university is in the same case for much the same reason: the costs are identical, and their sources of wealth, the legislatures, are feeling the general pinch caused by inflation and the rival needs of welfare. Besides, faculty salaries have reached a point where legislators, rightly or wrongly, are beginning to lose sympathy with "the underpaid college teacher." They compare his salary and workload with theirs, they think of the three-month vacation and the opportunities for outside consulting, and they are puzzled by the expensive cross-country bidding and switching. Articles in business journals that they read take for granted "the affluent professor."

The facts are not quite as represented. In real wages, university people have not caught up with their professional peers; that is, when *salaries* are compared.* It is the new opportunity of double and triple income that has made some academic men prosperous. The rest of them manage on what is a kind of welfare salary, and not lifelong affluence. I mean that in the middle years the professional income is increased by fringe benefits for housing, children's education, and high insurances; then it declines to a frequently substandard pension. Deferred compensation is for many reasons impossible, though book royalties sometimes produce an equivalent.

In the midst of these complexities, the state legislatures and universities are troubled about money as they never were expected to be by their once-envious private counterparts. Finding that the student demand keeps growing and brings many out-of-state applicants, the states have steadily raised their tuition fees for out-of-staters and begun here and there to charge or to increase fees for residents. And wherever legally permissible, state universities now solicit gifts and grants like the rest. "Public" and "private" are

* The AAUP report for 1967–68 gave the average salaries for full professors as ranging from $7,720 to $25,750, including fringe benefits. A study by the American Council on Education sampling the salaries of persons newly appointed for that year gives a spread that goes from about $9,000 to a top of $27,000. An interesting point is that subject matter is not so influential as formerly. The high salaries are not all in the sciences, but often in classics and the humanities. When pondering these figures it is also well to remember that not all professors are full professors.

thus no longer clear-cut terms in financing (though still an important distinction in governance), and both groups are alike in feeling that if "affluent" is the right term for the society they serve, the opposite term is the right one for colleges and universities: they have all joined the great order of mendicants.

The late Beardsley Ruml was the first to predict the bankruptcy which the presidents of the Ford Foundation and the Carnegie Corporation have recently declared imminent.* That imminence has been in plain sight for university administrators since about 1960. It has been a race among a few fundamental factors: (1) fixed costs rising, (2) endowment rising very little, (3) outside aid adding to expense, (4) tuition fees rising but not filling the gap.

Why is endowment not rising? The answer lies in the state of mind described in the preceding chapter: gifts nowadays are for purposes, not for universities. Some gifts may set up chairs, which adds to endowment only if the subject to be taught from that chair is not new, but already part of the program, and if the income is permitted to go to a man already on the staff. Otherwise the chair is a new gain *and* a new expense, for even at the high price of $750,000 a chair soon begins to eat into the *previous* endowment.† And so does a building even when fully paid for by the donor, which few are, owing to inflation working on original estimates.‡

The general situation is vividly seen in a comparison of the sources of income and expense for each dollar at a typical university during any of the past five years, the percentages being

* Beardsley Ruml in a speech to the Bank Street College of Education in February 1958; McGeorge Bundy reported in the *New York Times* for Oct. 14, 1967, and Alan Pifer, *ibid.*, Jan. 17, 1968.

† The income on that sum being $37,500, assume a salary of $25,000, which is average for a distinguished scholar. Fringe benefits add 22 percent, or $8,250, which leaves the meager sum of $3,750 for secretarial help and nothing for future raises in salary.

‡ It is not easy to build a cheap building and not possible to equip it sparely: the occupants want the latest facilities, including air conditioning, and so does the generous donor. Hence the ratio of annual maintenance to construction is at least 3.5 percent.

rounded to the nearest unit: endowment contributes 24 percent of the income; tuition and fees 40 percent; athletic and other receipts 2 percent; direct reimbursements (not government research, but hospital and other services) 5 percent; current gifts 29 percent. On the expense side, 70 percent of the dollar goes for instruction and the administration related to it; 5 percent for other administration, 10 percent for student aid; 6 percent for the library; and 9 percent for operating and maintaining the establishment. None of the receipts or expenses for government-sponsored research are included in these figures; they form a separate account, even though, as shown earlier, some of the outlays above supplement government money for that research.

Some universities, it is true, have endowments that bear a larger share of the costs; some have no endowments and live on fees; still others show a larger proportion of gifts. These differences are balanced by variations of quantity or quality in the sources of expense: support by fees means larger classes and cheaper instructional costs; more gifts probably mean more sideshows. Administration and maintenance are not easily alterable. For all institutions the only pure, holy, and absolute good is unrestricted endowment, which yields the most precious substance after uranium: university general income. Two important connections should be noted between endowment and tuition fees on one side and student aid on the other. The higher the fees the greater the number of students requiring aid, hence a larger amount of any fee increment has to be turned back to the needy students; also, in the older universities, part of the endowment is tied up in scholarships and is therefore not wholly free for meeting new demands.

BUDGETEERS O BUDGETEERS!

These things being so, the goal of good administration is to make the general income go as far as possible by finding ingenious uses for gift money within the terms of donation. Not all gifts are restricted with equal minuteness. The "annual funds" of the schools that were described earlier tend to be fairly free, though only for use within the specified school. The strategy of the university budget-makers is therefore to "put on a gift" every possible regular expense. But the university budget-makers are themselves not free: their strategy runs into the countermoves of the school and department budget-makers, an amicable conflict on the whole, but repeated, incessant, never won, like the battles of dead heroes in Norse mythology. In order to understand it and at the same time to appreciate the reasons why "business efficiency," "radical retrenchment," "cutting your cloth," etc., are inapplicable to a modern university if it is to remain great in its kind, a typical budget procedure must be described. It will also give an account of the improvement—the measurable efficiency—that was brought about at one institution during the period of our concern.*

In earlier days, it will be remembered, the president in successive interviews with some of the deans and some of the department heads put together a tolerable budget, well within the university income. At a later stage, the consultation was extended, and all the deans formed, with the vice-president, a budget group. It could not be called a committee, because it sat like a small legislature from November through February, its composition varying from hour to hour as other appointments took the members away. The budget book was gone through line by line from page 1, and decisions were sometimes made in the absence of the dean concerned. When he came back the decision was reconsidered. Between the debates on school needs, the chairmen of departments came one at a time to make a case. Orators and table pounders tended to have the best of it. In the end, the whole work might have to be revised, roughly and hastily, because the income estimates had meanwhile come in and the budget for the business side had been adopted by the trustees. A simple subtraction showed what was left for instruction, research, and their administration, and this remainder fell short of the deans' rival budget.

* The reference is, of course, to Columbia University during my administrative time.

Vice-President John Krout led and won the struggle for the principle that the entire budget must be made up at one time, President Kirk having on his side won over the trustees to the necessity of his being responsible for administration in toto and not just educational administration. These seeming technicalities permitted a modernization of budget procedures. It took about seven years, from 1959 to 1966, to modernize the budget. One way of measuring this progress is that in the latter year the time of discussion in the Budget Committee was half what it was at the beginning—98 hours instead of over 200.

Before anything else was done, the budget book was made clear and consistent. All items such as "Assistance" were broken up and attached to recognizable activities, e.g.: supervisor of the slide collection in art history or curator of the chemistry museum. All supporting expense was divided into a few categories, main salaries stated in full, and lump sums for clerical staff followed by the number of posts. Earlier, each school and department had used for these outlays a separate language of its own, whose vocables had to be interpreted and could be justly suspected of concealing ancient peculation and privilege: the totals varied unaccountably for similar services. By thorough "editing" the budget became readable at sight.

The importance of the budget to a university administration is not simply that of any budget to any firm. It does indeed forecast income and authorize expenditure, and it serves as an approved payroll; but every day of the year it tells at a glance to those in charge how the resources are distributed and what educational or supporting work is going on as a result. Turn to page x and you see that department Y is large, top-heavy in associate professors, stricken by many leaves this year, but not loaded with visitors, understaffed in clerical help, yet lavish in stationery and telephones. Other allocations, such as space, fringe benefits, and student aid also are stated or implied. If any changes are to be made in the work, wealth, or happiness of the department, they must start from a knowledge of this history embodied in cost items.

The budget, in short, is to be conceived as a document for administering,* as well as a prediction of solvency. It is generally agreed among leading private universities that as an instrument for the first of these purposes the budget is not in good shape. Too often, what it records is not a plan of judicious distribution but the upshot of faculty behavior.† To explain what this means one must follow the life cycle of a budget; the varieties, only a gifted zoologist could illustrate, but they are all of the dinosaur breed.

At Columbia, in late May, requests for budget estimates go out from the provost to the deans and chairmen.‡ Until a few years ago, the habit was to ask, What do you wish, dear friends? And they wrote back long letters with large totals. By 1958 a form was substituted, which was gradually improved into a pair of documents—one a copy of the division's budget sheets as amended for the current year, and a single page of instructions for organizing future wishes in five categories, promotions, salary increases, and new positions being the main ones. Comments in support of the schematized reply may also be submitted ad lib. All this material is due by early June in the Budget Office, where it is duplicated and tabulated for submission to the budget committee.

That group is no longer the indeterminate body of former days. It came to consist of the dean of faculties and provost (chairman), the vice-president of the university, the vice-president for business and finance, the coordinator of university planning, the vice-provost for projects and grants, the director of the budget, and the associate provost acting as secretary. It is they who spend the hundred hours between June and March reconciling all that they are urged to support, improve, and augment. The task is arduous and not merely monetary: it is about education, for it is in budgeting that the purpose and structure of a university exhibit themselves. Its *purpose* is to turn material goods into immaterial: the product is invisible, not susceptible of measurement. Hence there

* See the definition of administering given in the first paragraph of Chapter 4.

† State universities are usually no better off in having state rules to follow or individual salaries published like other civil-service schedules.

‡ Except Medicine, which has a different rhythm.

is no obvious yardstick for deciding between persons or between plans; there are no profits or losses to be read at a glance, no simple gauge of ability like the output of a manufacturing division.* The *structure* is such that hundreds of persons, having permanence, are equally entitled to press demands, not for themselves necessarily but for what they wish to do or to see done by, with, or for their colleagues. Without knowing it, the faculties and their deans form a perpetual lobby, which may not and must not be disregarded, for they are the university; what they desire (foolish fancies aside) holds in solution present and future greatness.

The budget committee in its turn holds the chief instrument of government and of change. By withholding a raise of $500 for an assistant professor of engineering, the university may lose a young genius (and his angered department head); or by the same act the budget committee may be creating a much-needed gap; or again, it may be reducing the cost of an overstaffed unit whose enrollment is dwindling. To help the committee know precisely what it is doing, various persons and groups are consulted: the deans are invited (or invite themselves) to appear and descant on their needs. The prepared harangues for these occasions tend to fall into familiar patterns, but the following "question period" is full of valuable information. Moreover, the heads of such offices as the registrar's, buildings and grounds, etc., supply statistical reports to back their claims. Finally, standing subcommittees of the budget committee enlist intermediate administrators to sift through requests for clerical personnel and other estimates of service expense, and draw up detailed schedules showing how the percentages of increase or the lump sums tentatively set by the main committee have been applied.

Another subcommittee, the most important, is that which works out the list of salaries and promotions in the departments of arts and science, roughly two-thirds of the university. It will be

* Accordingly, university accounting (a large and complex process that also requires improvement but cannot be discussed here) is cash-flow, not profit-and-loss, accounting.

remembered that these departments provide both graduate and undergraduate instruction, and since chairmen are in closer touch with graduate instruction, their plans need the corrective of the undergraduate deans. This subcommittee consists of the deans of the college, the school of general studies (adult education), and the graduate faculty, and their joint report becomes the groundwork of discussion for the budget committee.*

THE PIE AND THE KNIFE

The bulk of this sifting and weighing goes on during the summer months for the budget of the year twelve months ahead. Budgets come into force on July 1 and affect the work of education that begins in the September following, that is, fifteen months from the start of budget-making. This distance of time accounts for the endless revising which goes on up to the last minute, early April, when the trustees expect to adopt the great collaborative work. In the interval between June and the next April, the plans of many professors change. Leaves are canceled or asked for, acceptances of bids are withdrawn or postponed, grants and contracts altered —a perfect saturnalia of shifts that must be reflected in budget provisions. In this way, certainly, the budget follows the behavior of the faculty, but good budgeting means maintaining the outlines of the planned distribution—and with it equity—regardless of the chain reactions of change.

In early October it is possible for the treasurer and the registrar to give their estimates of income: the one tells of endowments, the other of tuition fees. The registrar, who first consults every dean for interpretation, bases himself on the current enrollment returns (those of the September just past); the treasurer studies the

* In a number of universities, notably Harvard, the dean of the faculty of arts and science directs graduate and undergraduate activities as one unit, the deans specifically assigned to the graduate school and to the college having restricted responsibility. There is something to be said for each system of coordination—and it is frequently said.

investment portfolio and the yield of rental properties. The coordinator of university plans has put together forecasts of the gifts to the schools and to the university. The grand total is always disappointing, but no matter. At that point the budget committee tries to make these funds match the lump sums it has tentatively allotted to the six or seven large subdivisions of expense. Much arithmetic follows, done by the office of the budget.*

If so much is given in promotions, increases, and new posts, so much additional has to go into fringe benefits: the ratio is 18 to 22 percent for academic staff, 9 to 11 percent for clerical and manual. If tuition fees are scheduled to go up, or the cost of room and board, then student aid must go up too. If the NDEA, or the Woodrow Wilson Fellowship Foundation, or the State Scholar Incentive Plan, or the Work-Study Program has announced changes of policy, then many calculations must be adjusted. If the power or water rates, the labor contract, or the state unemployment insurance have increased, the budget is further distorted.

Unemployment resulting from university action is extremely low—only a dean's murdering the president will get two people off the payroll—yet the liability under federal and state law may amount to $400,000 in a salary budget of $50 million. Likewise to be absorbed—or "picked up," as the phrase goes—are the rising contributions to social security, the premiums for several types of insurance, the casualties on "soft money," and—the most crushing blow—the maintenance for the latest building built.† Add to this the normal incidence of the unexpected—a new roof, a new boiler, the nemesis of deferred maintenance catching up and requiring the

* A good budget director for a university is one who learns the protocol of dealing with faculty members (they are not "employees" or even "personnel"), and who can, by studying the budget ceaselessly, eliminate duplications and produce comparisons helpful to the committee. These comparisons can never be mere percentages of dollar increase in various departments assumed to be all of a piece: he must come to know what is comparable and what is not.

† "Soft money" denotes the grants that expire after serving to bring tenure professors, who still expect to be paid.

total renovation of an old building—and balancing the budget becomes year by year a madder tour de force.

Especially anguishing is the number and kind of uncertainties. It is bad enough to have to guess about gifts and tuition fees; but government programs (say, about available loan funds), and government auditing as well, bring an uncertainty of the second degree. The university need of loan funds can be predicted to within a few dollars ($1,698,000), and the money has to be assured, because it must be promised to entering students months ahead. But the federal allocation comes at its own pace, after the fact. Similarly, the indirect cost allowance on contracts and grants is computed by rules that take months to apply to past events. In practice, the amount of the payment due is settled in the third year after expenditure. True, the government has all along deposited money on account, but in that third year, even after careful calculation, the university may be faced with a whopping refund. In short, the number of variables to budget is large and the range of each is like that of the weather in the so-called Temperate Zone.

Difficult as this trapeze work is in itself, there is one more feat to perform, one more deadline to meet, which is the late December sessions of learned societies and professional associations. These lofty gatherings, born of nineteenth-century faith in *Wissenschaft*, have become slave markets on the side, and each chairman and dean goes there with the beady eye of the auction buff. He needs young men to staff his lower ranks, and he is not above making advances to established scholars if he has an aching vacancy, perhaps well over a year unfilled. For his ends he must have from central administration the assurance that he can offer so many places at such and such salaries. The budget committee knows that it cannot assure anybody of anything, given all the variables, which always include the president and trustees. It knows too that without risking these assurances there may be a university in panic twelve months hence. The assurances are therefore given, wrapped in tentatives and stuffed with pleas for Levantine haggling.

Many chairmen do their utmost and nevertheless come back with overdrafts to be honored: they *had* to get those men; the budget-makers *have* to find the money; the university *has* to roll on toward deficit financing. Multiply these imperatives over an area populated by scores of activities and thousands of able persons, and the ride to the abyss begins to look like logic itself.*

Meanwhile, as sections of the budget take shape under incessant revisions, the president is shown the outline of what he will have to "sell." He takes the intermediate summaries home and broods on probable questions from the trustees. When figures become still more exact after second-term registrations in late January, the altered state of the stock market, the latest news from government agencies, the first slice of committed student aid, and the last throes of bargaining with coy outsiders, the president takes the encyclopedic volume home and goes over it line by line, seeking for opportunities to slash, combine, or melt down. He queries elevations too rapid and merit increases too generous. He brings to the work a shrewd and all-knowing mind that has not been abraded by contact with two hundred fierce claimants. In cabinet (which is the budget committee minus the recorders) all that he questions is discussed again and agreement reached as to "what can be taken to the trustees."

An explanatory memorandum of 20 to 25 pages is put together, each section of which is written by the cabinet member in charge of the activities forming a section of the budget. Then come two or more meetings with the trustee committees on education and on finance, at which the budget-makers justify their works. The joint committee acts, and soon the full board passes the budget. From it the controller prepares the payroll for the next fiscal year; the president and secretary send out pre-addressed letters to members of the university whose salary or rank has gone up. It is now the end of April. The budget committee has the month of May, the whole month, with nothing to do.

* For the parts of a large university, see Appendix B.

"AND WHEN HE DECAMPED/THEY DISCOVERED THE DEFICIT."

It should now be clear why the administrative heads of a large university had best come from the ranks of the faculty. The many tussles that ultimately produce a budget would degenerate into a class war if the two sides were not fundamentally of one mental species, fluent in the same language. It is helpful if some of the administrators still do a little teaching.*

The absence of this more or less close relationship is one of the many difficulties that make budgeting for the medical school different from the rest. The life of the physician, as teacher and researcher, follows different norms. The university medical man views his institutional role differently; he is paid differently and turns in such fees as he earns outside; courses are divided differently and taught by several hands; departments (headed by permanent autocrats) assign their staffs differently; grants and contracts are awarded and shared differently. Only an able medical dean, preferably without nerves in his body, can make the budget correspond to anything but the behavior of his faculty and its hundreds of satellites, known and unknown. And even such a dean can turn in a readable document only a few weeks before the beginning of the new year—a year, moreover, which lasts twelve months and not nine like the academic year. The medical budget is consequently autonomous, though cursorily revised by the budget committee.

In the minds of any faculty, of course, the budget committee exists for no other purpose than to "find the money" for what the faculty wants, though it is understood by the askers that the money cannot always be found *the first time*. In practice, the committee

* For the greater part of President Kirk's administration so far, two of the central group continued to give a seminar and one directed a scientific project. Among the twelve deans, six from time to time offered a semester course.

has deeper responsibilities. A good budget embodies many judgments that originate with the committee or the president. None is enforced; the divisions have the final say. Yet only the committee with its synoptic view can reward outstanding merit, mitigate the effect of obvious prejudice, redress old injustice, look out for the young, and gradually straighten what the accident of history has made lopsided.*

In this last effort the imaginative use of statistics can play a salutary part. The budget committee that emerged from the Columbia reorganization of 1955–1967 had the advantage of including as vice-provost Dr. Ralph S. Halford, professor of chemistry, who had long pondered administrative questions, notably the optimum size of Columbia College. As budget-maker, he contributed comparative studies of departmental and school staffs, of student-aid allocations, of rates of promotion and withdrawal (whether by retirement or otherwise), of endowment, salary, and cost increments, all of which enlightened the committee and supplied that "existential" basis for decisions which nothing else in university life provides.

Thus it was remarkable that without premeditation the most frequent distribution of staff among divisions was five tenure members and three nontenure for every 100 equivalent full-time students.† He also established the ratio at which the amount of student aid granted for tuition (not subsistence) ensures, or protects, the increment secured by raising fees. These norms from the recent past should not, of course, be taken as absolutes to follow. I said: the "imaginative use" of the figures derived from

* In the best book I know on the subject, *Finance in Educational Management of Colleges and Universities,* by Thad L. Hungate (New York, 1954), it is said that a good budget procedure is one that "assured wide consultation and participation of all concerned." The extent of concern knows no limits, so to get a budget done in time compels those in charge to deal with persons who *represent* all concerned. To interpret that representation and modify it if necessary completes the approximation to fairness.

† "Equivalent full time" means that two half-time students are taken as one full time, three one-third as one, and so on. It is a convenient way of merging the specials into the main body.

practice. The committee spent hours discussing the bearing of each chart before seeking in it a pointer to action. It is clear, for example, that the faculty-student ratio presupposes a commitment to small classes—8 to 100 gives 12.5 students per man.* The same ratio also suggests something about early promotion, which in turn implies young talent discerned quickly. But these are intimations to be verified by other tests and to be made into policies only when all related effects have been examined. In university working, the most persistent truth is that everything is tied to everything else; and "things" in that sense run the gamut from dollars to degrees, which is to say from the symbol of wealth to that of myth.†

What figures show in the most recent years is that the new university, when it is run on lines of decent self-determination and humane economy, cannot avoid a deficit. There is no waste as the world (and especially the government) understands waste. And there is no possible chance of enforcing retrenchment (as business sometimes can) and still keep a university. The reasons for that impossibility are several and, I repeat, intrinsic. One might as well hope to train a heavyweight contender on the diet of a coolie: a leading institution today needs what its members, after being cajoled and reasoned with, think it needs.‡ If they do not get it,

* The latest count (September 1967) shows that 86.6 percent of all Columbia classes had 40 students or fewer. This does not mean that larger classes up to 100 or 175 do not exist, but they are few and presumably occur by design.

† An ebullient critic and reformer, well known for his books attacking the establishment, was shocked when I told him that a university had to be run like a savings bank. He quoted the words as a confession of depravity, never grasping the fiduciary responsibility of the trustees nor the educational, spiritual, immaterial obligation of making every dollar account for its destiny. It was Emerson who said: "The value of a dollar is, to buy just things. . . . A dollar in a university is worth more than a dollar in a jail."—"Wealth."

‡ Reasonableness, as I have said before, is always there to be tapped, but much depends on the form in which questions are asked: always indicate limits! Several years ago a great midwestern university, afire with planning and prosperity, asked its responsible heads to study ways of improving, by both expansion and elimination, the work of their divisions. The proposals would have added a cost of $25 million a year to current operations. The eliminations of needless activity came to $3,000.

they leave. It is inevitable that in the conditions the world has created for research, each department should think it needs more men, and the very best. Every other department must stay put while *it* grows. It wants fewer students, all of them on full scholarships for the three or four years of the program. It must have more space, more library purchases, more secretarial help.* Its members need more frequent leaves and could use a bevy of research assistants and postdoctoral fellows, and finally, higher fringe benefits to cushion the abrupt change from a fair salary to a pension. After all, in their field they are—and are regarded as—top executives; yet they find themselves engaged in petty struggles over small sums. This discrepancy is one that the world has taught them to measure and teased them into thinking reducible.

A second and also sufficient reason why a university cannot cut back its costs is that they do not stand still for the cutting. With inflation and the normal system of promotion and merit increases, the budget goes up $2 million a year on an instructional-administrative base of $50 million; that is, barring all new activities, the cost of continuing at the same rate is 4 percent a year, or the equivalent of an annual addition of $40 million to the unrestricted endowment. No wonder the president and trustees concentrate on raising current funds, taking endowments as windfalls reminiscent of another age.

For completeness' sake one must consider a third barrier to penny pinching in the present situation. A good budgeteer can always go through the big book and by dint of ingenuity squeeze out, say, $300,000 to $400,000 in a total of $100 million. Once he has done this on paper, he has the task of arguing his need with a hundred or so persons, some of whom will resist with threats of

* In attempting to account for the increasing number of resignations from Harvard and rejections of its offers, a writer has picked up the complaint, among others, of "being stingy about secretarial help" (*Science,* vol. 156, May 19, 1967, 925). The point to note is that to academic men the administrative attitude is more important than the fact. They infer from any "niggling": hostility, neglect, or failing finances, the upshot of which is disquiet and possibly departure.

total paralysis, some accept reluctantly, and some readily consent, inwardly confident that overdrafts will take care of the little difficulty. Success here is a losing game. Academic workers agree with Robert Frost:

> Never ask of money spent
> Where the spender thinks it went.[1]

They cannot, in any case, be subjected to continual harassment; they must be trusted; and most of them are trustworthy, especially after it is demonstrated to them that overstating their needs and overdrawing their accounts nets them only trouble, which they hate. There are control points in university expenditure, but they catch errors and occasional wild acts rather than repress dishonesty and conspiracy.*

Assume that of $300,000 in savings on paper, $275,000 is made good in fact. It is not a negligible sum, but it does not bridge the abyss of $2 million. Moreover, what has been compressed in one year will regain its bulk the next, e.g., the tight stationery account left the department with a bare cupboard which has to be refilled. And the atmosphere of strain pervades and persists, to the detriment of good work, willingness to stay, and that *sense of possibility* which is by now bred into all who do research.

FOR EXTERNAL USE ONLY

Beardsley Ruml's speech of warning about college bankruptcy was the prelude to a small book (written with the late Donald

* The "education" given by the budget committee is decisive in creating or destroying morale. Disclosing all relevant figures, stating real reasons, and keeping promises show the constituency that the budgeting is being done for it and its work, and this wins its cooperation.

Sometimes that reward has to be tussled for, as when a great scholar-chairman kept putting in his budget salaries for visiting lecturers who never came. The money was spent for teaching aids of various kinds. Finally, he being a friend, I ventured in tête-à-tête to call him a liar and a thief. That was a new idea which, coupled with the assurance that he would get some money for teaching aids, led him to present and administer honest budgets. Until then he had sacrificed his mundane integrity for what he considered a noble cause.

Morrison, provost of Dartmouth)[2] in which Ruml proposed countermeasures, chiefly in the size and composition of the curriculum. Too many courses and too many men in the departments at a time of shortage of talent and cash were, he thought, a grave defect that only surgery could remove. The cost of "proliferation" is indeed high, but prevention and cure are difficult, as we shall shortly see. Abstractly put, the plight of the university, as well as of the college, obviously comes from their being unable to support a rising standard of living as industry does, by increasing productivity. True, a modern academic man works far harder and at more varied tasks than his forebears, and he may be doing more over a longer span for the community. But on the campus, as educator, his productivity has, if anything, fallen. He teaches fewer courses on briefer and briefer subjects, and his antipodean depth, which *is* an addition, does not speed the student turnover or multiply university income.

When one begins to think of multipliers, one wonders, Why not teach all the year around and thereby increase tuition receipts and make better use of "the plant"? The analogy with a factory, its output, and its overhead is obvious. But it will not do—not because the academy declines to be thought of as a factory but simply because it is not a factory. Universities that work on the quarter or three-term system have been disappointed in their hopes and hampered in their operations.

A university is unlike a factory in that the product is alive and has imponderable demands, which can be met only by suitable adjustments with the producers, also alive. The capital invested is not in buildings but in men and their development, which all-year-round university work damages or delays through confusion. Under it teachers and taught are coming in or going out like a crowd through a revolving door. The administering of examinations, credits, prerequisites, exemptions, fees, leaves of absence—the whole paraphernalia, which is complex at best, becomes a vast tangle. Numbers plague the soul. Supporting staffs must be increased, often disproportionately to added enrollments. Part of the tuition gain at once goes into more salaries, space, desks, but for less efficient working.

And this burden is as nothing compared to the problems of enlarging and deploying the faculty. Nobody can teach three terms consecutively without being let off one or two. Hence students that go through without a break are robbed of instructional continuity. This is bad for the supervision of the higher degrees. Again, for the university to offer all required courses and their sequels in all terms is a great expense; but for the students not to be able to jump on the assembly line whenever they wish is a great nuisance. To reconcile the two, one must recruit and house masses of junior instructors, which is laborious, if indeed it is possible. In a word, operation begins to supersede education.

And that is not the worst of it: to shift a two-term graduate faculty to three terms (let alone four) means that its present strength has to be increased by 50 percent. Where are suitable men to be found in such numbers to supply even one great university? How many years would it take to recruit such a body of five hundred men? And what would it cost?

These questions answer themselves. The scheme can be thought of, but it's unthinkable all the same.* The university is not a plant, beguiling as the prospect of automation may be: the student fed raw and young into the machine at one gate and emerging bearded and gray at another, machine-finished, qualified in a dozen ways, and even "Inspected by No. 23," just to keep the human touch.

Finally, learning all year long is as bad as teaching all year long, to say nothing of the needs of students who count on a free summer to earn money.† The learning mind needs intervals of

* The professional schools that have adopted a three-term year have found that in order to staff the curriculum as offered, they tended to overwork the faculty, pile up a backlog of leaves past due, and meet trouble in the recruiting designed to alleviate these two evils.

† For accelerating or making up lost time, summer sessions exist at many universities. They vary in length from two to twelve weeks (some run concurrently at one institution) and provide courses, mainly undergraduate, without dislocating the separate administration of the regular sessions.

assimilation and, in study time, surroundings more calm, not less, than they are right now. The ideal of efficiency has a place in the life of learning, but it is an efficiency of learning, in learning—not of or in production. The belief that with machines and arrangements everything can be changed and education will become administrable like penicillin is an illusion that has been repeatedly shown up by costly failure. And to return to costs, the laborious arrangements of continuous operation would leave a trivial gain in exchange for the sacrifice of coherent teaching and academic quality.*

For large universities there is one last resort, which is to spread the responsibility for financing to the constituent schools: each unit on its own bottom, as at Harvard. If a school falls on hard times, it can borrow from Alma Mater, which keeps a reserve for emergencies, then pay back in better days. Tuition rates are set independently, multiple-fund campaigns go on in counterpoint—in short, the federal union is replaced by an association of autonomous states.

Decentralized fund-raising does meet with success, because the alumni of each school feel that their gifts support exclusively what they are interested in.† But that advantage is qualified by certain social realities. Law and Business Schools appealing to lawyers and businessmen will fare well, and so will an undergraduate college with enough alumni.‡ But a School of Education or Library Service, of Dentistry or Divinity will probably be a perpetual pauper. If these end by being centrally supported, how soon will

* The three- and four-term systems are independent of the attempts to reform the calendar of the two-term year, beginning it early in September, or even before, completing the first term by Christmas, and ending the year by May 1. The pros and cons are intricate and tedious to discuss on paper. *Any* reform of the academic year, if it is to succeed, must be generally adopted, like choosing the side of the road to drive on.

† Until 1966, when the present university campaign was launched, fund-raising at Columbia was decentralized; budgeting never has been.

‡ A small college is obviously handicapped by having to call too often on the same few donors; the chances of finding benevolent millionaires rise with the size of the group.

the deans of prosperous schools continue to exert themselves raising money?

Nor is it good to have all of the deans desperate, some from poverty, the rest from being always in the gold rush and never at faculty meetings. Then, too, the power of a single school to resist alumni or donor pressure is less than that of a whole university; and in turn a university will not long keep its oneness if the member schools can say that they live on their own earnings, kindly keep out. Finally, the conditions that are bringing the university to bankruptcy are such that they will sooner or later overtake the schools—unless the schools withdraw from teaching and become research sanctuaries, like All Souls at Oxford, with an undergraduate body limited to four.

TOO MUCH EDUCATION?

The last comparison will not fail to put ideas into shrewd minds, especially if echoes of the Beardsley Ruml critique of the curriculum and of the Parsons College plan have already found place there.* What if the sanctity of the things done for students at universities were but an ancient ritual no longer necessary? Having seen the external conditions of expense and philanthropy, we should perhaps look at the internal uses of money by categories and see what they provide that is indispensable.

To judge aright, we must assume a fixed student body; for a growing enrollment entails more dormitories, laboratories, and instructors, which start a spiral of new costs at the highest prices and obscure present fact. Remember that each student who pays the full fee receives a hidden scholarship of 50 to 60 percent of the

* At Parsons College, Fairfield, Iowa, the "plant" keeps open all year, the faculty receives high salaries and teaches a heavy load; the students choose from a pared-down curriculum, pay high fees, and are virtually guaranteed good teaching. The college pays its way (*New York Times,* July 3, 1966), but it has lost accreditation, as well as its president and some faculty members (*New York Times,* Oct. 22, 1967).

cost of his education: the time of economy is not one in which to increase that subsidy.

The biggest item of present cost is instruction, let us say $42 million out of $70 million for education and maintenance of premises. Government research will add $60 million that we shall consider a "wash item," i.e., fully reimbursed (though it is not). Now, the salaries of professors, as we know, are set by the market, which is stimulated by raiding, by gifts to raiders, and by the AAUP annual survey of salaries.* This part of the budget does not seem a likely place to start reform; the brash institution that tried it would find itself stripped like a locust-ridden field. The most that seems feasible is to reduce mobility (and therefore cost, for the replacement is always higher-priced) by creating a vested interest in staying put. Judicious fringe benefits do this, notably housing on favorable terms and progressive pension contributions, e.g., for fifteen years of service, at the age of fifty, the university will pay the whole premium (15 percent of salary); at sixty and after twenty years of service, the fully paid premium goes up to 20 percent.† This is adding money to save money; it remains to be seen how strong the inducement will prove.

Clearly the bastille to storm is not the rate of faculty compensation but the amount of instruction offered and paid for. Every specialist wants his own course; all are specialists from an early age; the sum of these specialties swells the number of courses; the number of students is static; long division is bound to reveal that each course has fewer students. Each hour of instruction thus becomes more and more expensive, particularly after one adds the cost of teaching the lower reaches by means of assistants and preceptors, not yet in a position to claim "their own course."

* This is so computed and reported that it is not so much a ranking by actual scales of support as a lever for raising the salaries by distributing marks of approval and prestige. Thus an institution that spent most of its money on cheap "slave labor" at ranks not within the hierarchy might get a very high rating for its professorial scale, applicable to but a handful of men.

† This scheme, akin to a stock-option privilege, was put into effect at Columbia in 1966.

The first thing to be done is to show the departments and schools what they are doing with "their" money and how soon they will reach the end of it. This demonstration was brilliantly achieved by an invention of Stanley Salmen's, called by him the "course study."* In effect, it brings together in a few pages, easy to scan, the facts of the budget and of the registrar's office: so many persons teaching so many courses at such-and-such salaries. The name of each man is set down beside the numbers denoting his courses and the registration figures are appended for each term. The cost of instruction is thereby matched with the income from the related fees. Other departmental facts, such as prospective retirements, total allocation for the unit, and so on are added to give those in charge of the work their first look at the departmental metabolism.

At the outset the course study is found extremely offensive: Are we to infer that a professor must pay his way? Is the administration going to favor the men who draw big crowds? Can't you see it's a premium put on popularity-seeking, through easy grades, low jokes, etc.? The flurry subsides when it is shown that no philosophy of education is going to be derived from the bare ratios. Only the ordinary rules of prudence are applicable, and prudence is full of nuances.

For example, if the School of International Affairs needs to have students trained in Urdu, we shall continue to give Urdu, expensively, to five students a year, because we have decided that that is the right way to spend that piece of the endowment, unrequited as it is by tuition income. But here is department X, of central importance, which declares itself overworked and asks for

* One-time secretary of the Harvard Corporation, then director of the Atlantic Monthly Press and vice-president of Little, Brown & Company, Stanley Salmen was Coordinator of University Plans at Columbia from 1956 to 1967. The course study was only one of his many contributions to making the university conscious of its own practices and capable of intelligent change. If any future historian of the university should choose to linger over my own name, I would wish it recorded that my chief contribution is that I persuaded Stanley Salmen to join the central administration at a critical time.

a full and an assistant professor—say $30,000 more on the bill for next year. Turn now to the course study: in that department are Professors M and N, each of whom for the past three years has offered a course attracting only three students each. Total salaries prorated for that pair of courses each year: $13,000. Total tuition income: $1,800. (Keep in mind that instruction is not the sole expense.) What follows is not a conclusion but a question: are those courses by M and N essential, and (if so) to whom? The students do not seem to fight for standing room at the sessions. Unless the department declares the subject essential, it would seem that M and N might redirect their talents in such a way that the two new men asked for could be dispensed with, at a saving of $30,000—not a saving, actually, but a spared addition to cost. The one doubt is, where do the rights of scholarship end and the crime of extravagance begin?

It is a crime, because of the three-men-in-a-lifeboat situation which the academic world is now in. What any person or group within the academy wrongly appropriates cannot be made up for out of any cornucopia. To the credit of the faculties that first endured the shock of the course study, it must be said that they soon made changes in the light of the facts and dropped all talk of "bargain-basement methods." To put it on the lowest ground, they faced a self-contradiction: as professors claiming higher salaries they implied that money was important to the individual; as collaborators in the budget they could not argue that money was unimportant to the institution from which they expected to receive it.

ACCESSORIES AFTER THE FACT

The doubt that goes with any questioning of instruction is whether the administration is not top-heavy. Its cost, on the base chosen earlier, is $9 million, or somewhat over 20 percent of instruction. The reader is referred to Chapters 2, 3 and 4 for descriptions of the services desired on campus by faculty and students. As long as that corner is to be kept warm and swept, administrators of all ranks have to be hired.* Nor does the traveling critic find any university generally overstaffed. Even when an office here or there seems too full, it is probably a seasonal effect, or a false comparison based on the neglect of that particular function at home. This generality holds: university administrations are run ragged, day and night, in all functions, state and private, thirteen months a year.

One of the services does seem wastefully conceived: the Admissions Office. In order to get into one graduate department or professional school, an applicant must fill out forms for six or a dozen different places. Think of it! All the letters of recommendation duplicated, blanks about age, address, educational purpose, and nearest of kin filled over and over again. And on the receiving end, hundreds, thousands of dossiers to be scanned, many of which denote only a third, or fourth, or end-of-the-line choice.

Every application, moreover, is glued to a request for scholarship aid, which usually means the addition of an essay in proof of ability. Artists send canvases or scores; scientists (even when young) published papers. The sorting of this blackened woodpulp, the sitting on its ethereal contents are in themselves an incalculable social waste. I mentioned in passing the minute autobiography required for a chance at undergraduate student aid. Until all this hopeful, verbose, unreal matter is boiled down, there is no hope of ease for college and university and their students. A national clearinghouse, a one-sheet table of contents for documentation available *if needed,* are the prerequisites to sanity. Meanwhile, each application costs on an average $22 to handle, and most universities charge $12 to $15 for the service.†

Student aid itself is becoming a crushing charge, generated by the vicious circle of rising fees, as was explained before. On the

* The periodic Booz, Allen, and Hamilton surveys of leading universities show that administrative salaries are not excessive in relation to the rising instructional scales, rather the reverse.

† Only the medical schools make the fee prohibitive, but it doesn't prohibit. Students are advised to invest $200 to $300 in multiple applications.

chosen base of $70 million, it levies $6 million. In ten years—with government aid, to be sure—its total has risen 400 percent at one university committed to the proposition that no fee increase shall ever interrupt the education of a single student. If an ever-extending mass education is the national policy, then no college or university in these days should be out of pocket for student aid.

The next large item of cost is the Library, or as those in charge make a point of saying, the librar*ies*. For a university law library or science library is as massive an establishment as the public library of a large town. On our base of $70 million, the library cost is $4 million, and the sum is always inadequate. University libraries are *research* libraries, that is, collections always aiming at completeness in multitudinous fields, therefore requiring large spending budgets, specialized librarians, and elastic space. One thinks of the New York Public Library as a mammoth enterprise, but in one year the Columbia University libraries must not only buy but hunt down more books than the New York Public Library, in answer to pitiless demands.* The cost of putting any book on the shelf for users is now $10.08, whether the book is a pamphlet costing $.75 or a $12 tome. What is more, the research library is everybody's resort: the members of the university are matched, on some days, by the same number of qualified outsiders who ask for free use and obtain it, for learning is a freemasonry. Use has doubled for research libraries every three or four years. Net result for the budget: a quarter to a half million annual increase for book purchases and professional salaries.

Latterly, a mechanical counterpart of the library has staked a claim to campus space and general income: the computer with its housing and staff. The machines, from the ancient 1401 doing administrative chores to the 7094 for scientific research, and the gallant 75 (later 91) that will crown the "360" system, need a

* Daily attendance at the New York Public Library was recently 9,000; at Columbia it was 17,000. As for the buying of books, it should be noted in passing that many foundations strike out library costs from project budgets submitted to them, whether the purpose of the grant be instruction or research.

building specially cooled, a retinue of attendants always underpaid and footloose (because business wants them), and a presiding genius who can work out the costs, subsidies, and transferable charges while planning for the obsolescence of units not yet installed and, indeed, still in blueprint at the manufacturer's. The saturation of current equipment takes only five years, and scientists want the new model before the saturation of the old. Overnight, then, the specter of the devouring computer has come to haunt the administrator. It has been estimated, soberly, that by 1975 every leading university will have to spend $10 million a year of its own money for computers. The endowment thus tied up is $200 million.

To be sure, computer time is then "sold" to the users, who put the charge on the government contract or private grant subsidizing their research. But as with the Library, the feeling is strong that facilities are for those who need them, whether they have money or not. The computer should be available to the literary scholar doing a concordance, no less than to the geophysicist tabulating ocean cores, even though the former is backed only by faith. Hence the university must assume a large share of the annual cost of computers, a rising cost that the government demand for assessment contract-by-contract makes more burdensome than it might be.*

The computers on campus can partly redeem their cost by aiding administration. If a set of systems and programs can be devised to meet in full the needs of admission, registration, payroll, account balances, and budget work,† it might permit a saving in salaries of half a million yearly, while ensuring greater accuracy and speed at the same time. For this work a small portion of the

* Not long ago a leading western university threatened to shut down its computer center if a system of charges it felt more equitable was not adopted. Caught between Washingon and its own scientists, a university threat is a mere gesture.

† One of the impediments of good budget-making during the long gestation is the lack of "actuals," that is, a figure next to each item in the current budget showing how much has been spent so far and was spent the year before.

main computer in the 360 system or a separate unit, switchable at will, would suffice for a long time.

Whether the scheme should run to registration by telephone ("I am Tom Jones, put me down"), as has been proposed and tried out, depends on the degree of accuracy obtainable from people en masse when the coercion of bits of paper is removed. The present trauma of registering at a large university is everywhere deplored, by none so loudly as the students, but every move to make it easier—by preregistration the previous spring or by mailed packets of cards—runs into the fact that people "cannot be bothered" until the last minute. Early registrants write down courses at random, with no intention of taking them, thus increasing labor and error; and recipients of mail "cannot be bothered" to return the cards or follow instructions. The university must perforce deal with these free spirits as they are, which is to say, rather unperceptive about the freedom that comes from dispatching routines quickly and correctly, instead of tangling later with the inevitable red tape.*

A further hope of computer aid in academic life has inspired plans for library cataloguing, data banks, and the like, a technical subject in part, but not wholly so. What goes into the computer must at the outset be chosen by scholars, and the product must bear some relation to other scholars' capacity to use it. The machine salesmen and the intellectual middlemen—librarians and journalists—have too readily assumed that knowledge is the assembling of items found here and found there, the act of finding being research. The facts, the literature of a subject, the previous state of knowledge appear to them like goods in interstate commerce, which can be classified, shunted, and put in storage until wanted. The action of mind, if they think of it at all, will come afterwards, when the "retrieval" has been done automatically by the computer.

* The typical state of mind is "can't be bothered to send in a change of address," coupled with indignation that the new address was not supplied to an inquiring friend.

There are short cuts, undoubtedly, that the computer can take in behalf of scholarship; but their value diminishes rapidly. Much has been said with eyes aglow about turning up in a split second "all that is in print on the subject." But a man's search itself instructs him, his quick rejections along the way keep his vision clear; nothing could be more paralyzing to the mind than a thick wad of IBM paper in accordion pleats containing five thousand "relevant paragraphs" on something one wanted to know—or "a computer-based . . . personalized stream of papers," as some enthusiasts put it.[3] The attempt already made with legal cases bears out this predictable experience. Even the IBM experts were dashed when the results were submitted to good legal minds. The conclusion of the panel was: "the less likely you were to do research as part of your practical daily labors, the more likely you were to like the computer's cases."[4]* In a university of all places the tendency of systems to give ignorance an edge over mind must be carefully watched or it will bring about a subversion of one mental class by another, quietly and fatally.

TEMPTATIONS AND TOMFOOLERIES

In discussing data banks we are not off the subject of academic poverty, for educational idealism is ever ready for a sacrifice in what looks like the cause of knowledge. Sometimes the futility or impracticality of the thing is its badge of merit, as in some features of graduate (arts and science) or medical instruction. Again, a field chosen by few students is often held to be superior: real scholarship is abstruse. Or an adventitious duplication becomes a source of pride: "Just think! There are three courses on Dante

* There are also inherent difficulties in language: the computer selects cases by means of a list of key words given by the searcher. You can of course program the machine to supply references for "negligent" when the key word is "negligence," though that will turn up irrelevancies; but you cannot without superhuman work and prohibitive cost keep apart "appropriate" (verb) from "appropriate" (adjective). The notion that the computer reads the cases before printing extracts is a modern superstition born of bad newspaper metaphors.

being given!" That each has fewer than five students, and that this poetic eleven could huddle as comfortably and less expensively in one classroom is deemed irrelevant, close to sacrilegious. Yet small fields have become a grave administrative problem. Under faculty pressure universities try to "cover" everything. Each must have Korean studies, and Arabic classic and modern, and Uralic and Altaic languages, and Demography, and Central Asian Animal Art, together with Ethnomusicology and an institute for every region of the world. The experts in such fields are very few; the bidding for them raises their price; they do not like to be one-man departments and need coadjutors; finally, the cost of supporting small units is always high, and sometimes (especially in the "rare" languages) their clientele vanishes altogether for several terms on end. The argument is: we owe it to ourselves; they do it across the river, why can't we?

Some of these fields a foundation or an NDEA grant has helped into being. Others grow out of cognate faculty concerns, e.g., Korean out of Chinese and Japanese studies. The logic and the first money may be unimpeachable, but both lead to extravagance. The money is not more "soft" than the logic, for departments often change their minds about necessities. In view of these facts, attempts have been made to distribute the fields among institutions. Let the students go to Pennsylvania for Indian studies, to Princeton for Korean, to Columbia for Iranian. But departments balk, affecting to mistrust each other's methods. And there are material complications of residence and scheduling. Only among the Big Ten in the Midwest has coordination worked in any degree to reduce absurdly competitive offerings.

A similar growth difficult to check is that of publications. A great university may be giving space, money, and unaudited services to publish over two hundred periodicals other than catalogues.* Some are fugitive student efforts, but they continue in kind if not in name. Some are newsletters, a spreading plague.

* A recent census showed the annual money cost at Columbia to be $82,000 a year.

Others, the greater number, are learned journals, some of which appear once or twice a year, others quarterly. The distribution list may be 800 or 1,000; the subscriptions hover around 125 in good years. Every journal is indispensable—the department is said to gain immense prestige from the publication, though at times finding it hard to fill an issue. If a departed professor left a small fund for his colleagues' use, the survivors are sure he would wish it spent to spread their writings throughout the world; and the small fund being insufficient, the university must supplement it. Even within small departments there may be "nationalist" movements that burst out in review form, two or three such periodicals expressing divergent tendencies. Infanticide by the administration would be a capital offense; and once past the first year the journal lives forever. In the sciences the rate of growth is exponential. And altogether it is the periodicals bought and bound that make the library walls bulge.*

Under the heading of temptations one could describe a good many other university outlays, beginning with courses and student residences abroad. A brief sampling of the rest must suffice. "Memberships" consist of institutional payments to scholarly groups, whether societies, museums, archives, archaeological digs, or other expeditions. They too grow rapidly, in part because of the new restlessness about everything "established." Regular subjects are old hat: we must cut across them; the old society (founded in '96) is *impossible:* we need a fresh one. The same fear of offending the young and stifling the genius works to prevent any pruning. "Memberships" run into the scores and cost some $25,000 a year. Similarly, faculty grants must be made to young scholars, especially in summer. With these goes a large subsidy to the university press for publishing good dissertations and scholarly writings that have no chance of meeting their costs. Here we approach one of

* The predictions of the late Fremont Rider have come true, but his best proposals have yet to be made use of, notably the microcard in place of the periodical. See *The Scholar and the Future of the Research Library,* New York, 1944.

the topics of the next chapter: Is there a "knowledge explosion" or only a bulky imitation of one?

Finally comes the cost of being represented by one's scholars at learned congresses and other academic occasions, by now an acquired right of theirs, closely allied with that of getting a salary supplement when a national award or professorship abroad carries a stipend lower than the normal salary. A university pays for the honor of having a Pitt Professor at Cambridge or a Fulbright at Aix: there is no honorable way to avoid the tax.

SELF-DEFENSE AND INCOME-RAISING

With the final category of expense, the business critic is perhaps most familiar and most in sympathy. He believes in public relations and slum clearance, and therefore understands why an educational institution maintains a news office (with radio and TV divisions); an office of neighborhood services; an office of publications (catalogues), whose annual turnover (including stationery and forms) comes to $1,250,000; a legal department (sometimes a large firm on retainer); and joint or single representatives in Washington and elsewhere. As for defense against the elements, that is, maintenance current and deferred, it comes on our chosen base to $7.5 million a year for the current, including reserve, which means an appropriation of $1 to $2 million annually.

The attention given to the town or city takes the form of buying deteriorating houses and renovating them, after relocating or rehabilitating the unhappy tenants. These costs come out of capital, since they are to yield returns, however inadequate. In a large city it is easy to sink $15 million, perhaps in concert with nearby hospitals and charities, to remove in ten years the blight of the SRO's (single-room occupancy buildings, in each room of which, by law, not more than two families may live). Add to this the cost of a private night patrol—$30,000, as at Chicago in the worst time—and the largest endowment begins to look pitiful.

Readers may also remember the great fund drive. Is it not a

huge additional expense during the years of the main effort? The fact is that if well-run the campaign should carry itself by means of the interest on the gifts before they are used. The normal cost is 2.7 percent of the receipts. True, that figure covers only direct outlays. The help for carrying the strain on the university—as by more assistance for deans—is absorbed by the administrative budget and seldom separately measured.

It is a generality that cost accounting, which is an art of imagination at best, becomes on the campus a cause of despair and logic-chopping. Annual reports prepared by the controller's office show what each school costs, but the deans of those schools invariably protest. They cannot be "charged" for what they have no hand in spending. They object on colorable grounds to the prorating system for light bulbs and wet mops, or they maintain that the old roof belonged to the university and they replaced it with *their own* money, i.e., raised for the school.

Despite all quibbles, it is clear that the several kinds of education and training within a single university vary greatly in cost, the medical and graduate (arts and science) being the most expensive. When it is said, therefore, that a student pays less than half the cost of his education, the statement gives an average that buries the extremes. By the same token, schools and programs vary in the amount of their expenditure over revenue, but none—despite the deans' occasional hallucination of solvency—receives as much in fees as it pays out. The days are gone when some division, usually the evening classes or the summer sessions, "made use of the plant" and brought in a net sum.

These calculations and others naturally preside over the setting of tuition fees. Two considerations are dominant: the interference with education that may be caused by higher fees and the rates charged at comparable institutions. The latter is, indeed, an aspect of the former, since it is desirable that a student choose a college or university on other grounds than the tuition rate.* At present

* Parity is not so easy to achieve as might at first appear. For a long time the method of charging by the single course at Columbia resulted in making

the leading institutions closely hug the $2,000 mark and tend to favor an inclusive and uniform fee for all programs. They are reluctant to go up much further, but consider the rise inevitable. The question then is the mode of increase—regular on an announced schedule, in amounts of not less than $200 every two years, or regular at $100 a year, or irregular, or by a yearly alternation of increased tuition and increased room and board rates.

Deans and budget-makers pass anguished hours over these unpleasing choices, which are complicated by a price-linking among professional schools of one kind across the country. Their moves may not fall in step with the university's preference for a convenient uniformity within. However arrived at, every tuition increase requires a supplement to student aid of about 20 percent of the additional income. Contrary to a common impression, student aid has quadrupled while tuition rates doubled. Government scholarship and loan have contributed much of the increase, which still leaves many students preoccupied during their course or in debt after it. Graduate study is almost everywhere subsidized in such a way that the good worker can count on four consecutive years without worry. But it is this same group which is now threatened with interruption by the draft, thereby involving the schools also in deplorable confusion.

The real damage of rising tuition fees is just this interference by uncertainty. Though steps are taken to prevent a student's dropping out for money reasons, there are always casualties: some refuse to take a loan, others are upset enough in their calculations to resign in disgust, all are apprehensive—not the best prospects for an educated nation. The conclusion of a weary budget-maker unwilling to see tuition go out of sight and of reach is that, if the

---

the Ph.D. degree less expensive by a half or a third than the degree at sister institutions. To give up the course charge or to impose a flat terminal fee was equally resisted by the faculties, always tender to the student purse. Dean Ralph Halford solved the problem by the invention of "Residence Credits" charged for during six semesters and yielding a suitable return.

country wants the able to go to college and the ablest to be further trained, the most direct and efficient way is to make government aid to education consist of scholarships guaranteed for the length of the course and coupled with a substantial "cost of education" payment to the institution. This extension of the current practice might require diagnostic skill in sorting out the mere shoppers from the real students at the entrance to graduate and professional work, but under proper safeguards the subsidy would mean clean-cut support of what all profess to want supported.

A last word on the private-and-poor must go to the matter of investments. The suggestion has been made that, if the universities would only rub off their gilt edges and throw in their lot with growth industries, their income would float up with the inflationary wave instead of disappearing in it. This remedy is more easy to imagine than to carry out. To begin with, numerous states have laws prescribing kinds of investments for charitable trusts.* In the second place, the cost of the risk must be reckoned—and when is a good time to take it? In 1945 all the best economists predicted a severe recession. It is reasonable to budget a deficit and make it up by taking the capital gains on appreciated stocks, as a committee of the American Economic Association has recommended. But to do this indefinitely and with the rising deficits whose causes I have tried to suggest would call for financial acrobatics beyond the power of most trustees. If the rejoinder is to hedge with less spectacular common stocks, then the income problem remains. Safe issues will yield less than 5 percent and afford only modest gains.† Compared with them, mortgages and rental properties give

* The state universities, which are but little better off than the private, run into even closer restrictions. Indiana, for example, forbids a state agency to own common stock or benefit from patents, such as scientists and engineers sometimes turn over to their university.

† The Ford Foundation Annual Report for 1966, which advocates the investment in common stocks, estimates that a yearly improvement of even 1 percent would yield the colleges and universities $120 million a year. That this sum is twice what Ford gives to education and research does not make it suffice for the needs at hand. The Yale plan (*New York Times,* Sept. 25, 1967) for augmenting returns on the portfolio through a holding corporation will bear watching.

a higher return and are as steady. In a word, no bonanza is in sight.

So far, the new university desired by the nation has been stimulated by its suitors but not fed. That is why, from time to time, it is caught by the mirage of owning factories and handling patent rights, which might attach it to the pipeline of affluence. But it has no business meddling in such things, for it is not in business for business but for education.

7 The Higher Bankruptcy

The one thing not to be forgiven to intellectual persons is, not to know their own tasks or to take their ideas from others.

—EMERSON

But annyhow, degrees is good things because they livils all ranks.

—MR. DOOLEY

THE DISENCHANTED REPUBLIC

A social institution is like a mountain. It is huge, rough, majestic, ungainly, treacherous, ever-changing, and impossible to see as it is: it looks totally different from opposite sides, and even from a few paces to the right or left of the point of view. Yet we climb it, and it is one. For at the summit one sees other mountains on every hand, making ours a distinct, shining peak. So with the university when it becomes mountainous. It cannot appear the same to outsiders and to occupiers, to the citizen at a distance and to the one just welcomed in and bearing gifts. But having somehow climbed it—stumbled up it—as was our purpose in the preceding six chapters, we may see it now more completely than before. And yet something is lacking, There is a fog that blurs the distinctness from other social institutions. And when we ask those observers that have also seen it from the top, they report the same spectacle of diffuseness, the same lack of identity and radiance.

The critics assign different causes and point to different aspects, but even the most inexperienced and self-centered talk as from a sense of wrong, as if a great deception had been practiced upon them by speaking of a university, leading them to it, and giving them—*that!* Students are of course the bitterest in their disappointment, and they express it in unclassifiable ways. With the candor of youth student leaders at Stanford two or three years ago summed up the emotion I mean when they told the president: "We have no set policy. We are trying to reshape the University in the way we would like it to go. The American university is not Utopian. We are idealists, trying to build a Utopian University."[1]

They went on to claim administrative powers and planned ultimately to build a "free and loose society." That very association of ideas shows that they think the university has capitulated to the world and must now be judged with it as unworthy. This is the great common denominator of protest: the university as bad as the world. To make the point perfectly clear, let me suggest that if students came from the world they know to a monastic university, full of learning, devotion to teaching, and visible sacrifice to both, they would regain their piety and accept the most arbitrary regimen without a murmur.

There being no such university, almost all the attacks go with programs of liberation. The "free university" movement, which numbered as many as six "cells" within a year, offers an "egalitarian learning situation" run by students, no credits, low fees, and a curriculum that "answers their needs." They learn a "Marxist approach to art" and "definitive analyses of society, the world, sex, and freedom."[2] This effort is to undo the evil of the universities in which "students have been dehumanized for delivery to business and other bureaucracies."

Against these statements it is idle to argue the Marxist bias or the naïveté of "definitive analyses." Other students are saying the same thing differently, and their elders—indeed the wisest among them—are saying it also. It comes to this: the university has lost its magic. The word of complaint everywhere is: *impersonality.* The word denotes a spirit even more than a natural result of size.

That excellent critic of literature and intellect, Dr. Gordon Ray, calls the university's loss of touch with its students the "Achilles' heel" of the institution.[3] And he discusses Berkeley's seething thousands. But among the hundred or so of one graduate department at Columbia, and a rather cozy one at that, the same objection is made about the lack of opportunity for contact with the faculty outside class, which is ascribable to the "pressure to publish and to participate in world affairs."[4] The point to note here is that the literal fact is probably misstated, but the emotional one is not: faculty members can be seen and talked to, but speed and suspicion make the encounter seem as if it did not exist. I find significant the remark of a perceptive teacher of sculpture who says that he has given up addressing his class of less than a dozen "because they pay no attention to anything not said to each personally."

The general formula for this phenomenon was given by President Harry Gideonse when he spoke of the loss of organic cohesion in our institutions: what we have is "atomism packed tight."[5] A shrinking consciousness explains a good many traits of the new university, particularly the desire to form new and spontaneous groupings. The idea is to choose friends and build a little society with them, all the better if it is done in the teeth of resistance from "the establishment." Student societies in vogue are no longer the traditional ones, fraternities or literary and dramatic clubs; they are ad hoc and always new, being formed. The faculty yearning for institutes and centers and interdisciplinary groups shows a similar motive at work: we'll be by ourselves, doing what we want—nothing *regular!* In parallel with the dropouts from society, one might call these the "university hideouts." If the university is now the all-embracing merchant guild I mentioned on an earlier page, these groups are the nascent craft guilds seeking an autonomous life outside the walls of routine.

But what is the matter with the routine? Was the "routine" of a university not supposed to be elevated in purpose, inspiring in action? What has happened to this purposive action? It seemed guaranteed for all time by the character of those involved, but when the world approached them, full of devotion but also of demands, this character changed and took on that of the demanders. These still come, eyes aglow, voice and gait subdued, thinking they are within the portals of Love the Beloved Republic, but whether or not they discover their mistake, the university cannot help knowing that the republic has turned empire. It has assimilated itself and is only another institution like the rest, no better than it should be. Yet nobody ought to conclude that the university has been contaminated merely by contact, or that earlier its members were of finer clay now coarsened by mixing. Contact and communication in themselves are excellent, invigorating, but only if both participants keep their idea and identity. These may be usefully modified in meetings and partings, but they must not be given up.

The greatest theorist of university life, Cardinal Newman, pointed out a century ago that colleges (in the English sense) are "the corrective of universities. . . . By a college is meant not merely a body of men living together in one dwelling but belonging to one establishment."[6] We would say today: one enterprise. To be *one,* a university does need physical limits that can be grasped and a continuity that can be taken for granted. But both are consistent with a fairly large establishment, if the true idea pervades it. The association of older and younger in the enterprise of learning is that idea, that routine which is now despised because the disinterestedness of its effort has evaporated. The feeling of making, building, resisting, overcoming is gone. The young are sullen or indignant. They feel exploited, because they feel surrounded by the perfunctory, not *making* but making believe—casual teaching, mechanical scholarship, assembly-line research.

EVERY CAMPUS ON MARKET SQUARE

Some might say that "the students" referred to are but a few morose spirits, and that the faculty members who flee regularity are just as exceptional. Otherwise the campuses would have witnessed not riots but massacres. I judge the proportions of numbers and importance differently. Enough, indeed, has been seen on campuses to amount to the massacre of the university's dignity, and I include in the causes of loss the many public quarrels between presidents and faculties, regents and presidents, senates and administrations, young scholars and departments, old scholars and public officials—all the incivilities, bad logic, and bad faith, to the spectacle of which the public has been treated. These too are symptoms of a deep disorder, which is why we are looking at the university-mountain from yet another point of the campus.

To be sure, it would still seem resplendent if we looked only at the scientific work, the absorption of old and young in arduous studies, and the selfless behavior of the best teachers. There is still a company of scholars and scientists who, though scattered, have the vocation to continue their proper work, in the catacombs under the strife-torn crossroads; and it is they who for the time being sustain the university as an institution. And supplying unconscious support by their inertia is the greater part of the student body, the "mandarins" who work to "qualify." It is not from them that a renaissance is likely to come, but one must be grateful for their stolidity. None of this alters the fact that everybody who thinks, or has thought since the rise of the new university, is in disquiet.

By these thinkers' reckoning one or another vital organ is failing. If all were well, each day would not bring such a load of discourse on what is wrong and what remedies are right. If the discordant voices connoted the energies of life, they would not be so often querulous and impatient.* If within the institution all

* An experienced administrator, Dr. Alvin C. Eurich, says that our present practices are inadequate and that current ideas must be "desanctified, re-examined, revitalized" (*Saturday Review,* Sept. 3, 1960). A great scholar, Marjorie Nicolson, terms higher education "debased" by our educational leaders' capitulation, "first weakly, then wearily," to the demand for lowering standards and increasing output (*New York Times,* Dec. 29, 1963). An editorial writer says we must "light a fire" under education authorities so they will "assume a larger and more activist share in the fight against ignorance, poverty, and unequal opportunity" (*New York Times,* July 23, 1965). And the president of a great foundation condemns the leaders of higher education for "neglecting urgent action and being busy framing essentially self-serving statements for delivery in Washington" (*New York Times,* Jan. 17, 1968).

were happy and proud though insolvent, fresh supplies would probably not be hard to come by. But so much dissatisfaction and disgust is crippling and must be traced to its source, in the university and outside. The two, inside and outside, now form a conglomerate which the critics try to push this way and that and find immovable. The reason is that its footing is buried in educational ideas and social habits of long standing, petrified into a solid mass by their very contradictions and willfulness.

What is so stated must now be shown. The first obvious interpenetration is that of the university and the members of the college, who are products of the lower schools. The lower schools are a compromise between public expectations and professional educationist nostrums. Of these three, the college, being the universal joint between school, public, and the world of learning, requires our attention first.

In American society the college is the gateway to good employment. Every year the figure goes up that expresses the value of a college education in future earnings. Banks publish it, parents daydream about it. Depressed minorities view the college as the tunnel out of prison into economic freedom—it is the great equalizer, as Horace Mann said of all education. But now nothing short of college is education. Do we conclude that it is an instrument universally approved for preparing the able young to earn their living, delivering them duly fitted to "business and the bureaucracies"? Not at all. Though hundreds of communities are setting up local colleges—"instant campuses"—that will serve as such instruments,* going to college is a social much more than a vocational preparation. The newspapers speak of college students as ipso facto middle-class and privileged, and there are demands for making the public institutions more representative of the sur-

* E.g., in Baltimore, an extension of the University of Maryland, beginning with 1,800 students, plans for 20,000 in 1970. In Dallas, within eighteen months, a junior college reached an enrollment of 8,000. At the same time we are offered "A Junior High That's Like a College" in Newton, Mass. (*New York Times* Magazine, Oct. 29, 1967, 32). Obviously the parts of the system are "all through ither," like the inbred Scottish isle.

rounding population.* The college, we conclude, is a place where following an *exposure* to learning (such is the accepted term) a social stamp is affixed, the B.A.

Not at all! cries still another group. The college is not for either vocational or social ends. It is for education, which is bigger than social and vocational goods. Specifically, it is for injecting the necessary dose of the liberal arts into the undergraduate *before* he enters economic and social life. At this shaming reminder everybody begins to praise the liberal arts. They are indispensable—to what, is not clear: some say, the good use of the burdensome leisure that is coming; others, the inculcation of "values"—we need citizens, democrats, humanitarians; still others, the making of strong, critical minds for all uses; and yet others, the development of native gifts: we need artists and such people—creativity.

But what is a college, after all? As everybody knows, the answer is: almost anything, anything that calls itself so and is not blatantly a diploma mill. There is, in short, no idea in the name or reality of the college. This is not the same as saying that some colleges are inferior, others good, and the rest superior, but simply that colleges are not institutions of one kind (or even of two kinds, such as technical and liberal), and that of the greater number no particular good is expected except the B.A. This lack, this void of idea, which has for some time characterized the lower schools, now marks the college and is affecting the university.

It is no argument against the void that an institution can serve several purposes. In all endeavors there is product and by-product; and makers of college plans are full of notions about what their college will do to and for those who entrust themselves to it. "Objectives" are the richest crop in the world—all the virtues and the powers of man are promised, in perfect balance and vaguest language. This automatic blurb-writing only adds to the trouble:

* "Higher education in California in no way represents the total community of which it is a part." This declaration by a state senator was based on a disparity in percentages between students admitted to the state university and minority populations. The senator urged a change in standards and testing methods (Los Angeles *Times,* Jan. 7, 1968).

the country has decreed mass education but has never made up its mind what it means by it. The impulse is to give all the young the benefits of some presumed good. But supposing it were milk, there would be little awareness whether any given dose of it were the true sustenance, or half milk and half water, or liquid from the nearest ditch. It would be ladled out in the mood Shakespeare attributes to the misguided Brutus when he killed Caesar:

> . . . in a general-honest thought
> And common good to all. . . .[7]

BANKRUPT IN MIND AND PURSE

Around any idea, present or missing, allowance must naturally be made for fruitful diversities of structure and outlook. One kind of college does not mean a single pattern reproduced from coast to coast. But what are we to think when the dean of one of the oldest liberal arts colleges finds it necessary to proclaim that "America's educational system is in danger of becoming a vast factory committed to the production of specialists, technicians, and fact collectors . . . making it increasingly difficult for the college student to achieve a mature understanding of himself and his proper relation to society—to achieve, in short, a liberal education"?*

When the best and strongest institutions run this danger of subversion under "pressures" and "forces," one knows that not only the vast public but the experts also have neglected their duty. American educators—far more numerous than teachers—have to this day not managed to tell the nation what education is and where it can be got. The touted liberal arts are no answer, since they too require explanation. Academic leaders of opinion have wasted their wits in spendthrift, extravagant talk in public, and are plagued on campus by students in large numbers who grumble about "relevance" and want the curriculum in their own hands or in open scorn set up "free universities" on the spot. Is not all this,

* David B. Truman, dean of Columbia College, now vice-president and provost of the university, at Dearborn, Mich., Feb. 1, 1965.

one wonders, the fit reward of "educating for the twenty-first century," instead of simply educating?[8]

The relevance question is indeed a clue to the whole degradation of thought and language from which the academy now suffers. It is as absurd to try educating "for" a century yet unborn as "for" a present day that defies definition. Relevance is in the mind, a perception of the way ideas are related; it is not a connection between things. Siamese twins are connected, but not relevant. When students find no relevance in their studies, the cause may be one of several—they may have been taught by "fact collectors," whose bad example has not induced the habit of finding relevance; or they have been led to think that anything local, contemporary, or popular is ipso facto relevant (or "more relevant") than something not so present and hot;* or finally, they have been indoctrinated with the error that their "needs" are the same as their "wants," which means of course that later needs not yet felt, later relevance gradually disclosed, do not exist. By these errors they have been made restless, uneasy about whatever they are doing—"am I getting the real dope?" No wonder they do not act like students: they have been kept in the dark about the point of their own endeavors and turned into apprehensive malcontents.

Misled likewise by the phrase "preparation for life," students never suspect how indefinite this criterion of life is. College should prepare for what life and whose life? The life of the mind and emotions? There are fifty careers in a class of fifty and a dozen facets to each life: where is LIFE? Business executives and professional leaders know better; they keep saying to the colleges: "don't try to prepare your graduates for our techniques and routines, which may change overnight. In-service training will teach the tricks; you teach them to use their brains, work hard, and be

* Thus at an urban law school recently the students organized a course in military law, in which the curriculum was "deficient." The new subject was "relevant" because a war is going on, and "students will want to come here rather than go to their classes." When peace is signed relevance will presumably have shifted to the law of international treaties. (*New York Times,* Oct. 23, 1967.)

adaptable. Of course, B.A.'s should know *something,* but you'll attend to that."

In this confidence they are mistaken. The "needs" theory, coupled with the social and preprofessional intention, has overlaid what might have been, with suitable variations, a curriculum, a course, a program. These terms imply: a form and a point. Form and point are now obscured and nullified by innumerable "majors" in journalism, home economics, communication arts, creative writing, real estate, and "effective living." All are worthy activities, especially the last;* they require ability and training, but they are not educational subjects. They are vocational or professional subjects, the difference being set not by tradition alone, as some would like to believe, but by their nature: first, these subjects cannot be reduced to theory and principle; second, they look inward, not outward—they end in a delicious muffin or a well-drawn lease; they do not lead out to the great network of topics and questions about which the mind feels a permanent lust to know.†

It would be easy to show from history that when the cry of Relevance is heard, it is because the spirit has gone out of whatever is being taught. And spirit in education means also *spiritedness.* When the classics crumbled under the onslaught of science seventy-five years ago, it was because science was fresh and concrete and its proponents also, whereas the classicists had become engrossed in philological analysis and *were not teaching the clas-*

* In case anyone should think that subject an invention, I must record that I learned of its existence when, after a public lecture of mine, a young man introduced himself as Assistant Professor of Effective Living at a midwestern university.

As for college courses, their range of subject matter is infinite from "Cosmetology" and "Advanced Ice-cream Making" to "The Pleasure Horse: Appreciation and Use," followed logically by "Blacksmithing." After these, "Police Science" and "Fire Science" seem almost philosophic.

† I say "the mind" and not "the best minds" or any such snobbish phrase, because observation shows that all but diseased minds have a yearning to "know" in this sense, even when their capacity goes but a little way. Soldiers in camp, workmen along the road, strangers in a stalled bus will, given the chance, wonder about matter and God, discuss the nature of love, or grow vehement about justice and the criteria of truth.

sics. The revival of the classics (and the "great books") in the past twenty years shows that they had neither gained nor lost relevance, but merely found convincing interpreters. From Bacon to Robert Hutchins and taking in stride Woodrow Wilson and Jeremiah Day,* the lesson is the same: the subjects of learning underlie the subjects of information. You can forget the details of history or chemistry and have gained immense profit from learning them, because by learning them you have become a different being; but forget the details of real estate management or ice-cream-making, and you have nothing.

No doubt it is because educators secretly know this nothingness, this educational futility of practical courses—no good to business, no good to the student—that they never cease covering their nakedness with grandiloquence. "I like to think of education," says an able college president, "as a process as large as life. It seems to me that learning is a process . . . as inescapable as breathing."[9] Very true, but in the sense in which it is true there is no more to be said, it will happen; we can go home. Meanwhile what the student picks up from such truisms is a mixed attitude that is unfortunate. Having all of life to "educate" in, he can indulge himself a bit; and he misses the spur of difficulty. There is nothing in front of him to do that must be done. For what others sing to him is in the same vein: Education must release the potential of creativity. Education is "to gain new insights into the self and the lives of others." Education "develops aesthetic experience and capabilities"; and of course helps to acquire a "set of values," which sounds like a box of chessmen to play the game of life with. Educated parents themselves catch this habit of speech and praise the college of their

* Professor at Yale in 1828. He wrote in a famous report of that year: "Our object is not to teach that which is peculiar to any one of the professions; but to lay the foundation which is common to them all. . . . But why, it may be asked, should a student waste his time upon studies which have no immediate connection with his future profession? Will chemistry enable him to plead at the bar, or conic sections qualify him for preaching? Or astronomy aid him in the practice of physic? The answer to this is: . . . 'Everything throws light on everything.' "—T. R. Crane, *The Colleges and the Public, 1787–1862*, New York, 1963, 89–90.

child's choice as an "experience . . . that enriched his capacity for both living and giving."

The concentration on *experience* in all these partial definitions is the great flaw. Because "values," "creativity," "living and giving" lie in the realm of experience and are good, it is supposed that they can be "given" directly, taught as experiences, and that the college is the institution to contrive all this: have a syllabus on effective living, take a course in effective living, and then say "I've had effective living." This is but a slight caricature to light up the deepest rooted error of American education: for thirty years we have inverted the sensible order of things. We have tried Instruction to instill Virtue, and Experience to remove Ignorance. I contend that Ignorance is best removed by Instruction and that Virtue is best instilled by Experience.[10]

The next worse error is the related one that Experience (in the sense intended) can be contrived. The truth is that when education ceases to be itself and tries to ape life or to forestall it, it turns false. And the attempt is at best entertainment and at worst anti-educational. For it casts upon all of education the coloring of make-believe that past adolescence youth most resents. An educational experience is an experience of education, not of life—except in the sense that anything in life may be said to be of it. In short, regardless of vocational training or education, or both, nothing will fit a youth for life except himself.

For lack of such obvious straight thinking in the faculties and in the catalogues that they write for the public, college education is regarded and judged either as dull, grim training, or as a series of moral and aesthetic experiences ("STUDENTS LEARN THEOLOGY BY LIVING IN EAST HARLEM").[11]* No wonder many students take to drugs and sex as more genuine experiences still. The cliché that

* The love of confusion inspires clichés which keep common sense at bay, for example, the cliché about the teacher being educated by his students as much as they by him (perhaps he should pay the fees?) or that about the new need of our age for people to return for "more education" throughout life (in which case one's education should perhaps be *rented* from the college, like a telephone).

education never ends thus virtually ensures that it doesn't begin, confusing as it does the proper and finite activity of an institution with the infinite possibility of a man's own development.

The upshot is that the college and its contents remain "a problem," and because this amorphous experience-education is hard to keep fresh—let alone nutritious—hundreds of conferences are held in order to examine it and devise "innovations."* Articles are written on "new approaches to the liberal arts"; good money is spent to "make college meaningful" and "break up the routine by field trips and seminars" that shall be "exciting"—the desperate activity of people trying to revive a lifeless body. And while teachers of Freshman English, having tried everything but hypnotism, declare their subject a lost cause, college administrators wonder where the money to keep up the show will come from.

PREPOSTERISM

It will occur to sensible people that, if college is growing weaker and fuzzier, the university is bound to correct the deficiency for educable minds. In graduate work, surely, they will find intellectual order in the system imparting intellectual habits in the learner. One of the strong passions of youth is to be treated as mature, and intellectual subjects are the first and best medium for the equality they seek. The so-called gap between the generations is only increased by efforts to bridge it on the level of emotion and experience, for obvious reasons. If that gap seems today so wide, those

* In one conference report, "Innovation in Higher Education," which was the outcome of long sessions and generous subsidy, the recurring theme confirms the generality above: "The main push was away from teaching writing through rhetorical techniques, and away from teaching discrimination or taste in literature through literary history or literary forms, toward finding ways to enable students to grapple with literature and with their experience directly" (Tufts University, Dec. 10, 1965, 9). The reader had been prepared for this by the preliminary statement that "the pressing task was to involve the student in intellectuality, in evaluating experience, in connecting theory and pratice. Emphasis on involvement reflects an emphasis on the student as doer, as being plunged into the underbrush and making his own way out." At this point college is obviously superfluous.

efforts may be the cause. Unfortunately, the role that a university plays in its college is no corrective to the deficiencies of experience-education. But before explaining why not, two things must be made clear. One is that the description of the college so far given is not a roundabout plea for a particular type of college; it is only an argument for putting the right name to what one is doing. If the country wants vocational colleges, well and good. They can be excellent in their kind. If it wants experience centers, in which the students will be chiefly engaged in outside projects, experimental learning methods, and new "approaches" to old subjects—in "cutting their own way through the underbrush"*—that too can be justified. But the result in either case will not be an education: it will be training in the one college and acculturation in the other, both desirable.

Why bother, then, with education in the strict sense, the cultivation and tempering of the mind so that it becomes flexible and strong, and acquires control of powers that are enhanced through learning to control them? Control includes being able to summon up these powers, and put them to work at one's pleasure or under examination by others.† And this command of one's mind goes with important arts now thought trivial accomplishments: the ability to talk and write coherently, to notice detail and be accurate about it without being enslaved to precision, and to depart, not on principle but with judgment, from conventional opinion or practice, holding all the while a fund of knowledge with which to acquire more. Why, it is asked, go in for "that great postponement, education" which, as Glenway Wescott goes on to say, "is expensive"?[12] The only conceivable reason is that many

* See preceding footnote.

† No person by way of being educated resents examinations; they are so instructive. But I sympathize with the modern student's revolt against them, both because they are often multiple-choice tests that affront the thinking mind and because the modern discussion course is no preparation for the orderly mustering of subject matter. The teacher sets an examination based on a systematized treatment that he possesses (or finds in the book) but has never imparted.

people are born who want it and are capable of it.* The benefit they confer on the nation is obvious but incidental.

The second matter to be clear about is the trick of thought by which modern educational practice is bedeviled to its own destruction. It is the preposterous fallacy, which I have called *preposterism* to save it from suggesting the ridiculous, for it is rather sad. That is preposterous which puts the first last and the last first. Take the disastrous outcome of having used for three decades the "look-say" method of teaching reading. Educationists had observed that people who read do not proceed letter by letter to form words, but take in the whole word as one outline. From this true proposition about reading at last, the false one was inferred about reading at first: children learning to read were expected to follow the adult example—*cat* all in one glance, with a picture to help. The scheme led to every absurdity—"reading-readiness," the horrible repetition of the Dick-and-Jane books, the limited vocabulary doled out like a dangerous drug through every grade, and finally the illiterates-by-training, who in high school still confuse *tall* and *talk, advance* and *askance*. That anyone emerged from the long ordeal liking to read is a sign of man's unconquerable mind.

Now, preposterism is the principle that explains what otherwise would appear madness in college and university. To jump from beginning readers to Ph.D.'s, consider the assumption behind the highest degree: it is noticed that trained minds who investigate a subject and write a book about it sometimes make a contribution to knowledge. Valuing knowledge, we *preposterize* the idea and say to every intending college teacher: you shall write a book and it shall be a contribution to knowledge. Since the Second World War, as everybody knows, the mania has become endemic: everybody shall produce written research in order to live, and it shall be decreed a knowledge explosion.

* ". . . but this John [the lawyer] would not be quiet, but he must be a Scholar too. . . . Being then ten years of age, he learned to reade, and at the year's end entred into his Greeke grammar."—Aubrey's *Brief Lives,* ed. O. L. Dick, Ann Arbor, Mich., 1957, 168.

An explosion it may be, of print and paper pulp, but the knowledge is extensively imaginary. One has only to listen to the private confidences of the ablest scientists and scholars, and to have oneself some familiarity with a given subject to be persuaded that an enormous amount of the research output in all fields is: (1) repetition in swollen fragments of what was known more compactly and elegantly before; (2) repetition, conscious or not, of new knowledge found by others; (3) repetition of oneself in diverse forms;* (4) original worthlessness. In the midst of all this matter there are of course good books and true discoveries, but they do not come to life because of the surrounding mulch, and their worth is not the result of the general compulsion.

Endless illustrations of preposterism will occur to every reader of educational literature. All the schemes for "enlivening" the curriculum are based on the belief that you can get the wished-for byproduct first, in isolation, and drop the product. The drive to Excellence is a case in point. Excellence is what other people say you have achieved after the work is done. In the doing, the energies should be bent on the task and not on excellence. There are no externals of excellence to be appropriated by going after it or them.†

In still other situations preposterism can be defined as the confusion between role and duty. For example, it is an observable role of the arts to convey moral ideas and generally to "make men more moral." Even the violent amoral art of today is by its very stance intensely moralistic. But as soon as that role is laid on art or artists as a duty—i.e., putting first what comes last—art ceases to have any effect at all; indeed, it ceases to be art and becomes

* E.g., the young scholar who knows he must produce quickly and impressively to earn his promotion will stop in the middle of writing a book so as to make a little article of an interesting point he has found, instead of slipping the point quietly into a footnote to the book. He does this three or four times if he is wise. The need for more journals and library buildings springs from this excess.

† The words "excellence" and "excel" may needlessly confuse the issue. One may strive to excel, i.e., do one's utmost, surpass oneself or even another. But to go looking for Excellence as a separate commodity is to chase a shadow.

preaching or propaganda. The curse of this inversion in curriculum-making we have just seen. It could be called "engineering" in the bad sense; or again, contempt for the difference between a transitive and an intransitive verb when applied to human beings: nobody can "broaden somebody else's horizons"; the somebody else himself doesn't broaden them—*they broaden,* perhaps after the learner has learned something which can be taught and which fits itself to his whole previous mental organization.

To believe anything else is not only conceit on the part of the teacher or the college, it is also mistrust of the student's inner power to fashion "values," "aesthetics," social conscience, and the rest: whatever of these may be engineered into him has the perishableness of whatever is done by mimicry and gimmickry.*

The best liberal arts colleges have resisted this error as well as the jargon with which it is garnished in a vain effort to appear distinctive. They have kept a strong grip on solid subject matter and trusted to its broadening, deepening, and thickening effect. They have also held to their faith in teaching, have insisted that the brilliant Ph.D. proffered by the big university be able to keep the class awake and moving through the syllabus. On the strength of these merits, they have latterly maintained that they might prove the salvation of the university college, where the liberal arts are in danger, as we know from Dean Truman's warning and others'.†

A GUILT-RIDDEN PROFESSORIAT

The neglect of teaching in the university we have glanced at in an earlier chapter. It is a side effect of the drive to "produce," that

* ". . . college might help to change the individual himself, to broaden his horizons . . . to give him a new sense of identity. These changes . . . occur especially where education is seen as a total experience embracing not only courses and examinations but opportunities . . . to try various styles of life . . . Such planning of a total educational environment, etc." —Nevitt Sanford, *Where Colleges Fail,* reprint from the Introduction, San Francisco, 1967, n.p.

† See Harry D. Gideonse, "The Purpose of Higher Education," in *The College and the Student,* ed. L. E. Dennis and J. F. Kaufmann, American Council on Education, Washington, D.C., 1966; and also Appendix D, Nos. 95 and 114.

is to say, print, and of the outside activities that go with expertise. What was not mentioned in the previous discussion is that the best college teaching has traditionally been done by the men in the lower ranks, and it is they who now have to compete the most fiercely through research. They are thus deflected from the time-consuming and energy-draining art of instruction. What is more, they have acquired from the new system suspicion and distaste for courses in the liberal arts: every subject is "too large," and they do not know enough for the philosophical treatment of small ones. An experienced, well-stocked mind can take a single book, author, or small period and make the scholarly virtues of thoroughness, accuracy, and precision accompany the discovery of ideas, facts, and suggestive relationships. But it is much easier to teach these same subjects from a "professional point of view," that is, to go through the work or works of the poet as if one were supplying the notes to a new edition, taking form, ideas, imaginative marrow for granted.

Or again the historian, the economist, the anthropologist can teach introductory and intermediate courses as so many steps in technique, as if technique ahead of purpose introduced anybody to anything except boredom. The very same technical instruction ceases to be boring as soon as the student has decided that he wants to become a historian, economist or whatever, but as freshman or sophomore he has evinced no such intention, and he will hardly find it budding within him if, swamped with bibliography and method, he never even gets a glimpse of what the subject is. No matter, the misguided young instructor, from pride or fear or laziness, makes his teaching reflect his newly acquired professional skill, thinking perhaps that the department is looking over his shoulder. And the older scholar may teach listlessly what does not feed his current "research interest."

The mood that leads to these misdoings is a compound of several emotions. There is the desire to be as scientific as science,*

* It is an academic irony that in the natural sciences teaching is taken more seriously, often in a spirit of broad understanding coupled with professional minuteness. Older men of high standing volunteer for teaching the

the wish to remain a professional at all times, the missionary urge to make converts to "the discipline" and sometimes—alas—the inability to do anything but pass on the professional technique. No more than the graduates are faculties now disposed to think of themselves as intellectuals, with all the obligations that ensue. In becoming the great producer of research, the university itself has turned into a specialist, a big industry, suitably diversified, whose members honestly believe it gives good value and will go on forever as it is. It follows that they could not do better for the next generation than to introduce them to the approved techniques.

In this atmosphere it was logical for the mandarin system to grow and flourish. From the graduate school this profitable professionalism has descended into the college, which is why the university is not its savior. In the upper college years, the bright student specializes; he does "independent research"; he makes useful working contacts with an elder. In the lower years, he gets the general education requirement "out of the way." With the advanced placement program permitting the ablest college entrants to start as sophomores (the high schools having successfully pre-empted what used to be freshman courses), college work is squeezed flat, a thin partition between the improved high school and the professional university. Naturally, the partition comes to seem an annoying obstacle to be got rid of. Bright students are impatient, from youthfulness and from encouragement, to be apprentice specialists. To be asked to serve as assistant to a scholar and help him verify footnotes is the first step on the ladder that leads to the status of postdoctoral and sure-fire grant collector. And what is thus contrived with care and skill in the best colleges is imitated more or less foolishly elsewhere. But no matter where, the cycle seems designed to prevent an excess of well-educated persons in the university faculties, in college teaching, and in the nation at large.*

---

freshman course, and recently some have taken an interest in devising introductory courses for students who know they will not become scientists.

* An engineering dean asks of a graduating class and their friends, "Why do not university graduates readily consider themselves intellectuals? Or conversely, why should some feel a slight tinge of uneasiness, or even insult,

I say "the nation," but this new phenomenon only happens to be more conspicuous in the United States than elsewhere because of the sharp and sudden contrast with our tradition of the liberal arts college. In the entire Western world, as Ortega y Gasset pointed out some years ago, "the contemporary university has developed the mere seed of professional instruction into an enormous activity; it has added the function of research; and it has abandoned almost entirely the teaching or transmission of culture."*[13] The question is how long the public, in spite of its suspicion of pure intelligence, will accept a training university instead of the teaching university that it thinks it is supporting.†

There might be no objections worth heeding if everybody up and down the system were cheerful and lively about his place in it and the results of its operation. But the opposite is true. Young faculty members are abnormally nervous and glum about the future, despite what is termed a sellers' market. In intimate gatherings of the middle-aged and old, the most frequent utterance is that if they

---

in being so addressed?" and he gives as a reason that "there is very little respect evident for pure intelligence."—Wesley J. Hennessy, Class Day Address at the Columbia University School of Engineering, May 31, 1965.

By contrast, an anonymous "New Assistant Professor" at Dartmouth, writing a "Love-letter to a College," justly praises his students for being "not 'professional' about learning, but eager amateurs, less smooth but also less bored, innocent in the full sense of the word. Some teachers prefer to instruct junior-grade graduate students. I happen to like . . . the Dartmouth undergraduate, who I believe is capable of seizing on the heart of the matter precisely because of his openness and worldly insouciance."—*Dartmouth Alumni Magazine,* April 1965, 14–15.

* One observer at a midwestern university thinks the disaster already consummated: ". . . the faculty and lower administration have been divided into all sorts of distinct interest or professional groups which have little or no intellectual or social unity. . . . We don't really have colleges, we have many departments in search of a college [and] . . . no department or division has responsibility for the total intellectual life of the student."—John Weiss, "The University as Corporation," *New University Thought,* Detroit, vol. 4, no. 2, Summer 1965, 37.

† Out of every hundred youths of the right age, forty go to college, half of them reaching the B.A.; five carry on to the M.A. and .8 to the Ph.D., M.D., and other professional degrees. It would seem elementary to order things somewhat differently for the forty from the way they are ordered for the 5.8 who have different aims and are from four to six years older.

had their lives to live over they would not enter the academic profession. Allowing for temperament, which may dispose men to dream of repeating or of changing their careers independently of the facts, the recurrent bitterness will strike anyone who can remember earlier talk on the same subject. A good judge says:

"The most pervasive academic corruptions . . . are of a less tangible and more tragic kind . . . the everlasting angling for place and promotion . . . the overemphasis on specialization, minutiae and trivia, and the refusal to look at the larger consequences of one's work, its place in the larger whole. . . . 'But these [you will say] are the corruptions of life itself, particularly in our kind of industrial society.' and I reply: 'We yield the good life more often than we need to.' My wish for you, Rip, is that you will [be] true to the instincts that brought you into the academic profession in the first place. . . .

"What a change has come over the academic world since I entered it over thirty years ago! How quiet, unworldly, and innocent it was then, how modest the material surroundings and rewards, how few the opportunities for glamorous careers. College professors were a kindlier, more unpretentious, more humane, more earthy, less sophisticated breed. Remember, . . . you are now entering what has become one of the bitchiest professions in the world."[14]

AGAIN, WHERE ARE THE DISCIPLES?

As for the graduate students, whose peculiar work at the top of the tree of learning is presumed so blissful that it deserves to be imposed on the college, they and their mentors alike agree that the life is not simply hard but an ordeal. They must study and prepare for oral examinations while they work for their living, usually by acting as assistants or readers or "section men" in classes that "do nothing for them," and for which they consequently do little.* It is

* From an anonymous letter recently received by a department of graduate study: "A friend of mine is at present 'grading' final exams for a

dinned into their ears that *research research research* is the aim and end of life, and they know at the same time that a teaching post in a college that pays well is the need and means of their proximate life. The "post" is thus only a job, one for which they have not received one half hour of training and one which in itself has no future. Success comes only through recall to the mother university, for published work.

That phrase reminds them that after the orals a dissertation has to be written—how and on what matters less than how quickly. For many topics Europe or other foreign parts are inescapable and disheartening!—Fulbright, children, wife working (or also a candidate), more library work, and in a foreign tongue—it is a nightmare. Besides, except in science, the good subjects are all gone, pre-empted by those bastards in power in all the departments. One is reduced to "Danish Newspaper Opinion on the Death of President Kennedy" or "Machiavellianism in Hotel Employees"—the artificial flowers of learning; or else, if one wants to indulge a critical taste, one risks a subject that may turn out not to be one, such as: "Banality as a Destructive Force in the Novels of Dostoevsky"—another potential petard in the knowledge explosion.

Nor is this intellectual maladjustment the worst, for some graduate students are not after academic jobs and hardly belong to the university. "Our new-style students," says Professor Richard B. Hovey of Maryland, "are bringing to graduate school problems which neither the faculty nor the administrators are prepared to cope with. . . . It is no longer the exception when a graduate beginner starts his interview with the adviser . . . by explaining that he is free only on Tuesday and Thursday evenings and Monday and Friday mornings. . . . The reason is that only on two evenings is he free of his job and only on two mornings can his

---

large course. This individual has attended none of the classes and has at best a scanty knowledge of the subject. Yet this person has no intention even of making a show of grading the exams, but has secured the grades given for the midterms (which were graded in a most haphazard fashion) and is simply affixing them to the finals. . . . I am sure my friend is scarcely the only graduate student who indulges in that sort of thing."

working wife spare him from baby-sitting. . . . [There] are [also] students who are on leave of absence from their jobs for a year or so and who must complete their work within that period."[15] The writer draws the educational moral by comparison with the old-style graduate student: "He might have been hard up, [but] most of his working hours went into study . . . it never occurred to him that courses and requirements could be tailored to his private schedule." He had *fellow students,* with whom he exchanged gossip and ideas; he was part of an academic community, and "his circumstances enforced upon him a harder attitude toward his scholarly discipline. . . . Almost never did he expect graduate study to be easy . . . our new-style students have built-in expectation that the institution [will] take over tasks and responsibilities it never used to assume."[16]

For most students, then, in college or later, the shift has been from *study* to *qualifying*—a new form of initiation congenial equally to the university and to the world, for the world has allowed itself to be academicized in all but its manual work.* The technique of research, of footnoting, of long reports in jargon, of covering the "literature" before starting to think (or instead of it)—all these relatively recent ways of getting on, and sometimes of getting things done, are products of the *ménage à trois* that unites business, government, and the university.† The young mandarins accordingly pawn their intellects at the institution for a number of years and expect on retrieving them a passport to the available affluencies.

Nobody should feel surprised at this outcome, for an institution necessarily reproduces its kind, and the young qualifiers reflect in

* Or as a friend puts it who finds "academicized" a tongue-twister: "The university has macadamized the world."

From a radio advertising bureau pilloried in *The New Yorker* (June 26, 1965): "A meeting was set for next week . . . to evaluate plans for the initial study in what is anticipated will be a chain or sequence of pilot studies leading up to a major study in which several measurement methods will be compared simultaneously."

† See Appendix D, No. 70.

their persons the scholars in orbit—a further proof that the faculty members *are* the university and guide its course, in so far as the heavy traffic around it permits. The further replication is in the subjects of study themselves, which in the last few years have been the occasion of shaming indictments. The humanists are accused of having betrayed the tradition in their keeping by slavishly imitating the sciences and ignoring meaning in favor of technique; and the scientists have been called "campus mercenaries," hence also betrayers of science, for allowing themselves to be led by the nose in response to the smell of money.*

Since there is self-criticism and a live memory of better ways, why is there no redirection of effort? What keeps the great imposture going? One motive power has just been mentioned: money. We looked at its appetites and affinities in the last two chapters. With federal support for education going more and more to "create new centers of excellence," the current system of research and training will be extended and strengthened, not reformed. Unavoidably imitative, the new centers are seeking and getting, in science, the contract-bearing men they want, and in other fields the big names, suitably sterilized from teaching by offers of a salary without duties. The aim of the new centers is to turn out "desperately needed" Ph.D.'s,† for which purpose programs are improvised somehow, without adequate staffs, library holdings, or experience.

But a second and still greater power propelling the American

* See "The Shame of the Graduate Schools," by William Arrowsmith (*Harper's Magazine,* March 1966); "What's Wrong With Graduate Literary Study?" by Louis D. Rubin, Jr. (*The American Scholar,* Spring 1963); and the report of an address by Mr. Gerard Piel to the American Philosophical Society, in the *New York Times* for April 25, 1965. (Also: Appendix D. No. 119.)

† The Department of Labor has for three years been sounding the alarm. In its Manpower Report of 1965, it called for 185,000 new Ph.D.'s before 1975, including a substantial number not choosing teaching. The yearly output is far from uniform in quantity, quality, or tenacity, but with the new programs it should be possible, by 1975, to satisfy the Department of Labor.

university is Prestige. This is a postwar invention. For prestige must not be confused with reputation or greatness and glory, which existed before. Greatness and a glorious reputation descended on institutions after a long course of remarkable achievements. Prestige is preposterous, i.e., it is acquired first instead of arriving last. Prestige means choosing faculty appointees who will look stunning in the press release. Prestige means getting the man or the line of goods that has just come into prominence. Prestige means picking up the top people in mid-career so that nobody can fail to see their beauty, instead of farsightedly judging the young and future kings. Prestige means image-coddling for maximum visibility.* Prestige means getting a good rating in the surveys and polls of excellence, and avoiding trouble so as to appear in the press both frequently and favorably. Prestige, in a word, is commercial advertising.

The late William C. Fels, president of Bennington College and a true educator, published a brief but definitive castigation of blurb-writing for colleges simply by quoting from the catalogues of the best known: each claimed in unctuous prose all conceivable advantages and promised parents and students programs so closely fitted to the figure that Fels was driven to conclude: "Fortunately, progressive colleges no more than traditional colleges do exactly as they say."[17] Catalogues are now the least of the instruments of self-praise. Slick descriptive books with pictures of students studying and frolicking, of faculty members thoughtful or in paroxysms of pedagogy,† alternate with leaflets and brochures detailing the

* A useful formula is: $ViP = \frac{2p + 5n}{f}$, or Visible Prestige equals twice the number of Pulitzer prizes plus 5 times the Nobel, divided by the total number of the faculty. Said a university relations officer at an intercollegiate gathering: "We had to reorient our image to make it visibler."

† A public relations firm, advertising itself, makes the point: "During the past decade a quiet revolution has occurred in college public relations. Ten years ago, the majority of publications released by colleges and universities were graphically unexciting—drab examples of the publisher's art. . . . Then [they] woke up to face competition. . . ."—Circular from Wm. J. Keller, Inc., Buffalo, N. Y., 1967.

merits of individual departments and programs, together with the fellowships waiting to be plucked there.*

The loss of dignity is patent. To notify the public is one thing; to gurgle on and on about oneself like a complacent dove is another. The language of most academic publications is no longer academic.† Under the influence of the news office (which in some universities employs as many as twenty or thirty experts), the development office (the money-raisers), and the faculty authors of foundation projects, sobriety of speech has come to look like surliness. The belief prevails that public expectations must be soothed by advertising what cannot be: we are distinctive and yet typically all-embracing; we are ruled by plan and yet growing madly in complete freedom. Self-praise rots judgment, false standards usurp the mind—it is the drug experience.‡

DR. JEKYLL AND MR. HYDE

In the turmoil of seeking prestige, of pursuing lucrative and noticeable outside work while juggling with the unwelcome kind inside, faculty members and administrators can hardly be supposed to think much about the idea of a university. No clear contrast with the college, which has mislaid its own idea, is there to help them. Graduate students, as we saw, have also lost their innocence and press no *educational* claims that might act as a brake. Publicists encourage the chaos with their loose talk of

* As graduate dean, I have myself been the instigator of such leaflets, from seeing plainly that in the clamor of claims a good department would pass unnoticed if on distant bulletin boards its existence was not signalized by a piece of print.

† E.g., a document from a professional school that had to be censored in galley proofs: "Increase your self-understanding! . . . This novel educational experience which is both powerful and controversial, etc. etc."

‡ From a Catholic college of otherwise good repute: "—has long recognized the importance of the sciences in a liberal education. Ranks third (according to a federal government survey) among the nation's Catholic colleges and universities in the production of graduates who receive science doctorates. Ranks seventh . . . in the percentage of graduates becoming physicians. A scientist would call this objective evidence."—Advertising in *The Catholic Digest,* July 1967.

relevance to the problems of the age being the sign of vigorous and influential universities. And on campus the dogma of free choice for students is used to condone waste in professional and nonprofessional studies alike: that only half the entering engineers graduate in engineering, that leading schools of international affairs send only 10 percent of their products into international affairs and 20 percent into teaching (most of the others going into government work in no way international)—all these commonplace occurrences are taken as part of the order of nature. Administrators would be pilloried if they spoke out. Meanwhile "the average faculty member . . . like the average student [is] concerned with his private career . . ."[18]

This scholarly individualism has gone so far that no chairman or dean would attempt to control it, and no public opinion among immediate colleagues does control it as it did as recently as six or seven years ago. One reason is that this new independence is not cynical but expressive—it expresses the drift of the institution itself, which has no time or energy to concert measures. All feel that there are enough committees as it is, and that "participation," if it were possible, should rather affect policies that affect individuals. It is only fair to add that the flight from the institution, like the flight from students, is a response to a universal skin disease: the need to avoid more contacts. Communication—except within the profession and its comforting lingo—is exhausting, and the effort only worsens the sense of nonaccomplishment which possesses everybody.

In professional work itself the prevailing bent of mind is not toward the concrete, which requires judgment and compromise, but toward the abstract, which is clear-cut and proceeds by deduction. From the new math to the social sciences, all is categories and "models." The sociologists scarcely soil their hands with a living example. The humanities themselves, linguistics in the van, are straining toward the mathematical form. Philosophy is language analysis. In a word, the university—barring those crass people, the historians—is in the hands of Platonists.

That fact might be thought encouraging to whoever is looking with Diogenes' lantern for the idea of the university; but alas the idea of a university is not a Platonism, it is a principle of discrimination within the flood of concrete events, a continuous practical choice between what fits and what does not fit the purpose of higher education. President Gideonse has worded with blinding clearness one of the questions that a university should ask and ask until the multiform standard becomes second nature: "Are we in positions of educational responsibility really engaged—as we say —in the 'promotion of learning,' or are we involved in the competitive merchandising of social status?"[19] And he goes on to show, with examples, the related need of "toughness in the exposure of moral or social illiteracy in high places."

Again, John W. Gardner states what should appear a commonplace but is not, because of our determination not to distinguish anything from anything else: "Properly understood, the college or university is the instrument for *one kind of further education.* It should not be regarded as the only passport to a meaningful life or the sole means of establishing one's human worth. And we have come perilously close to that."[20]

If judgments linked with the idea of a university were at work, some body of university men would have prevented—or at least challenged—the relabeling of dozens of incompetent institutions as "universities."* What a thoughtful (and intelligible) sociologist calls "The Protection of the Inept" has, on his showing, much to be said for it in our industrial system.[21] But unless the American university as a collective force is finally accepted as but another industry, this protection should be denied to the upstart institution that also qualifies as inept.

In another domain the university should have led the way in

* Here is the head of the Social Science Department in a midwestern teachers college enlightening a widely attended workshop in his putative subject: "Social science is defined as more than a collection of facts but as effective and harmonious social living. Or, still another way of putting the same idea: social science is the art of gracious living. Those steeped in the social sciences can live this dynamic idea better than those not so steeped" (Report of the CHSCCI, 1959). That teachers college has since become a state university.

ascertaining and publicizing the difference between the useful and the deceptive: I mean the clutter of machinery, the so-called aids to teaching. Some are excellent, like the equipment of a language laboratory, various projector devices, and certain films for scientific or medical demonstration; others are fraudulent or futile.* Too often the visual aid is to teacher and student what the coffee break is to the office worker. And still worse than the canned lecture is the mechanized mass meeting—800 students in one room and 400 more hearing or seeing a lying replica of the event in scattered places. At some institutions the disheartened student may even stay away and borrow a tape. Zeal and mastery by borrowed tape has yet to be proved.†

WHAT IS ACADEMIC? WHAT IS ART?

An institution that justifies itself by its output of scholarship and wants only the best should have learned to distinguish between journeyman and original work; and—no less important—between academic and nonacademic work. A writer in *Science* deals with the present shape of the first of these failures when he points out that "Basic scientific research is concerned with new ideas, new concepts, new principles"; from which it follows that "the overwhelming majority of scientists are not capable of performing basic research to any significant extent. . . . Hence there has arisen that form of self-deception in which the scientist reasons

* A film that professes to teach a portion of physics in twenty-seven minutes is probably useless, even though not a word or fact is out of place. The slickness prevents instruction, just as the pace prevents taking notes on what the lecturer says or writes on the blackboard. The performance meets the standards of commercial television, not those of the classroom, where halting, thinking, and even starting to say or write the wrong thing does the instructing.

† Senator Paul Douglas says of his own university days: "But the greatest inspiration came from men outside [my] department, notably John Dewey, Charles A. Beard, and James T. Shotwell. Beard was at the height of his powers and was the finest university lecturer I ever heard. Every one of his lectures was a finished performance and threw new light on past events."—*University on the Heights,* ed. Wesley First, New York, 1968)

that if his work is 'undirected'—not directed toward a specific goal—then it must be basic research."[22] *

It would not be difficult to find the counterpart error in the assessment of work in the humanities and social sciences. That large bodies are bound to make mistakes and mix mediocrity with merit is no rebuttal to the charge that in the new university the prevalence of "courtesy" and laisser-faire nullifies every measuring stick, even though everybody keeps prating of standards. Privately, there is recognition of true worth; publicly, the impatient young prestige-hunters go by fashion rather than intrinsic merit. They do not hesitate, for instance, to dispossess or disaffect older men of high achievement if the "line" has "gone out of date," thus conclusively showing that they do not understand the part which continuity and the presence of embodied talent play in the life of a university. They act rather like alert sales managers, who drop and take up lines as the grapevine suggests. Whatever company they work for is not a company of scholars.

Indeed, the latest breed of unattached, uncommitted university men should rather be called Sophists; and this is only to say that they come under Emerson's stricture, quoted at the head of this chapter.

Pondering another tendency of the past decade—the mutual involvement of the university and the fine arts—a sanguine observer might hope that it would bring to the academic world a renewed sense of the genuine, a firm grip on the nature and nurture of talent. Regrettably, it is not so. On the one hand, some of the new faculty artists encourage the anarchy they find, mistaking it for freedom and creativity.† On the other hand, neither they nor

* This is what Lord Rutherford meant when he said that every good laboratory consists of first-rate men working in great harmony to insure the progress of science; but down at the end of the hall is an unsociable, wrong-headed fellow working on unprofitable lines, and in his hands lies the hope of discovery (traditional in Cambridge).

† At one conference seeking "innovations" to break the deadlock of freshman English, the livelier half, composed of young writers, would not tolerate any doubts that every gifted writer could teach. Such doubts were met by slurs against "reactionary chairmen of English departments." Just

the university have given thought to the difficult question of merging the creative with the academic. The problem has long plagued the conservatories and art academies of Europe: the true creator is likely to go his own way from the start, to be strictly incommensurable, usually unrecognizable. He looks at first like a bad artist. But he ends by showing the world why academic art is a term of reproach.

Now, there is no trouble about equating great art (even a beginner's) with great scholarship and science. But besides being hard to assay, great art is very rare. Hence the university inspires—and is called upon to judge—merely competent art. Is that good enough? On what basis is it to be judged? In academic scholarship or science, technique suffices and questions of doctrine or tendency rarely interfere with a fair judgment. In art, technique is not enough and tendency is at once all-important and productive of passions. There is in art a principle radically opposed to the principle of the academy. Between the two there can only be a *mariage de convenance,* which turns out to be one of great and perpetual inconvenience.

On the workaday plane of hours and credits, the conflict continues: is a course in scene painting the "laboratory" equivalent of a course in chemistry? Scientists and humanists well-disposed to the arts think they detect a difference; the proportions of theory in each are not the same. And again, young artists want to do little else than their chosen work: they are professionals by instinct, and what they most like to do uses up long stretches of time. Should the university bend its schedule and requirements accordingly, while denying academic students the same right to skip the uncongenial? In short, what is the meaning of the common degree?

Perhaps the culture's new favorite, art, can be acclimated to the culture's new catchall, the university, but the attempt calls for

---

"liberate" the freshmen as only a real writer could do, and we should be seeing themes, stories, poems in profusion, not all great or even good, but *genuine,* and sufficient to pass the requirement. Exceptionally hard cases could talk into a tape recorder and, hearing themselves, become writers.

thought much more than for friendly feeling. And the first product of that thought must be a conception of what university work is. That idea once in the public mind and communicated to interested parties, the student of an art will know whether he does not after all prefer the concentration of a conservatory (or dramatic or art school) to the balance that a university must require between studio work and the normal academic requirements. Even in graduate school, the practice of the art for the university student will have to be matched with the theory, history, philosophy, and sociology of his art.

That is but one example, perhaps the most obvious and appealing, of the kinds of judgment by which the new university must define itself anew, and by a series of such choices reach its idea. There is of course no guarantee that it will succeed, given the load of demand and complaint it receives from the modern world and the corresponding loss of will to maintain its form. Let us recall the provinces from which it has abdicated: the unity of knowledge; the desire and power to teach; the authority and skill to pass judgment on what claims to be knowledge, to be a university, to be a scholar, to be a basic scientist; finally, the consciousness of what is properly academic—a consciousness which implies the right to decline alike: commercial opportunities, service assignments for industry, the administering of social welfare, and the bribes, flattery, or dictation of any self-seeking group.

Having said this, one must add that there is nothing in an idea, or in a criticism based on an idea, to compel reform. History shows that independent Sophists loosely attached to schools can continue their work for generations, do some incidental good and bring some light. But men who are prudent if not wise should avoid *hubris* and always be haunted by the possibility of an iconoclastic movement from disenchanted followers, when "the love of many shall wax cold" and material support stops. For everything has its limits, and as Lucian—a Sophist himself—imagines the Moon saying about the big schools of his time: "Be sure you tell all this to Zeus: I can't stay much longer where I am if he won't stop the mouth of Dialectic, raze the Porch to the ground, set fire to the Academy, close the Walks, and put an end to the Aristotelian discourses there."[23]

Shall we side with the Moon (which we need anyway for young love and cold war) or shall we keep the Academy from burning? The choice may soon be forced on us, and not in the weasel form of a priority.

8 The Choice Ahead

Education, longer and longer, eating up life—and death on time.
—STEPHEN LEACOCK

Let us not burn the universities—yet.
—H. L. MENCKEN

"WATCHMAN, WHAT OF THE NIGHT?"

The preceding chapters should have given the reader a sufficiently detailed account of the American university for him to understand the choice it now faces. The new university can get newer and newer, that is, larger in scope and numbers, drifting with the demand and only occasionally using the tiller or backing water.* It will in slumber dream of itself as a great national force and call itself a multiversity, which at first only a few will see as a contradiction in terms.† And for a while all will seem well enough, that is, in a state of trouble. Federal transfusions of cash

* The terrible modern fear of the word "back" applied to action is quite groundless: there was nothing but approval when Columbia backed out of the cigarette-filter enterprise and admitted a "well-intentioned mistake" (*New York Times* Editorial, March 1, 1968). Any other view of *going back* or *taking back* implies infallibility.

† Robert M. Hutchins: "The multiversity does not appear to be a viable institution. There is nothing to hold it together, and something that is not held together is likely to fall apart."—"The Next Fifty Years," American Planners' Institute, October 1967, 12.

will keep the great heart pumping; friends will rally round and bring jam (rarely meat); and commencement speakers will administer with a free hand the drug of self-praise.

Then the parts will begin to drop off, as the autonomous professor has begun to do; or go into spells of paralysis, as the student riots have shown to be possible. Apathy and secession will take care of the rest, until a stump of something once alive is left to vegetate on the endowment or the annual tax subsidy. The change will be gradual enough for everything to adjust to it, and *varsity,* neither *uni* nor *multi,* will survive, in utility a vestige just next to the Electoral College. Some will think the two connected, as the names suggest.

None of this would mean the end of higher studies. Private nonprofit technical institutes, business and government programs (already very numerous), free groupings of students and citizens, will have created substitute centers during the debacle. The professional schools will go their separate ways, as they think they would like to do now. The character of these studies would of course be different. They would concentrate on advanced training of all kinds. Research, applied or undirected, would be carried on at the best and richest places. Learning and fundamental research would go into limbo.

If something like this were to happen, it should not cause surprise or railing at providence. The harm will have been self-inflicted. And this too is natural. The idea of the university, which I used in the preceding chapter as a reflector to show where we are going, has been tarnished many times. Take as indicative Oxford and Cambridge. In the early 1600's Cambridge was under a cloud for giving degrees scandalously to barbers and apothecaries who never attended. John Donne got his by royal order.[1] A hundred and fifty years later the poet Gray of the "Elegy" was made professor of modern history, again at Cambridge, by ducal influence, and "following custom . . . delivered no lectures."[2] He paid a deputy. At Oxford in the first half of the nineteenth century, "lectures [were] regarded as a joke and a bore. . . . As for modern literature . . . its existence never dawned upon these youths, none of whom knew any language but English."[3] In short, between the early great days and the radical reforms of 1850, most people agreed with Carlyle that those eminent in learning had not gained "their proficiency . . . through the aid of their pastors and masters, but in spite of them."[4]

The history of these aberrations establishes the reality of two things: decay *and* reform. We are not quite at the first but in need of the second. The baroque university that we have built is causing more and more people disquiet and discomfort: those whom I have quoted are an infinitesimal sample. The suspicion grows that diversity, generally deemed a sign of corporate strength, has for *this* institution become a means of escaping responsibilities, a means which all alike employ—students, faculties, and administration.

For my part, I keep—in the words of Newman about the Church—an "unruffled faith in it, coupled with a conviction of the miserable deficiencies that exist."[5] I have, for one thing, seen how a university with the will and the mind can reform itself administratively in little over a decade—hard work, but no miracle. For another, it is a fact that university problems are at last seen to be common problems. No university is now able to thank its stars that it is not as others are. All are poor, beset internally, belabored from outside. This fellow feeling should not only warm the hearts for action but knock heads together, and from the concussing a conflagration of new ideas may burst forth.

The many practical minds that seem to me to regard aspects of the present state much as I do—among them John Gardner, Robert Hutchins, Kingman Brewster, Harry Gideonse, James Perkins, Allen Wallis, Robert Cross, Roger Heyns—do not in the least give up the possibility of change. They define and redefine the idea of the university which in their eyes obviously continues clear and controlling. Grayson Kirk, who presided over the changes at Columbia, has a perfect grasp of that same idea, has backed every move of his associates in support of it, and has shown himself ready and eager for progressive changes.* Four years ago he made a number of predictions—about the higher degrees, the shift in subject matters and allegiances, and the preferability of new forms to old routines[6]—which again proves that the picture of the conservative old universities clinging to their rituals is a caricature.

"Yes, but they *don't* change!" In the large, that is true too. They are held back from all but operational changes by their public role: the clients call for change and restrain it. I have shown how government, foundations, donors, alumni, critics, and, latterly, students feel free to impose their ways, their routines, their notions and expectations upon an enterprise of which they know only parts and upon which they levy for their own selfish or elevated ends an incessant blackmail. Charity and public opinion are ruthless. Tackled singly as the universities are, they cannot help being defenseless. Competition has them by the throat.† "If we refuse this grant for some principled reason, X will take it, and we'll be in the foundation's bad books." The "independent" university is a myth, or rather a memory. Which leads me to the principal point of this chapter: *if the university is to save itself by making the changes that it is already eager and able to make, it must act not singly but in groups.* As regards changes in the Ph.D. degree, for example, no great university can afford to modify it, lest rumor call the change a "dilution" and the value of its own degree go down, followed by the ship's rat effect of students and professors fleeing the sinking hull.‡

* The work of the Macmahon Committee (see Appendix A) is one example among many of how universities can criticize themselves when they put their minds to it.

† E.g., at a meeting of representatives of seven comparable universities, someone proposed that they report to the government all direct and indirect costs on contract research and see what that might secure in the way of better treatment from the Bureau of the Budget. Taken aback by the idea of concerted action the representatives mostly shook their heads.

‡ Sometimes the threat of perdition is a useful spur. The regeneration of Teachers College under the brilliant leadership of John Fischer was probably helped rather than hindered by the intellectually inanimate state in which he found it.

REPUBLIC OR EMPIRE?

After the root idea of concerted action—different groupings at different times for different moves—the next most important is the idea of a center, of university wholeness and oneness. It leads to, and is presupposed by, all the other ideas I am about to suggest. Newman long ago stated the spiritual necessity for a center. A university is the kind of institution to which people of like purpose come from all parts of the world. A great university is at once local, national, and international. The motive for going to it, even as a visitor, is that it *is* great. And it is great because it brings together the lives and works of the best in a certain kind. Since the best cannot be everywhere, and since they work better in groups, centers arise. That is why "greatness and unity go together and why excellence implies a center."[7]*

The phenomenon of the city embodies the same law of human aggregation. The university is a city, or a city within a city.† At the same time it is not merely a crossroads or a convenience. The restrooms of large terminals are also visited by a great crowd from all over the world, but they are nothing except conveniences. The danger of the multiversity is that it will be a terminal and not even a restroom, because those who will come, and are already coming in large numbers, are not people of like purpose. Given the like purpose, the results are not to be thought of as added together but as multiplied and enhanced. Contact and collision strike fire from the individual mind and bring out of the total effort an achievement greater than could have seemed possible. When this happens steadily, it is a great age of the university and of the nation too. Of

* See page viii.

† *Universitas* originally means a group, a collection, a community, not necessarily related to study or teaching. Indeed, in medieval documents containing the words *vestra universitas,* the translation could be simply the pleasant southernism "you-all." But by the same token, a *universitas studiorum* means a grouping of studies, hence a community of learners, bent upon corporate life and action.

all the educative forces this perpetual making of a city of the mind is the strongest.

The reader will have seen in earlier allusions that the life of the university goes on at three levels, as in *The Divine Comedy.* Below—unmistakably the Inferno—is the day-to-day struggle with disorder, confusion, and penury. Next above comes the meritorious work of students and faculties overcoming the disabilities of their state and surroundings. At the top is the realm of high fulfillment and realization, which a wanderer through the first two realms can imagine and may be rash enough to desire.

But the sight of possibility, paradise, utopia—whatever its proper name is—must not blind us to pressing needs. Actual institutions are always bad, but some being much better than others, the goad to immediate improvement is ever-present. That is why under the same heads of discourse that I used before (scholars, students, and the rest) I set down here a variety of suggestions, large and small, immediately practicable or utopian. I do not mark the two kinds, for I (or anyone else) may be badly deceived in the event. Utopian things happen daily while practicables are resisted for years.

In any case, whoever wishes to consider or apply these notions born of experience and reflection, will, I trust, be generous enough to remember a few details about their form and my intention in making them: First, they are set down dogmatically—they are insufficiently qualified—so as to be brief. Second, they are clearly not equal in weight nor do they make up the plan of any "university conceived," much less a "university demanded." Lastly, they are not hints to my own university any more than to any other. They indicate possibilities, ideal and practical, for all universities, as well as a direction I think indispensable to the survival of *the* university in America.

I say a *direction.* Here and at all times, I mistrust in human affairs the ready-made design fashioned in the hope that fine adjustments can be obtained by merely describing them. "Policy-making" is an empty word; only daily acts give policy reality, and people do not act conformably to policy until consent and practice have bred habits. These are always conditioned by the past: on one floor and in one department people will declare unworkable what is actually working next door.

Again, the adaptation of an idea to a particular situation requires means and opportunity, like a good murder. Seizing on a recent and well-known situation, preferably embarrassing, will speed novelty—if both are rightly handled. The right means, in a university, consists of the right proposer and the right channel. A skillful administrator will know how to choose both, just as he will know the pace he can maintain and the degree of interest he should show (or conceal) as to the outcome. All this makes flexibility of judgment imperative, especially in matters of formulation, except when the very heart of the proposal resides in a word.* Many a good scheme valiantly striven for has been edited out of existence.

Now, a "really great administrator thinks not only of the day but of the morrow; does not only what he must, but what he wants; is eager to extirpate every abuse and on the watch for every improvement. . . . Administration in this large sense includes legislation."[8] I quote Bagehot not to cover my poor proposals with the mantle of superior worth, but to excuse their legislative tenor and uninhibited scope. Good or bad and regardless of their author, they are the logical extension of administrative thought. These coming suggestions also permit me to recapitulate, as is fitting in a final chapter.

I begin, therefore, by saying yet again that a university should be and remain One, not Many, singular not plural, a republic, not an empire; and that no matter how old, large, rich, or conceited, it should from time to time join with other universities to introduce ripened innovations. Universities have too much at stake to risk heresy alone, and they should make public the grounds and meaning of any changes introduced in common. But they will also

* E.g.: *not.*

maintain differences, even in their innovations—there is no need of strict copycatting. Right now, the "uniform" Ph.D. varies not solely in quality but, even where quality is assured, in requirements and administration.

I. *Teachers and Scholars: Education, not "Life"*

1. *The faculty, which is the university, must convey at every turn what education is; therefore must reduce and disdain the opportunities for professional cant.*

In the literature of criticism and reform three topics in particular bring forth cant:

(a) "Education occupies (or should occupy) all of life. Education is life; only life situations educate. Education is self-education. What you learn formally is the least of education. This teaching that I do educates me more than it does you. It will take you all your life to educate yourself." The wise physician also believes that you cure yourself or that nature does it for you, but he does not continually pooh-pooh his art and his attentions—else how can he count on your cooperation?—and he does not say "this treatment does more for me than for you." *To bring in life every time education is mentioned is to play on words.*

(b) The "life" theme goes with the emotion theme. "Education must be exciting; the good teacher gives an exciting class; part of the excitement is that he loves his subject and in addition loves his students." He loves and they love or nothing passes between them. Teacher's love moreover understands everything and so forgives everything, particularly laziness, incompetence, and delinquency in meeting obligations, academic and financial. The excitement of love and love of excitement go with a desire for liberty, "profuse of bliss and pregnant with delight," as Addison says.[9] Any formal, regular arrangement is a constraint; education must catch the student unawares. Whence permissiveness, "self-scheduling," knowledge only when called for—like room service in a hotel. It follows that where circumstances are not suitably contrived to promote this love connection between teacher and taught, education is not possible or not good.

These are objectionable assumptions because they dismiss communication in favor of communion and make emotion compulsory. But communication is essential and must take place with or without love and excitement. As for compulsory feeling, it is a kind of self-abuse, an offense to the dignity of the individual, who is thereby made a means to an end. We talk a great deal about this dignity nowadays; let us find out what it is before we talk more. In teaching, respect will be found quite as effective as shallow, promiscuous "feeling." Indifference, real or feigned, is also pedagogic, and dislike has moments of utility as well. Nothing said here is to prevent friendship and affection between master and pupil. It is the oldest and most natural thing in the world—as long as it is natural.

(c) The third piece of cant: *elite*. The fear is that the presence of an educated group in our midst will "form an elite," surely a bad thing. If this is really so, that an educated group equals an elite, then why educational institutions? Or should we have them only so long as they do not educate anybody? An elite in the sense meant *is* a bad thing. But before it arises those forming it must literally form it, organize it. For an elite is a self-conscious political or social force exerting itself always in one general direction: army officers, the peerage, big landowners, city merchants, leaders of revolutions, can be elites. How could "the educated" resemble them? Where is the common interest? the leadership? Education is too diverse for the basis of a clique.

The real danger is the envy that hides under the cry of elitism. People who think others look down on them with the secret thought "I have a degree and he hasn't" suffer from a pathetic fantasy probably not curable. Educators and educated should not strengthen it by a show of democratic vigilance against the imagined dictatorship of the postdoctorals. The remedy against the growth of envy is educational opportunity. The chance to learn is in theory denied to no one, and in practice it is being steadily enlarged. What would be bitter would be to have those who make use of that chance branded as elitist because educated.*

2. *To keep a university in a time of centrifugal skedaddling, the slogan throughout must be* SIMPLIFY. The very complexity which stands in the way and seems permanent is the reason for simplifying. The method is *austerity,* planned and sought out, not forced by a crash like 1929. That condition of free choice makes "austerity" the wrong word for my thought: What I am urging is *sobriety.*

3. In the new university too much goes on, and not enough; too many courses are offered, at an insufficient density of instruction. If the goal of coverage—departments straining to "give" everything—were abandoned, it would lighten the teaching load and (in explanation of the change) inform students that it is possible to learn a portion of a subject without taking a course in it. "Independent work" has come, absurdly, to mean a research paper; it should also mean studying.

4. There is too much teaching in another sense. Most classes meet from 26 to 30 hours a semester. Most of that time goes to repeating more or less accurately what is in the books of the library. The rest may be new knowledge and interpretation. Therefore:

5. *Abandon the survey; substitute the short course:* such a course should begin with an introductory lecture or two outlining scope and strategy and commenting on the required reading. Six weeks later the class is examined on the reading. Students who pass are admitted to eight or ten lectures scheduled close together (say within three weeks). The rest of the term provides opportunities for questions and discussions in office hours.† In some courses, a short paper—not more than five pages—to show understanding, not scholarship or bulk. One thing more: bearing in mind

* A comparison: after 4,000 years of higher education in China, the first deaf student was recently accepted at a university in Hong Kong. Women have been admitted to Asian higher education only since the rise of the American Christian colleges about 1900.

† A first attempt, which I am now working on, will be tested in practice at Columbia in the spring of 1969.

what Roger Bacon told Clement IV—that he could teach in three months what had taken him forty years to learn—all graduate courses to be one semester long; undergraduate and professional one or two semesters at will. Only by reducing the present "stand-by" use of teachers can the university deploy where needed its now overworked and underused talent.

6. *The load further lightened by being choosy about new projects.* All new projects are interesting. This is well known—each is a "fascinating idea." On the day of approval, months later, it's marvelous, wonderful. After three years it's old and dull. I refer to the peripheral and scholarly ventures. Many instructional innovations of the past thirty years have resisted time's tooth, or served their purpose, e.g., general education. But the cross-country fertilizing, pollinating, or "exploring" has cost much with little gain. The chief item of cost is faculty time.

7. Just as advances across old boundaries have been made by individuals, by a piece of work, not a piece of mimeographed paper, so "studies" and conferences rarely advance learning, because largely paper efforts. The working committee may instruct itself by a study, seldom others. As for conferences, they are the waxworks of the intellectual world. The subjects are old and stiff, and the papers have already been written many times. They should be read by machine in some empty ballroom, to permit the absent listeners to stay at home and work. In time, the thought-clichés would settle at the bottom of the vat and be forgotten. (None of this applies to the meetings of learned societies.)

8. Projects with one foot outside the university and one inside can be kept down only by a campus committee on subsidized research. The members must be intelligent, scrupulous, puritanical, and must carry heavy life insurance. Logrolling has to be suppressed, as well as temperamental attachment to the tried-and-true and good-enough. The committee must work for the *university*—for themselves only through its preservation—and they must see its salvation not in prestige but in performance; not: "every full professor is entitled to his sideshow"; rather: "what will *this* side-

show contribute to teaching? to knowledge? How many of its size can we carry at one time?"* For the new university's worst lack is an elementary notion of housekeeping.

9. Good economy might lead to utopia, thus: from weighing the worth of proposed research, the academic mind might come to revise its feelings and words about it: I say feelings and words because academics *think* quite justly on the subject, but do not believe or act on what they think. They believe what they *say*, speak of "production," a "productive scholar," ask of a young man as of a farm animal, "has he produced?" For *university* purposes, not their own, they gauge the product like an exciseman, by volume; they know the idea of output comes from the factory, where it is entirely proper; they forget that it's Benthamee and philistine outside it.† It is preposterism to require research under threats to livelihood and with rewards in that livelihood, the practice being that when the academic peons have turned out *something*, it becomes possible to give them rank, grants, leaves, and a friendly good morning.

10. Reconsider research, and benefits to the university will include: less general anxiety, less preoccupation with money, fewer arrangements—to interrupt teaching and go away, to get research assistance, to get printed, etc.;‡ and further: smaller subsidies to university presses for useless books serving only the author's claim to more salary; libraries and journals relieved from the pressure of having to cope with what comes out of the foundry under forced draft: we are perishing from publishing and must keep down that which is premature and that which is artificial.

"But if a man doesn't produce, how do we know he's a scholar?" Answer: "How do you know now from reading titles?"

* On this topic the writings of "Grant Swinger" (D. S. Greenberg) in *Science, passim,* are an education in themselves and entertaining as well.

† "Productivity" is tolerable as a measure of teaching, perhaps, because it is work expected at certain hours by persons who have paid to get a predictable amount of it. But research, which we idolize, must necessarily be free, a gift of nature, not a tax due at regular intervals.

‡ See Appendix D. No. 110.

In the end, you take the fact on faith from close observers who know the man. They could just as easily tell you even if he never published a line. Teachers in college and university should be scholars. But scholarship and publication are not identical. Of the two, higher education should prefer scholarship. It is not as visible as jaundice, but it is often far more visible in one man's lecture than in another man's book. The teaching scholar should be able to say what Loup de Ferrières wrote to Charles the Bald: "I desire to teach what I have learned and am daily learning."[10]*

11. Ostentatious research comes from lust for prestige, not individual merely, but departmental and corporate, for prestige is thought to rub off indefinitely far. We saw how much faculties want presidents "prestigious." I suggest that instead of *prestige* we use the Hindi word *izzat* and see how absurd we are: "Has he *izzat?* Have we enough *izzat* in the house? Our friends across the way are getting ahead of us in *izzat.*" Newspapers could then rank institutions *izzat-wise.*

12. Better still: give nobody any such chance. "Surveys of excellence" by departments and schools are as dubious as TV ratings and cost good money twice over—in compiling and in overcoming their results. To be sure, as long as the university furnishes "public service" and will not furnish it quietly, prestige remains legal tender and popularity the measure of wisdom.†

13. In his parody of the explorers of his time Rabelais says: "We sailed for three days without discovering anything." If the university could acquire the same patience, the perennial problem of Presence and Absence might be solved and teaching improved.

* One can find in the beneficent Morrill Act of 1862, which originated the land-grant colleges, the distant germ of justification-by-production. Section Four requires that "an annual report shall be made regarding the progress of each college, recording any improvements and experiments made, with their costs and results."

See, in addition, "A Loyalty Oath for Scholars," Appendix D, No. 28.

† In any case, ratings by eminence and by departments tell nothing about the worth of a university's working divisions. For example, a "great" western university may have a college inferior to possibly several independent four-year institutions or smaller university colleges. And the higher quality of the latter will owe as much to the ability and drive of the students as to the teaching talents and administrative arrangements of the institution.

Leaves might become less frequent, and be taken primarily for study.* From this would come less hurried writing, hence shorter, better-digested books, and the elimination of inflated articles.

14. Next comes the raison d'être of the university as *guardian* of learning. In the miscalled knowledge explosion the university has only tried mechanical organization—putting the stuff into bales. A few journals occasionally commission an article reviewing a decade of scholarly work. Otherwise, there is no conspectus of any science or subscience, any field or backyard. If the public knew of this it might shut down the universities. Philosophic minds should sift and organize the mass of data in periodic assessments: "The Present State of Studies on ———." Criticism and supplementation would follow, both useful. These small works—not tomes—should have wide dissemination; reading them would become a point of honor and writing them a cause of it. In time, each scholarly sect might learn its place and purpose in the learned world, and the haphazard mental images of "our field" might gain in consistency.† As things are, the "knowledge" cast up by the index or computer represents statistical frequencies of approval or interest, just like the "surveys of excellence."‡

15. Implied in the foregoing is that academic scholarship turn serious about its significance. "Serious" is here a technical term, the opposite of solemn on one side and make-believe on the other. Scholars are on the whole conscientious and diligent, and they give of themselves as fully as any other profession; but this is not

* William James noted: "Fifteen months is too long a vacation for a man like me to take. Teaching is such an artificial discipline that one loses the habit of it immediately and seems to forget all that one ever knew."—G. W. Allen, *William James* (New York, 1967, 369). James's leave was of course not a vacation, but his remark holds.

† A scientist, much bemedaled and who desires anonymity, said at our last conversation: "Science as now organized is a huge superstructure of specialties floating above nothing at all—like the dome of St. Sophia" (Oct. 30, 1967).

‡ See a judicious critique of "citation indexing" in *Science* (vol. 156, May 19, 1967, 890): "The basic motivation underlying the citation index . . . is the desire to find methods of information retrieval . . . that reduce the need for scholarly work. In the long run, however, there can be no substitute for good . . . analysis based on a knowledge of subject matter."

enough. Learning demands continual thought about its *seriousness* in order to avoid pedantry at one end and mere business at the other. A piece of work may be scholarly and altogether misleading. Form and technique are no guarantee of truth: details can be correct and conclusions missed or purposely disguised. Scholars should so inform the young, who are sanguine and trust "method." The role of teaching as an aid to verification is also a truth to impart. Going over the same body of material in class deepens one's knowledge of it and even generates new ideas. Compared with such pondering, "production" born of a one-time survey in the library is thin. Here as usual scientists are better off in having daily give-and-take with their laboratory squad.

16. Scientists and reading scholars alike have a last duty to truth, which is to know that it is not separable from expression. Lip service is given to "good English," but just complaint about student writing continues. What it records is not a wounded feeling for prose; art or elegance is not the point. The point is *falsification*—by ambiguity, confusion, and nonsense. The point is also that no one has a right to make another toil at deciphering. Bad writing violates the university ideal of *access* to knowledge. To scorn expression as trivial compared to the "real subject," as if it existed independently, is to fail to take that subject seriously.*

17. To move toward these suggested goals, it is imperative to teach the 3 R's at every opportunity, from the first school grade to the Ph.D. Mass education without reading, writing, and counting is

* An inquiry into the quality of writing which I addressed ten years ago to the departments and schools of my university brought responses mainly helpless. "What's the use?" and "Why bother?" (to sum up lengthy memoranda) alternated with proposals for remedial courses (if money could be found) and the usual denunciation of the lower schools.

As to these, more and more are aware of their failure ("Most City Schools Lagging in 2 R's," *New York Times,* Oct. 21, 1965) and desperate for remedies. At a conference of school superintendents from all parts of the country held at Aspen in August 1967, the suggestion of one of them that schools "concentrate on a strong minimum program of 3 R's and give up the compulsory-high-school requirement" struck the group as apt and congenial. Higher education should not rule the schools, but at points of common interest, such as reading and writing, the higher educators have a self-serving duty to make their weight felt.

only mass deception. These fundamentals of all learning are in fact the only thing that we can be sure serves the needs of our students and will serve the needs of the twenty-first century.*

To restore the tradition of such teaching, it would also be desirable to establish or convert centers for advanced study. The Institute which bears that title at Princeton, and which was formed as a work place for Einstein, has (I am informed) benefited mathematics and physics by bringing together for a year the great masters and the young talents. In other subjects, it has done the more familiar thing of providing a retreat for research. There are at least five similar research centers in the country, and innumerable fellowships and grants of like purpose. Nowhere is the Oral Tradition of learning transmitted. No one has thought of any other good than the research sanctuary, to "free people to write their book"—an Aid-to-Prisoners Society.† The thing missed in the present system is not the rudiments of pedagogy, important as they are, but the intangible contents of the scholarly succession.‡ The quasi-apprentice system of an older day used to assure this continuity. Now the most conscientious department is too busy to converse with itself, let alone with the young. The young, equally busy, are also rather toplofty. Only a center of scholarship could induce the rapport I desiderate.§ Well-staffed, it would come to carry with it a trifle of *izzat* for both old and young, and create an esprit de corps that no longer develops naturally. Partial imitations might

* The lack of literacy seems to be universal. A scientist at the University of Paris addressing his colleagues says: "[we] know that by far the greater number of students do not know how to express themselves, do not know how to learn by reading, and do not know how to compute." (V. Kourganoff, "De Quelques Idées Reçues sur la Recherche et l'Enseignement," Montreal meeting of the AUPELF, May 5–15, 1967, 4.)

† The despair of a year off and no book written is a subject for a playwright of modern life.

‡ A student, newly Ph.D.'d and with his college teaching appointment in his pocket, remarked while saying good-by: "As far as I can tell, the five characteristics of a scholar are accuracy, thoroughness, taciturnity, inaccessibility, and TIAA" [pension rights].

§ A. Lawrence Lowell, as I know from his own lips, hoped that the Society of Fellows which he founded at Harvard would perform this office while also dealing the Ph.D. a death blow. But, although desirable friendships thrive there between older scholars and newcomers, the Ph.D. still spring up within the reading departments of universities. The sciences, by nature gregarious, are thereby wiser: their weekly colloquia afford the beginnings of such a relationship.

18. The previous suggestions variously relate to a chief predicament of the new university—how to reproduce itself; it is a common plight; every profession could use 200,000 more men. There has not been such a shortage since the Black Death, when the clergy recruited itself by simply shaving the crowns of likely youths. Well, what is here proposed—reducing the teaching load and the course offering, coerced research and project-making, grant-hunting, and the agitation and transportation incidental to conferring and speechifying—should make the impressment of citizens on the street unnecessary.

As a by-product of the change, the men sought out—and women too, since we award them 2,000 Ph.D.'s a year—would differ in kind from the present breed, chosen so exclusively for yield, *izzat,* and visibility. The unobtrusive but tangibly present man and scholar might be a great addition to the campus. He would, for one thing, relieve the strain on the departments of perpetually having to fill gaps with paragons. Anxiety to find and fear of making a mistake have surrounded professor-hunting with all the apprehensions of indissoluble marriage; for tenure is marriage, and without any pledge to obey and cherish. The resulting fussiness of choice is pathological; the paragon eludes every institution; he does not exist.

19. This being so, why not permit open applications for professorships, as in England? The excess of postulants could be held down by publicity, and the number of acceptable candidates would rise: there are good men stuck in poor institutions; but to lift one of these out of his trap and into a respectable college or university now runs into the fatal question: "But how did he ever get *there?*"—so rooted is the faith in appearances.

---

commands the latter's allegiance as a union card and diverts their energies from the desired communion.

A last word to dispel a possible misunderstanding about the serious teaching scholar. The suggestion that he divest himself of many obligations he has slid into during the heedless growth of the new university is not a suggestion that he isolate himself from the world. The austerity proposed is not monastic; it is secular, practical, therapeutic. It is designed to keep him out of the executive treadmill, and working instead at his chosen task. Outside work may still prove useful to him, but it must be seen to be so, not just assumed to be; and any loss to the university and its students through the defection or depletion of the man must be stopped, by him or by the university acting on an ethical conception of higher learning.

The distinction between the university and its free-ranging members is important because of the vague ideas afloat about the German universities' surrender to Hitler. Professorial aloofness is blamed for that collapse, but the verdict is unsound. Not all academic men were aloof; and, more to the point, subversion and tyranny always take forms adapted to the national culture, so that many are deceived until it is too late. The intellectual defeat in Germany should be attributed rather to the semieducation of discontented intellectuals, as Professor Fritz Stern has shown,* and to the misuse of the university for a combination of political ends and pure research, as Nietzsche and Burckhardt foresaw. We came back to the proposition that it is dangerous when "specialists usurp the rank of philosophers and educators."[11] Whether the American professoriat would resist better than the German in a comparable situation no one can tell. All one can affirm is that it has learned, not as yet very wisely, how to resist administrations and how to protest side by side with students.

II. *Students: the Work in Hand*

20. A university redirected would make fresh choices affecting all parts. The college in particular would change, and with it the

* See *The Politics of Cultural Despair,* Berkeley, 1961.

aim of its students. Already the liberal arts no longer belong exclusively to the college; a group of independent secondary schools is studying the possibility of adding one or two years to their curriculum.* There is much to be said for this new division of labor, by which the university college would consist of two years of "propaedeutics," i.e., work suitably specialized to lead to one or more professions, including the branches of pure scholarship and science. That is what university scholars want right now—and act on when they can and shouldn't. In grades 11, 12, 13, and 14 the liberal arts would be taught by men who know how to teach boys and care about the subjects. Junior colleges would parallel this offering and send their average products to community or other four-year colleges, and their best to the university. The great independent liberal arts colleges would, one hopes, continue as they do—a model, a reproach, and a blessing.

21. The introductory college courses being eliminated from the university, the task of staffing the lower ranks of departments would be simplified. The younger scholars could "stick to their subject" instead of dabbling in general education. Result: end of strain between deans, chairmen, segments of faculties, old and young. (Utopians of the next wave would have the opportunity of periodically pleading for the restoration of the four-year college, with the liberal arts at the masthead.)

Who should go to college is for the nation to decide. It is not easy; Plato himself gave a contradictory answer. All men, he said, can develop an appetite for knowledge, which he called "the food of the soul." But, he added, they must be sorted out at various stages and sent into different occupations. This is how we proceed in an unplanned way, and we shall probably continue. It is a good working contradiction as long as envy does not raise the false cry of elitism.†

* I outlined this suggestion five years ago while addressing the faculty of one such school, at which time it seemed by common consent (mine included) utopian. See Appendix D, No. 111.

† The rights of minorities should hold throughout society, but they rarely do when it comes to a minority thought "superior." Yeats observed when he

22. But to extend *education* as far as is wanted requires first that we reduce the fever of mandarinism. Cutting back the course offering should help. As long as students strain to qualify, they need the 1,001 courses leading down the various paths to jobs: always new courses, too, because pseudo-professions multiply. The curriculum becomes a bazaar: the student turns buyer with set tastes: "I need a topic that I can work on in my local library, because my time is limited." That topic, a hurdle in the way to earning a living, must be made as easy as possible. Who can bar the way to a man's livelihood—and not to his subsistence alone, but the wife's, the puling babe's? Every teacher with a heart accommodates, often at his own great inconvenience and loss of integrity.

It could be wished here that the example of athletics came to the rescue of education, for whatever else sports do, they make it clear that a deed is a deed. Good intentions, honest effort, sudden appendicitis are not performance. Granted that in a four- or six-year program, this fact cannot be invoked like a nemesis, the consciousness of it should prevail. It is the very law of truth that one thing is not another, and truth is what learning is after. In institutions of learning it should become possible once again to say: we are sorry that you cannot give the time, but we cannot out of good will falsify the truth.

Misplaced kindness also falsifies names and intentions. Much of what passes for education today would not deceive a child—for example, so-called adult education or continuing education. They can be genuine, but those in charge are often practiced self-deceivers, and even in good places activities bearing those names are but pastimes or saunters through the cloisters.*

---

was speaking against censorship in the Irish Senate: "They . . . cannot understand why the good of the nine-tenths that never open a book should not prevail over the good of the tenth that does."—*The Senate Speeches of W. B. Yeats,* Bloomington, 1960, 179.

* Another weakness of "higher education for all" is that the money supplied to make it possible becomes a temptation: being a student is a way of life. Youth enrolls in order to get cheap meals and rooms and an

23. In the same spirit let us be sober and skeptical about "methods" supposedly affording a livelier education, really designed to process refractory material—the seminar, the dialogue, the class turned over to its members in turn, the small panel leading the larger group—all for "involvement." These devices create temporary interest but increase the ultimate sense of make-believe; they give the *impression* of learning but deny it coherence. Gadgetry and other aids tend the same way. Learning is hard, continuous, attentive work. Those "innovations" whose merit is to "break things up," enliven through "unconventional" means, rob learning of its essence, which is precisely the convention, the *convening,* of studious minds better than our own, who compel us to change ours. Genius may upset that convention, but only after thought and study, not on the first day of the course and for the sake of "dialogue." With these tricks the simple demand of knowledge is not met; a student does not know anything until he knows it. When he knows, he can describe, explain, relate, reproduce the configuration of a significant portion of the field. To have heard of it, seen a film about it, recognize references to it, own paperbacks or "interact" with a computer about it is not knowledge. And some of these substitutes may well prove permanent impediments.

24. If educationally motiveless people must haunt the colleges, then there should be open to them the equivalent of the British "pass degree," and the number of such students should be kept low enough not to discourage the workers. Unfortunately, the tendency to inflation might bring about the counterpart of the British reality, which is that the passmen creep into the ranks of low Honors degrees, nullifying the meaning of honors.* The best solution is to

---

allowance, as in France. The last time I saw the rector of the University of Paris, he said casually across the luncheon table, "I have 140,000 students; how many have you?" The spontaneous thought is: "There *aren't* 140,000 students!"

* "They do not welcome the existence of such undergraduates at Oxbridge: but they do not take the only step that would rid the Universities of them. . . . Year by year, the examiners deliberately set questions that do not expose the weakness of candidates; year by year they allow semi-literate

make admission to an honors college sufficiently exact to prevent the waste of mere "exposure" to learning (more often a collision or sideswipe), and by reducing attrition for academic reasons save the time, money, and pride of the won't-be student.* In a two-year propaedeutics course, there would be no degree and no honors. A certificate of completion would afford entrance to the appropriate school or department, and at last Thoreau's injunction would be heeded: "Let every sheep keep his own skin, say I."

25. The next nut to crack is the Ph.D., and for this I urge a radical device. The best would be: give every native-born American a Ph.D. at birth and start from there. In any more immediate scheme the aim would be double. First, to weaken mandarinism, in parallel with the ideas that Mr. S. M. Miller expounds in a recent Ford Foundation reprint under the title: "Breaking the Credentials Barrier."[12] His thesis is simple: "We have become a credential society in which one's educational level is more important than what he can do."† The second intention is to unburden scholarship of an incubus that probably spoils more talent, and sours more good nature, and breaks up more homes than any other purely abstract invention.

Everybody knows about the ordeal of the dissertation. Since I described it twenty years ago in *Teacher in America,* the only sign of betterment is that which President Kirk mentioned as a prediction

---

and totally ignorant undergraduates to slide into an honours degree."—*Camford Observed,* by J. Rose and J. Ziman, London, 1964, 142.

* The lower schools have difficulties that lead to complete permissiveness about the completion of work. This latitude breeds bad habits. In college or "continuing education," time is of the essence. Some students cajole instructors into giving them the grade of Incomplete for a missed examination, which provides another semester or two in which to learn and pass the course. Again, adults will argue that because they seek no credit, they should be allowed to tune out of the course for three weeks here and three weeks there (accompanying husband on trip) and receive from the instructor the missed assignments and a bit of coaching on their return. These exceptions are not in the least "educational." They are connivance at misdemeanors.

† See also Ivar Berg, "Unemployment and the Overeducated Worker," *New Generation,* vol. 50, No. 1, Winter 1968.

in 1964—that it will in future be considered not an addition to knowledge but "a trial run in research."[13] Sensible departments so regard it, but tacitly. There are now limits to length as well. Compassionate sponsors will not let a student choose a life's work to be done in five or six years. At Princeton, a decade ago, the president requested the graduate dean to find ways of reducing doctoral work in all fields to four years or less, and by Sir Hugh Taylor's exertions this was largely accomplished. But none of these palliatives takes care of the social and intellectual preposterism of the requirement. The candidates have been sitting and reading since infancy—twenty years or more. They have just passed a searching oral examination for which nothing in their long training had prepared them. And now, the last great barrier leaped over, they are enjoined to start work without delay on an important book: "Go on—discover something, and be quick about it." The candidate is married, has children, and little or no money. The wife (or husband) supports the menage and the other's ambition —what a setting for thought and inquiry!

Some drop out for good. Others linger on as A.B.D.'s—"all but dissertation"—the label has become quasi-official.* Pending the birthright Ph.D. I have proposed, interim measures are urgent. Several previous moves to create a new degree for young scholars who lack the dissertation have been wrecked by the general insistence that only a Ph.D. is good enough for a college or university teacher.† We thus lose much talent and throw down the drain all that has been fed to it. The obvious remedy is: *award the Ph.D. immediately after the orals,* provided that the candidate can

* Bare numbers are apt to mislead in these matters, but here is a suggestion of ratios based on recent figures. In History (all branches) 9,000 students are enrolled in programs leading to the M.A. Registered Ph.D. topics number 1,674; 300 receive the Ph.D. annually, of whom 20 are women. This work goes on at 75 institutions, of which 25 have feeble and fitful programs. Twelve more aspire to give the Ph.D.

† The M.A. is being rejected as insufficient even in the newest colleges, or else the job is given on the condition of a subsequent Ph.D. The M.A.T. serves secondary school teaching. The M.Phil. at Yale has not yet had a long enough trial to find its level. (See *New York Times,* May 13, 1966.)

show "technique"—a passable M.A. essay or Senior Thesis. For that is all the streamlined Ph.D. of today will test in any case.

The contention that the dissertation shows whether the student can organize a book and write exposition may be disregarded. Organization *and* writing are more often than not the work of the sponsor. He edits, rewrites, and annotates several drafts. Only the rare student works by himself. All others start as would-be Ph.D.'s without the three R's. Consequently the dissertation proves nothing; it comes out of a last-minute tutorial in essay writing.

The logic of the reform is clear: the graduate student is a scholar before being a writer and he should be so certified—a Ph.D. fit to be hired. It would be splendid if he could be given a quick run through the art and ethics of teaching as well, but we must not be double-utopian. Let him go and teach, free in mind and time to prepare his courses adequately, and really earn the money he will be paid.

The gain to the sponsor will be enormous; no longer a diffident ghost-writer who is never sure of the dividing line between fair coaching and unfair assistance, he saves hours of drudgery. Also, the new regularity in graduating Ph.D.'s will give fresh impetus to a process that has latterly seemed less like turning out young scholars than like dislodging a bone from the throat.

26. Provision is needed, however, for the free offering of a student possessed by an idea and capable of giving it form. Let him do research on his own, do his writing on his own.* When he has a book of his own, or a substantial monograph, he presents it to the department, and after approval is examined on it. If the book is satisfactory, he receives a second Ph.D., "with honors"—or whatever additive or superlative formula may be devised. For this submission and award there is no time limit. He may take his chance four years after the M.A. or when he has one foot in the grave. In either case he has been *on his own* since the ordinary professional

* Of course his former teachers may help, if asked—as they would a colleague. That means modest demands, and only as a last resort.

Ph.D. The later dissertation only shows that for the first time in his career he has done independent work.

27. There remains the student life, the tendency of which, once again, should favor *student* rather than "life." Life is too precious and too complex to be engineered, too demanding and too expensive to be institutionally fiddled with. The present student life suffers from mental overcrowding, partly due to the mandarin urgings, partly to the unconscious mirroring of the institution in the student mind: if *it* must solve urban problems, so must he. But this commandment imposed by public opinion can only lead to the neglect of studies, to confusion and waste. The all-purpose man in an all-purpose college negates education. If a youth feels a vocation for social work, let him either prepare for it through study or drop studies and go use his talents in the midst of life. The plea that present emergency demands both together is not valid. In an emergency the only hope is to divide the tasks and not get in each other's way; and difficult tasks should be done by those who know how.

28. What if college and university, through not demanding enough of the right things in the right way, have brought on the unrest and yearning for genuine difficulty and pain and thus disrupted the institution? That would confirm other doubts previously expressed. Now, all the university can demand is studentship, it must indeed enforce it: academically in class, and by discipline where appropriate in other situations.* Otherwise, *why are we all there?*

Many have lost the answer because too much artificial "life" has obscured what the campus is for. It is for the *educational* relation

* The cult of individual talent, which starts very young, does much to confuse students about what a student is. Here is high school: "Teachers, counselors, and even a few professional writers have told me that I have enough talent to become a professional writer. These people told me that I should practice writing every day. But this practice interferes with my homework . . ." (Letter in the Chicago *Daily News,* Aug. 22, 1967). When is anybody told that a life is made up of choices—leave school and write: postpone writing and get through school; work twice as many hours to manage both?

of person to person, which warms the mind and makes it receptive. Students, as all know, learn from each other if they have time and fit places. Hence the traditional arrangements for a common physical existence, preferably managed by the students themselves. This is not "playing house" if the purpose is serious, if it is education. When education becomes secondary or marginal, it is understandable that students should seek seriousness elsewhere—in social work or premarital housekeeping. At many institutions today, students declare their alienation from college by taking apartments, re-creating there a society in small groups. If the movement persists, the university should abandon dormitories: *colleges* or nothing.

29. The University has no obligation to provide quarters that are more and more regarded as convenient places of assignation and that serve no educational purpose beyond. For older students, professionals or propaedeutics, the residences should be designed to permit small, natural groupings to form within the larger wholes, which should be self-governing to the utmost extent compatible with good order. If these students too abandon the campus for apartments, then let us have the Continental university of former days—all learning and no housekeeping. Modern youth is socially mature enough not to need domestic proctoring.

30. Under stress of violence and outcry, the proposition has gained currency that students are "full educational partners."[14] It is hard to know what is meant by this. In *education,* they are full partners by definition. In the administering of education, their student status would seem to imply a self-disqualification. What have they as yet done to earn a voice in making the curriculum or promoting their teachers? Both are faculty matters which neither trustees nor administration meddle with: why should students? As for the business policies of the institution and the external activities of its members, why (again) should students be given rights contrary to law? The fiduciary duties governing business policy are by law the trustees' alone; and the lawful actions of individuals, even in a university, are guaranteed from interference by the

Constitution and the courts. If these rights are to be given up under threat, the institution has "gone Japanese" and lost its raison d'être. It is being taught rather than teaching; the campus is nothing more than a resonant soapbox, and it will not be long before all who care for learning—scholars and administrators—will gladly look for other employment.*

It is no mitigation of the destructive intent to wrap it up in democratic forms. The university is not a political unit and therefore is not a democracy; it has members appointed for various tasks, not citizens voting for their governors—the president, treasurer, trustees, and so on. Moreover, it is in practice extremely difficult to get from student bodies either a significant vote, or a council or committee that is representative. Campus apathy being as great as campus agitation, students who profess to speak for the whole delude themselves and others. Add that student newspapers have long ceased to purvey anything approaching a public opinion, and it is clear that democracy is the last name a political scientist would apply to the government by outcry which has lately gained favor as an extracurricular activity.

All of this leaves—and indeed preserves—*Lernfreiheit* as sacred as *Lehrfreiheit*. The two traditional academic freedoms so painfully fought for protect learning and teaching. Because it is often difficult to see the boundaries of these acts, freedom in the university must stretch to include any reasoned and reasonably civil complaint or expression of opinion. It is for this purpose that campuses have a "Hyde Park Corner" for public harangues, picketing rules for protests, and as many societies for special causes as are desired. So much corresponds to the grass roots out of which useful changes come, but it gives no warrant for turning the university into a forum. What goes on in the university is as important and as delicate as the surgeon's work in the operating

* Chancellor Heyns at Berkeley had to warn his Academic Senate in 1965 that the "diversion of faculty and student energy away from academic and scholarly pursuits" might have "effects on recruitment and retention of faculty" (*Daily Californian,* Nov. 9, 1965). The need for this reminder to an Academic Senate is in itself a grave symptom.

theater; nothing but shambles will result from pursuing the idea that in each of those places there is plenty of room left over for a mass meeting.

31. The campus nevertheless needs a new outlet for grievances, the *Ombudsman* of the Swedish welfare state. Transplated to the campus under any other name, he would perform functions that no large institution can afford any longer to overlook. Threading one's way through bureaucracy is difficult; the girl at the window is (or seems to be) always new or ill-tempered. A student's time is precious and his patience thin. Worse, if he has suffered injustice from a rule or a clerk, he should have redress. Experience will determine how the benevolent Om should go to work, with what staff and under what conditions. The one danger is that his office should become a second administration duplicating and interfering with the separate offices. His best role would be educational—teaching by example what we neglect throughout modern life: why a large institution has to act as it does, and how to get from an institution what one is entitled to.

III. *Friends and Fellow-Citizens: Help with Understanding*

32. The slogan *Simplify* will have widest play in the university's external relations; hence there is no end to possible and desirable changes. A few hints must suffice. Bishop Berkeley, himself an educator, has a question in his *Querist* which runs: "Whether an expense in building and improvements doth not remain at home, pass to the heir, and adorn the public? And whether any of these things can be said of claret?"[15] Gazing at recent "improvements," I think the time has come to opt for claret. The institution doubtless needs buildings, which do stay at home and pass to the successors, but for their very sake the university must not put itself in pawn to improvers. Concentrate on claret: it is the wine of discovery and meditation, which the university does not merely lay down in its cellars but makes yearly and gives its students to grow strong on.

33. Both public and private universities, in short, must regain their independence, cease being the firehouse on the corner answering all the alarms, many of them false. To recover freedom of choice takes two virtues—courage and self-knowledge. Acquiring the second means repeating on campus and abroad: *not all good things are good for us.* (Examples: professional performance in the arts; full-scale museum keeping; competing with industrial laboratories; taking on the functions of city government.)

In all this, cost must turn educator: the university must learn to foresee and to demonstrate the crushing burdens attached to "munificent gifts," no matter who at first is offended. Bankrupt as it is, the university has nothing to lose and everything to gain. Institutions must also learn to recognize subtle exploitation under guise of "opportunities to cooperate." If a manufacturer of ultra-modern machinery settles near a good physics department with obvious designs on technical advice from the faculty, the university must be ready to submit a bill for development costs. The fees paid to the scientists themselves do not cover the choosing and assembling and improving of their talents, now appropriated by the newcomer.

34. By concerted action, universities can establish a charter of their rights and duties, an ethical code governing these and kindred situations. The leading institutions can become the conscience and strong right arm of the less secure. In dealings with government at every level the code will protect both the university and its members. Why should a scholar administering a foreign-language grant have to report the number of movies shown in his program, with an "evaluation" of each, title by title? If the agency head cannot distinguish between proper accounting and fatuous paper work, the university's charter of duties should inform him.

And the code should include an article against the giving of facts and opinions about students to investigators from the several branches of government. The American Council on Education has urged a number of good grounds for noncompliance with such requests;[16] the best would be that, just as in ordinary life, questions about persons should be asked and answered in writing. Anything else becomes uncontrollable hearsay, quite unscholarly.

35. In the moot matter of social responsibility to neighbors, the education of the public will take time, but the conclusion is in no doubt right now. President John Perkins of Delaware put the point with finality when he explained why he established a separate division within his university to apply the urban redevelopment funds given him by the Ford Foundation: "The secret of our success is that we didn't give the money to the professors. We hired people for specific missions."[17] These words of one syllable, or nearly, define by a left-handed compliment the role of a university: it cannot, except badly and dangerously, do things—however good—for which it is not equipped and organized. Education is a full-time task. University endowment or state subsidy is for education; it is misuse of funds *and* talent to embark on other than educational efforts.

This definition, as was made clear earlier, does not preclude research in urban affairs or training in that knowledge like any other; it does exclude the middleman role President Perkins took on.*

36. Nothing keeps the university from another kind of cooperation with the world. At many places, following the initiative of Professor Frank Tannenbaum of Columbia, "university seminars" have been established which bring together scholars and qualified laymen to discuss a topic of permanent significance. The Economics of Distribution; Genetics and the Evolution of Man; Population and Social Change; Modern East Asia, etc. These discussions among equals afford mutual benefit. That is the test for such undertakings, since every loss in any of the university's resources —time, men, money—is a loss to all of society. The supposition that a charitable institution should dispense charity, like a private person, is based on faulty reasoning. Nobody expects a hospital to

* President Thomas Robinson of the Glassboro (N.J.) State College knew his own role when, after the meeting of President Johnson and Premier Kosygin had distracted his campus, he said: "Running a summit isn't our business; running a college is" (*New York Times,* Sept. 26, 1967).

give out Christmas packages to the neighborhood poor. But learning seems both an insufficient gift and an elastic commodity, which beds and drugs are not. Hence the great expectations, which are bound to end in dismay and ingratitude.

37. That illusion about knowledge might be dispelled faster than seems likely if a further change in university practice were brought about. I refer to the conferring of honorary degrees. Leaving aside suspected quid pro quos, the honorary degree as now commonly dealt out has lost its point. At least it makes no academic point. Rather, it perpetuates the ambiguity in the word "knowledge": it is knowledge to know where the post office is; it is knowledge to know the history of the French Revolution. The university is a judge of knowledge only in the second sense. Its degrees *honoris causa* should therefore go to persons outside the academic profession who have done intellectual work of high quality—the free-lance historian, the learned judge, the amateur archaeologist, the profound critic, and the like. This happens now, but not exclusively. I think honorary degrees should not be given to academic scholars who already have "the highest degree given in course." Still more obviously, the university should not mark with an academic symbol its possibly justified admiration of a business or political career. The Chairman of the Board of General Aphrodisiacs may be all that is said of him in the citation, but it is not a judgment on which the university should set its seal. These considerations are too reasonable for instant use, but some things have to be said so that at some future date they will—quite simply—have been said.

38. Last under external relations is the duty, now totally forgotten, of making it clear that education is also "public service." The notion that only when the university helps in garbage collection is it serving the public is by itself almost enough to account for its present precarious state.

IV. *Officers of Administration: Educational Maids-of-all-work*

39. The necessary counterpart of the students' helper Om is the regular surveying of administrative grumbling—not questionnaires,

but inquiries. I do not know of its being done anywhere. But it is obvious that the institutional maze bewilders and demoralizes the bureaucrats as much as the bureaucratized, so the periodic discharge of ill-humors coupled with apt suggestions would enhance the common good.

40. This inexpensive idea occurs first because university administration must be still more centralized, not less. The "360" computer system should be made to carry all it can of the routines, as well as supply the facts and figures necessary to good management. It is a matter of devising systems that will fit as many situations (schools, departments, functions) as possible, and forcing none. Exceptions can always be made provided everybody does not want to be one. Never will administrative imagination and tact be more needed than in introducing the modifications of habit that will precede the transference of the enormous paper work to the broad back of the IBM machine. Naturally, the work must be well done, the routine easily changeable, and the results readily intelligible to those who depend on it. This last characteristic requires intelligent clerks throughout, from which comes the exacting advice: hire fewer and better servants in the lower reaches of the administrative system.

41. To be one and centralized, the university must have a structure. It may have been true for the ancients that "things refuse to be mismanaged long," but to rely on that maxim in the university of today and ignore the demand for a tighter fabric would soon bring to a halt activities which its members at home and across the globe already find impeded by loose connections. Administrators know where the gaps are, namely, at the points where administrative information should reach the faculty and receive its consent or amendment. One such point, already mentioned, is the administrative-assistant post. Its function must be much enlarged and the places filled by capable young men and women ambitious of advancement. The transmission of information between center and periphery must, with their aid, be assured in both directions and reach as far as the students. Otherwise, moving levers and pedals leaves the car immobile, the engine idling; and this is true whether

the levers are moved by the "participating" faculties or by the delegates known as administrators.

42. The second gap occurs between governing committees (instruction or curriculum, appointments, executive) and the membership of schools, faculties, and departments. Grapevines work better on rumors than on facts and must be supplemented. The need is for a coaxial cable through which decisions and questions can be disseminated and objections and suggestions returned, the give-and-take to be regular, by means of *posted minutes* or other digests prepared by a (nonfaculty) secretary *and nailed to a board.* Sending mimeographed paper by mail is futile; it will not be read. Luther knew this: he lived in a university town, and we must follow his example.

43. With increased information would come an increase in the feeling of participation. Knowledge *and* discussion would then be a safeguard for the next innovation: the converting of the main faculty committees into action committees; some already are. The role of an action committee is: to act. Ordinary committees discuss and report, *hoping* for action. To know that policy would be made as soon as decided on would shorten discussion, increase responsibility, and save a step in administration. Each committee should naturally observe exact terms of reference and its work should be reviewed often enough to give the constituency a chance to propose new directions. Perhaps under this plan academic minds would relearn *how to transact business,* in place of matching opinions about hypothetical situations.

44. For certain administrative matters that require prompt action and are now held up by full-faculty deliberations, a faculty review committee is indicated. Acting as retrospective guide, it could not undo what had been done by the officer it approached, but it could redirect his future acts. For the rest, *all committees must be notified of their purpose and powers in writing.* An incredible amount of time is now wasted in discussing the question: what are we supposed to do? Vagueness is in order only when someone appoints a camouflage committee—to give the

impression of seeking advice but hoping the advice will defy analysis. But I am not concerned here with the tricks, rather with the sinews of administration. To be sinewy, committees must be small (five to seven) and seldom representative of special interests. Put everybody on who has any the least vested concern and stasis is sure.

45. Deans must continue to be recruited from the faculty, for the reasons I gave before. The best inducement to secure them is a university that works well and the promise of a termination of service within a reasonable time. Ten years should be a maximum; six will perhaps best serve both institution and man: he spends one year in learning his job and gives his measure in five. The help he needs consists not of many clerks but of a few first-rate "career men" as associates. And after six years he has not altogether forgotten how to teach and read a book, though he may find that the march of science has passed him by. For this reason a scientist probably accepts a deanship only when he feels that his scholarly work is done.

46. The academic vice-president, dean of faculties, or provost needs two things that should be but are not generally taken for granted; he sometimes obtains them on his own. One is a central fund with which to counterbalance outside grants. It is incredible that an institution dedicated to research should depend mainly or even largely on the resources and the judgment of outsiders for promoting inquiry. The provost's aim would not be to hand out consolation prizes to grantless scholars but to exert (with advice) a university judgment on those of its members best able to fulfill this great university responsibility. If the powerful foundations do not wish to have sole authority in directing the intellectual life (as I believe they do not), they can express their conviction by maintaining in the private universities central funds as described.

The provost's second prop is more easily come by. He needs, in addition to the "course study," a number of "reference books" in which he can see the university under various aspects: faculty and junior staff; salaries; leaves of absence; summer and visiting appointments; resignations and retirements; rates of promotion and salary advancement; research projects; costs of instruction by department; areas of faculty residence; size and distribution of classes within the work week; number and kind of instructional units—these are but a few of the headings under which he should be able to read comparative figures giving him an idea of the slope (up or down) on which he is treading. The computer will supply the raw materials, but the organization must be his, adapted to his university and his educational goals.

47. In the whole university the administrator most deserving of change is the president. He needs to be rescued, "simplified," and returned to his post as *head of the university*. He and he alone gives the tone to the whole and strength to those who make it go. He should be visibly at hand, but not badgered by decision-seekers who should consult directly that administrator to whom referral will in the end be made. Many think that it is money-raising which pulls the president away, and indeed it takes time and energy. But it is rather the incessant demands on his value as a social animal—the few words after dinner, the receptions and committees, the speeches as local or national spokesman—that ruin at once his chances of consecutive thought and his digestion. Yet he is not appointed to keep a large public happy by his presence but rather to do very precise and difficult things. Let him become sober like his university and see what happens.

48. Although administrators do not possess tenure, the removal of any career man (other than a dean) is rare and difficult. Supporters rally round threatened heads. The university accordingly should set aside a fair sum annually for a prompt separation from poor administrators. The money would be easily recouped in efficiency and morale and possibly in gifts.

49. Last comes the task of cell control: how many units can be fitted into a structure? As in cancer, there is a tendency for new growths to metastasize. Soon programs and "centers" are all over the place, making the university resemble the God of Empedocles —"a circle whose center is everywhere and circumference no-

where." In the long run only the faculty will decide what a university shall be, but in day-to-day administration the deans singly and together with central administration must require all things, even of the best kind, to show cause why the fabric should be strained to admit them. Once again, the privilege of such admission cannot be paid for. And this statement does not mean "should not"; it means *can not.* Even if gifts and grants should by a miracle be enlarged to pay for direct, indirect, and hidden costs *in perpetuo,* the burden left over would be that of *increased complexity*—not measurable but easily felt and subtly destructive.

v. *Money, or Education Stricken by Affluence*

50. Poverty is not a blight; penury is. The difference between the two is the difference between an adjustment or balance and a life always on the verge of disaster: only the *solvent* poor inherit the earth. One of the curses of the modern inflationary economy is that by making it impossible to be poor, art and education are condemned to unrelievable penury. Those concerned are like the daughters of the horseleech, always crying, "Give! Give!," to the detriment of their minds and judgment. When found, money establishes a higher level of expenditure, which cannot be reversed short of the asceticism I have advocated here.

It is clear how the drain occurs. A writer in *Science* put the matter definitively: *"The simple facts are that we sell our research, we sell our educational functions, we sell our social service to the community—everything—at a loss."*[18] (Italics in the original.) The remedy is equally clear: stop selling so much. That calls for gradual change, naturally, but possibilities suggest themselves. Medical schools need affiliation with universities but do not need to be on their budgets: turn these schools into close but independent affiliates.*

Similarly, giant research can only be carried on by academic

* Perhaps schools of journalism and of social work should follow the same path. The administrative efficiency of Princeton University is due to its freedom from expensive professional schools and research laboratories, as well as to its excellent body of administrators.

staffs, but "big science" does not have to go on to eternity as a university expense partly reimbursed. The laboratories, multimillion-dollar machines, and attendant personnel can be detached and made (through contracts) the full responsibility of the government—as is in fact the situation of such an establishment as the Brookhaven National Laboratory. The administrative machinery for an affiliate and its linking with the universities are already tested by experience. The formula can be applied again and again with variations to any division of the university that bears a like relation to government or foundation demands.

51. In that category I place the whole apparatus of exchanges—students, teachers, researchers, visitors, books, and equipment. A government agency could effect a huge social saving by centralizing and simplifying these activities. Each new exchange set up at the request of a government agency uses up—as I can testify—half the time of a junior administrator for week after week, so many and variable are the details. The phrase in common academic use to justify the expense of *adding* activities applies better to dropping this one: "We can no longer afford . . ."

52. The federal government has begun, through the Library of Congress, the cataloguing of new books, published here or imported. Either this service must be made comprehensive and the library cards dispensed at cost to the universities, or a consortium of universities must see to it. The present duplication is wasteful and soon the trained personnel will be wanting. (This particular suggestion is not original with me; it is being worked on; I include it for completeness.)

53. A similar clearinghouse for admissions work is more difficult to design, but we shall have to come to it, on a regional or other basis. If the College Entrance Examination Board has succeeded in examining throughout the nation, it or another agency can help admit by handling the tidal wave of college and graduate school applications.

54. Before accepting private gifts for special uses the university must establish a schedule of costs by categories of purpose, and

demonstrate to the donor of good will what part of his contribution must be reserved for hidden costs before the remainder can support the new activity. A Columbia trustee, Mr. Lawrence A. Wien, has proposed (and acted on) a formula whose intention is parallel: any gift to endowment—e.g., for a chair—would provide that the capital gain on the fund should go to current income after the principal has been increased by a percentage equal to inflation. Money for buildings should of course provide for their maintenance. Present practice in this last regard must soon lead to starvation amid palaces.

55. Since the growth and shift of academic specialties is now rapid, some provision must be made for obsolescence. A depreciation charge on the budget for, say, 10 to 15 percent of the course offering would give the means of bringing in new scholars. The sum in turn could be used as an upper limit for expansion under that head, thus holding down faculty extravagance. For activities originally promoted from outside and now perishing, the foundations should be sought out as advisers and, in some cases, as contributors to the cost of terminating or reviving the effort.

56. Mention has been made of costly printing, much of it for boastful lures and competitive claims. The self-denying ordinance earlier proposed would need enforcement by the group adopting it, until it became a point of academic ethics, as among physicians. If the increasing number of students and a central application bureau do not bring about a wider and more accurate public knowledge of universities, there is no hope for either students or universities. Ordinary catalogues should be available in public libraries and mother wit should do the rest, putting an end to primitive advertising.*

57. The high cost of higher education has, it appears, begun to

* Jefferson to Dunglison, Nov. 17, 1825: "I send you the plan of a new Medical school. . . . It is also a specimen of our proficiency in the art of puffing, shewing that if others will not declare that we are the first of the human race in science as in everything else, we can declare it ourselves."—*The Jefferson-Dunglison Letters,* ed. John M. Dorsey, Charlottesville, 1960, 42.

affect the birth rate.[19] Even well-to-do parents plan and restrict in order to be able to face, twenty years later, the drain of their children's college bills. In the private institutions, we saw, tuition fees stand at or near $2,000 a year. The resulting income for college or university amounts to less than half the measurable expense. When tuition goes up, it is not in order to recover more, but simply to stay in the same place in the teeth of inflation. Yet it is a question whether tuition can go up indefinitely at a rate that will maintain even this unsatisfactory ratio. At each increase there is protest; students (or parents) drop out, and the lot of those who continue becomes harder: jobs and loans add preoccupations that should not exist for youth at its studies. The high price, moreover, strengthens the public prejudice against a "privileged class" whose supposed wealth gives it a monopoly of higher education.

Every aspect of the situation is detestable: the poor student of high ability must be helped through by a full scholarship for his tuition and a job and loan for his keep. The student in moderate circumstances is asked to take a larger loan, to supplement his partial scholarship. Both students leave college with a debt, just at the time they contemplate marriage. Sometimes the married partners both have loans outstanding and one or both want further professional training—more loans and more moonlighting; or else one is employed full-time while the other studies. These may be necessary conditions; they are not decent conditions. They may resemble the self-help and self-making traditional in this country; they are in fact much worse, because more complicated and charged with anxiety. They do not simply require ambition, hard work, and long hours: they require nerves of steel. The strain, while wiping out the pleasure of study, turns learning into an oppression made up of unendurable, arbitrary demands. And in the "credentials society" the four-year stretch of the college degree is lengthened by two to six years more of professional education.

Three desiderata suggest themselves that go beyond the problem of keeping tuitions within reach. One proposal was outlined in Chapter 6: abundant federal and state scholarships bearing with them a cost-of-education grant payable to the institution.

58. Two: shortened programs. We have discussed the excess of courses and its link with the undesirable vocational system of overparticularized training. Boiling down the curriculum, splitting off the liberal arts from professional propaedeutics, dividing among institutions responsibility for small fields, and granting the Ph.D. after the orals would permit compression. If properly planned, the course need not give a sense of rush—on the contrary—nor need it be assumed ahead of time to be an unsubstantial "quickie." It is just as plausible that our present programs are inflated "lengthies." It is a sobering thought that Descartes finished his studies at fifteen and the French historian Lefebvre at fifty. The cry of "Too much education" has in fact begun to be heard from observers worth heeding. For the public is noticing that educational deficiences are invariably met by "more time!" instead of "we'll do better." An assistant principal in New York has not hesitated to assign as a cause "the bankruptcy of ideas that exists today."[20]*

But to be of any use the new programs, arts-and-science or professional, must be carefully put together by masters of the field.† The principle of reduction must be brought to bear on the contents and organization of the subjects, and not merely on the collection of ready-made packages we now assemble and require.

59. The third proposal is to extend the practice of canceling educational loans for students who establish themselves in professions where the pay is moderate—librarianship, teaching, the church, etc. It is evident that loans incurred in preparation for these callings cannot be repaid without hardship in any reasonable time. The lawyer, the physician, the engineer, the business-school graduate stand a better chance of earning immediately a salary that permits prompt repayment. Since the country needs to fill the ranks of the several professions faster than laisser-faire is doing it,

* See also Dr. Hans Rosenhaupt, Director of the Woodrow Wilson National Fellowship Foundation, in his address at Texas Christian University, Oct. 1, 1964: "Can Education Be Too Much of a Good Thing?"

† Some ten years ago the American Chemical Society devised a model four-field, six-year Ph.D., counting from the college freshman year. One might risk the question, Is the third year of law school indispensable?

the investment of private or tax money in cancelable loans for education seems socially wise—at least as wise as using it for the relief of unemployables.*

60. John Gardner, when Secretary of the Federal Department of Education, held conferences with university administrators at which he broached the idea of alliances between small colleges and large universities and, alternatively, of several colleges in what has come to be known as "cluster colleges." Physical nearness would determine either type of association. The aim in each is both educational and economic. Small colleges need the expensive scientific installation of the large university. The latter may conceivably want to maintain the atmosphere of an undergraduate college that bigness destroys, by putting a branch of its own college "in cluster with" the affiliate, rather than by expanding it on home ground.

The thorny problems of colleges for women and their recent round-the-clock closeness to men are also capable of solution by this scheme. For women's colleges find the recruiting of first-rate science teachers very difficult, and yet women majoring in science are numerous. In the clusters the way to economy is to avoid duplication—in facilities as well as in staff. In the half-formed outline of this development one can discern a resemblance to the traditional English universities: groups of colleges using a central source of teaching as well as their own. As changes loom for American higher education, this model (with adaptations) appears as likely as the Continental model mentioned earlier, in which the university leaves the student life to the student—he being twenty-one—and concerns itself only with his higher education. Nothing in history or in the present would or should prevent both types from developing side by side. Differentiation indeed can only promote suitability to taste and means, provided that the notions of education and university remain high and vivid.

* A small point, but an important one: the word "forgiven" should not continue to be used for *canceled* loans. The educational borrower has done nothing that demands forgiveness; he deserves praise and thanks.

VI. *New Functions: Education* in partibus

61. To that visitor from Mars whom we have all been waiting for, nothing on earth would seem more paradoxical than this: the new university's concern with the outer world ignores all concern with what people in the world think about education. The university now attends to the dark places of the earth but not of the mind. Academic men can perhaps not be expected to bother with the ancient superstitions of astrology and cheiromancy, or the new-fangled cults flavored with Eastern religion or Western psychology. But the great and far more dangerous push of the plausible and pseudo-scientific they do nothing to resist. It conquers the public by default. For certainly common intelligence and a college education are no safeguard against what unknown Ph.D.'s and others put forward as the latest results of research or the sweetest methods of learning.

The neglected university duties under this head are too many and varied to be listed. They form the one function of criticism which some honestly believe they fulfill when they merely express disagreement. Criticism is not a duty of the university in its corporate form—that would be impracticable, and anyhow too close to the detestable tactics of censorship by group action. Rather, the university as a company of men of knowledge should make it its business to watch over the public's intellectual diet and interpose a corrective when called for.

62. On education itself, for example, there has long been a need for severe astringents. Individuals and committees, privately or officially designated persons—often of the highest qualifications—allow themselves to drool about education, its duties, contents, and possibilities, in a manner injurious to the public mind.* Why

* For one book like the excellent *Education and the New America* by S. T. Kimball and J. E. McClellan, Jr. (New York, 1962), there are hundreds of deplorable volumes, e.g., a certain *Philosophy of Education,* published some ten years ago, which winds up with a section on "Ultimate Questions in Education" that includes paragraphs on: Human Nature, The Ultimate Nature of Things, The Cosmic Process, The Aims of Education [so late

interfere? Well, whoever teaches is also said to educate, therefore must know what education is, just as a lawyer knows what the law and the judicial process are. All who teach therefore have a duty to expound the simplicities of education, if they can. They must help sober up the multitude who intoxicate themselves with educational talk, the most dangerous brand of word-alcohol. Possibly if the university (in the distributive sense just stated) had been vigilant thirty years ago, the country would not have run into the fiasco of reading instruction. Belated thought about this "programed retardation" is even now conveyed to the public by newspapermen, rather than by the highest educational authorities.* Meanwhile, extravagant promises of speed-reading continue unchecked for want of anyone's explaining the difference between scanning an interoffice memo at a mile a minute and *learning* what Hegel says in the *Philosophy of History*.

63. Both learning as an activity and scholarship as a result stand in need of continual critical attention. Every few months a new method brings "revolution in the three R's."[21] Sometimes it is listening to phonograph records before sleep that will transmute the dull mind, sometimes it is an injection of "brain substance" (ribonucleic acid) or pemoline and magnesium hydroxide.[22] Whether followed by a report of failure or quietly forgotten, the tidings leave the impression that students can learn without work. Another form of deception comes from studies of remote or irrelevant facts, e.g., *Noisy Girl Babies May Be Brighter* or *Pupils Do Well When Teacher Is Told They Will.*[23] With such ideas and the frequent announcements of tests that "predict pupil failure," there is enough in the air to persuade the reasoning young that fate or drugs hold the key to their education. Looking at it with Martian eyes, I prefer to believe that *Right Side of Brain May Not Know What Left Does.*[24]

---

in the book!], Good and Evil in Education, Holiness, and so on. On page 549 we are told that the "problem of aims in education is a problem of *values.*" Verbiage is the educational medium par excellence.

* See John Chamberlain's column "These Days," *Journal-American,* Aug. 13, 1963.

64. There is need, but not space, to discuss in detail the harm done to scholarship by the prospect of its transfer to the storage units of computers—another "revolution" which "should put at the fingertips of *anyone* who wishes to be a modern-day Faust *all the knowledge he desires* without selling his soul to the Devil."[25] (Italics added.) An occasional lone voice raised against such an utterance by a respected scientist in a Phi Beta Kappa publication is not enough to discourage barbaric misconceptions. Unexpectedly, it is in a journal of statistics that that lone voice is heard preaching the aptly named "doubt interval" to "deter us from joining what seems to be emerging as a Data Cult." The caution is simple and clear: "Data cultists believe that all data are beneficent commodities."[26]*

65. Nor is traditional scholarship exempt from the influence of the cult. It was left to a scholar not of the academy, Lewis Mumford, to show the perversity of the mind that edits the works of a writer into a cipher. The instance was the new *Journals* of Emerson, in which so many interruptions of words and sentences by diacritical marks occur that Emerson cannot be read.[27]† The purpose of the marks is to indicate variants, originals, errors, and the like, which, as Mr. Mumford points out, will be consulted at the source just the same by future specialists, and which meanwhile render the new edition a parody of written thought.

66. Two other concerns fall within the university's legitimate interest: the tendency of the entire educational effort and the performance of any one part that comes into notice through innovation or improvement. Here too we need a departure from indifference. For, like the well-being of the individual, that of institutions calls for attention to what is in one's domain without

* The science-bred habit of correlation, admirable in its place, tends to corrupt other disciplines: "If the birth years of the 92 composers in the 1938 poll are plotted, the median birth year falls in the decade of the 1720's. But if the criterion [*sic*] of eminence is made progressively less stringent, the median decade will move, for a time, toward the present. . . . Unfortunately, there are few guidelines to tell us what music will be like a century or more from now. . . ."—*Psychology Today,* August 1967, 43.

† It is curious that in the age of microfilm and Xerox this urge to print textual minutiae is given free rein and large subsidies.

being in one's purview. So far as I know, during the discussion of the new constitution proposed for New York State, no educator put side by side for the public the provision looking to a college education for all and that which removed the literacy requirement for voting. A *New York Times* editorial did regret the loss of an incentive to "full integration in New York life" for foreign-born citizens, but comments by others regarded the demand of literacy as "discriminatory to a minority."[28] What does higher education think?*

67. As for the university's indifference toward its own constituent institutions, it is deep enough to explain the public's invincible ignorance of the whole subject. When a long article in a daily paper proclaimed that New York University was stiffening its academic requirements, the reporter made a point that *Few Outside Educational Field Notice Change:* he was being kind to the field. Reports of such changes are deemed exaggerated or unimportant; nobody inquires or cares. The natural consequence is that the institution making the change is driven to advertise it—in this case justly and modestly, thanks to President Hester's judgment and tact. Higher education need expect no public knowledge of its importance, no public trust in its pronouncements and preferences, until it steadily demonstrates its quick recognition of merit—or fraud.

Today, business and politics are far better known than education. The facts are not aired and sorted out. This is not to require from universities either mutual admiration or mutual denigration, but a critical literature that does not, like the comparative ratings, add up estimates of research productivity by departments or, like accrediting groups, certify minimum standards.†

* And what—on a broader scale—does higher education think of the textbooks used in the nation's schools? Scholars sometimes write them, but scholars rarely review them.

† William C. Fels: "It would be delightful if . . . applicants and their counselors knew enough about colleges to distinguish between them on the basis of real and significant differences, but the plain fact is that they don't."—Memorandum to Admissions and Educational Policies Committees, Bennington College, Feb. 13, 1959.

68. Finally, the university must make up its mind and choose between two attitudes, which go with two messages now incessantly heard. One is: "Behold our eminence—it deserves your support and affectionate regard after you have attended and shared our greatness." The other is: "We are a public utility like any other—drop in any time." Both messages are spoken by the same voice and both, perhaps, should remain unspoken; but the first should secretly inspire the "university conceived." Let it be clear: The choice is not between being high-hat and being just folks. It is not a question of hospitableness—a university should be hospitable; it is a question of style, reflecting the fundamental choice as to what the university thinks it is. It can, from generous but misguided motives, yield to the assimilating effect of cooperation with the world. Then a big grant for a noneducational purpose brings out scholars in a goldrush, though they do their best to keep the rest of the show going not too badly. This defection has occurred before. "In my time and my country," says Montaigne, "learning has a salutary effect on the pocket, rarely on the mind."[29]

But the combination of Swift's Floating Island of projectors with Bacon's House of Inquiry is not a stable one. One or the other prevails by making converts or accomplices. At the present time the House of Inquiry still has great claims to our respect, particularly in natural science. If it is to set the tone, a new feeling of noblesse oblige must pervade the whole. The university should not be afraid of its own dignity: as Chapman says, it is the roof that stretches over man's whole intellectual kingdom; and if dignity is good for individuals, why should a company of them affect the slovenly style? Dignity as an attribute is also educational, especially for those of whatever background or capacity who have been lured into thinking that there is no mystery about education and that it comes like a soft drink out of a vending machine. Far better to be somewhat hushed, to be given pause by the spiritual grandeur of a place which can never be bought prefabricated for assembly like a service station. Students would not be wrong, would lose nothing by first being overawed, as at Chartres.

The foregoing incomplete string of imperfect suggestions, tentative in spite of the way they are put, takes for granted one premise: that the nation wants a university in the honorific and not in the service-station sense. To be sure, the nation acts as if it did want the real thing. It seems to be choosing such a university when it speaks of science and learning as contributing to the nation's greatness and of newborn talent as the richest of its natural resources. But it is possible to imagine a society thriving for a considerable time while repeating these words and harboring opposite feelings.

What develops then is a proletarian culture, by which I do not mean the culture of intelligent and cheerful workingmen exclusively, but one in which the prevailing tendency is to suspect *height*—standards of work and degrees of achievement, except in sports. Learning, the search for truth, high art are then gradually discarded in favor of practical training, applied research, and consumption art. The full professor is intelligent and cheerful too; he responds to the common agitation, discontinuity, and excitement of the mass culture; he prides himself on not being an intellectual, though he enjoys the "finer things of life" in a widely shared attachment to "gracious living."

The difference is marked, but not reprehensible. Nothing yields mankind a full beaker of bliss. At any time a society affords joys that are incompatible with their opposites. That is why nations and individuals must *choose* and, having chosen, strive to remember what goes with the choice made. I have tried to sketch, the latest and least interpreter in an ancient line, what choosing to have a university entails and what a great nation may expect from it—indeed must require. I do not doubt that the United States today still possesses the makings of a university, as I do not doubt that if circumstances send the institution into eclipse, the idea of it will survive into another day.

APPENDIX A—AN ORGANIZATION CHART (*JUNE 30, 1967*)

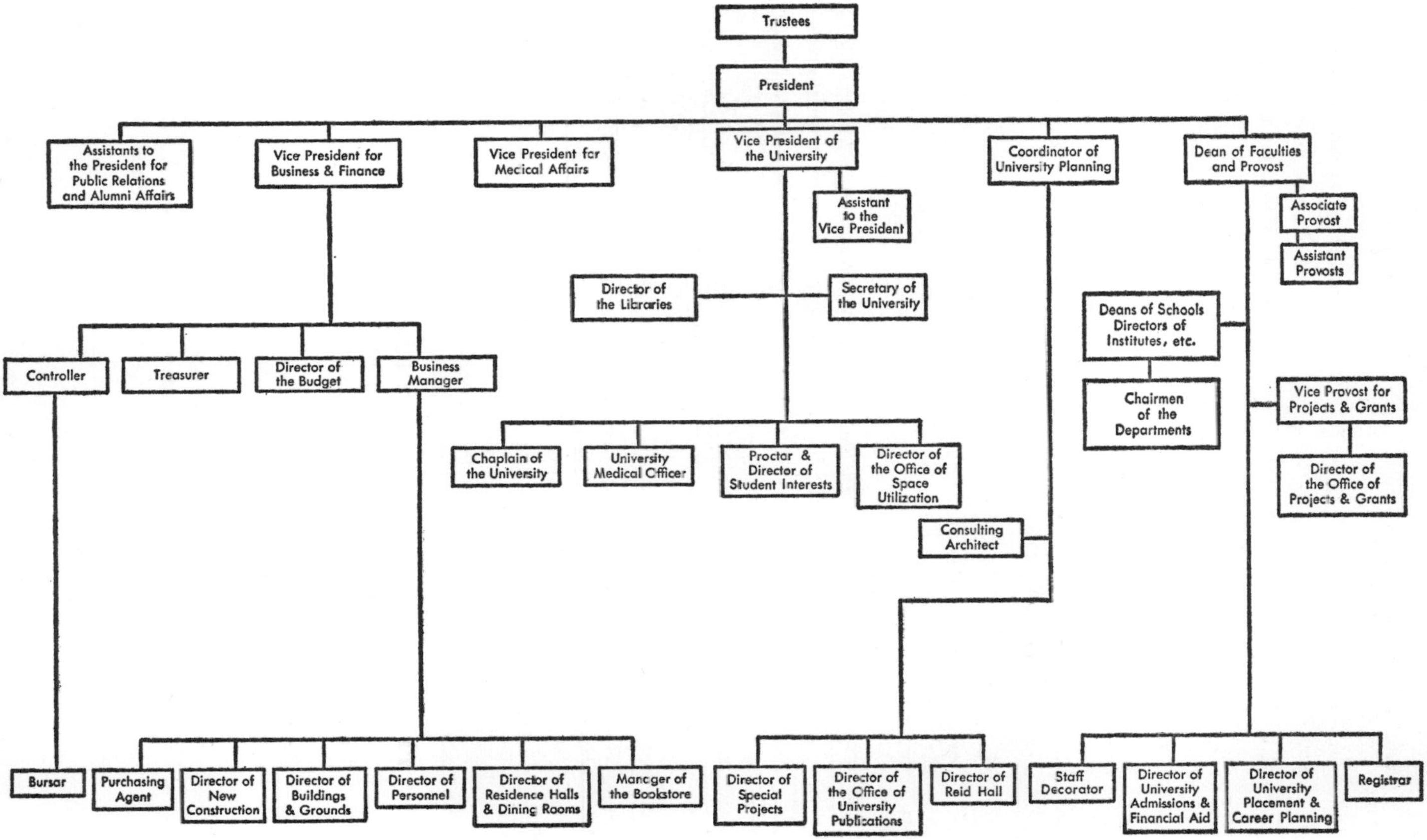

Appendix B

The Parts of a University

Departments of Arts and Science (44): Anatomy, Anthropology, Art History and Archaeology, Astronomy, Biochemistry, Biological Sciences, Chemical Engineering, Chemistry, Civil Engineering and Engineering Mechanics, East Asian Languages and Cultures, Economics, Electrical Engineering, English and Comparative Literature, French and Romance Philology, Geography, Geology, Germanic Languages, Graphics, Greek and Latin, History, Industrial and Management Engineering, Italian, Linguistics, Mathematical Statistics, Mathematics, Mechanical Engineering, Microbiology, Middle East Languages and Cultures, Mining, Metallurgy and Mineral Engineering, Music, Naval Science, Pathology, Pharmacology, Philosophy, Physical Education and Intercollegiate Athletics, Physics, Physiology, Psychology, Public Law and Government, Religion, Slavic Languages, Social Psychology, Sociology, Spanish and Portuguese

Faculties of Arts and Science (3): Faculty of Political Science, Faculty of Philosophy, Faculty of Pure Science

Undergraduate Schools (2): Columbia College, School of General Studies

Professional Schools (12): Architecture, Arts, Business, Dental and Oral Surgery, Engineering and Applied Science, International Affairs, Journalism, Law, Library Service, Nursing, Public Health and Administrative Medicine, Social Work

Institutes (14): Institute of African Studies, East Asian Institute, Institute on East Central Europe, European Institute, Institute of

Flight Structures, International Institute for Human Reproduction, Institute of Latin-American Studies, Middle East Institute, Institute of Nutrition Sciences, Russian Institute, Southern Asian Institute, Institute for the Study of Science in Human Affairs, Institute of Human Environment, Institute of War and Peace Studies

Programs (3): American Language Program, Executive Program in Business Administration, International Fellows Program

Centers (9): Electronic Music Center, Foreign Student Center, Inter-American Law Center, Center of Israel and Jewish Studies, Center of Pakistan Studies, Center for Research and Demonstration (Social Work), Center for Research and Education in American Liberties, Center of Turkish Studies, Center on Urban Affairs

Interdepartmental and Interfaculty Units of Instruction (6): Camp Columbia (Engineering), NROTC and Naval Science, Language Laboratory, Parker School of Foreign and Comparative Law, Summer Session, University Seminars (41)

Research Units (31)

A. Natural and Applied Sciences: Armstrong Laboratories, Chemical Engineering Research Laboratories, Computer Center, Institute for the Study of Fatigue and Reliability, Hudson Laboratories, Industrial Reactor Laboratories, Lamont Geological Observatory (2 divisions; 2 ships), Marcellus Hartley Electronics Laboratory, Nevis Laboratory, Pegram Laboratories, Psychoanalytic Clinic for Training and Research, Radiation Laboratory, Watson Laboratory, Yale-Columbia Southern Station

B. Political Science and Philosophy: Bureau of Applied Social Research, Research Institute on Communist Affairs, Conservation of Human Resources Project, Council on Atomic Age Studies, Economics Research Centers, Hispanic Institute, Research Program on International Economic Integration, Research Project in International Economics, Research Program on International Organization, Legislative Drafting Research, Research Program on Men and Politics in Modern China, Research Project on National Income in East Central Europe, Oral History Research Office, Sackler Fund for East Asian Studies, Research Program on United Nations and World Affairs, Research Project on Vatican Diplomacy, Research Program on World Music

Affiliates (3): Barnard College, College of Pharmaceutical Sciences, Teachers College

Appendix C

The Macmahon Committee and Its Administrative Implications

The Committee on the Educational Future of the University was appointed by President Grayson Kirk in October 1955, following a resolution of the University Council. The members of the Committee were Professors Charles H. Behre, Jr. (Geology), Charles Frankel (Philosophy), Maxwell Gensamer (Metallurgy), Arthur W. Macmahon (Public Law and Government) *Chairman,* Ernest J. Simmons (Russian Literature), and Howard R. Williams (Law). As the president's representative, Stanley Salmen, Coordinator of University Planning, attended the meetings. The report in book form, *The Educational Future of the University,* was prepared during the summer of 1957 and sent to press on November 1 of that year, after a two-day conference with a large faculty group at Arden House on October 11–13, 1957.

The report takes up in 282 pages the matters indicated by the following headings: Distinctive Obligations and Opportunities; Union in Diversity; Departmental Structure and Organization; Faculty Structure and Administration; Over-all Procedures (Budget, Admissions, Educational Planning, Tenure Appointments, Promotions, Assignment of Personnel, Graduate Deanship, Interdisciplinary Relations); The Central Structure; The Undergraduate Programs (Columbia College, Science and Engineering, General Studies, Relations with Barnard); The Graduate Programs (Nonprofessional departments; Residence and Tuition; Collateral Needs, Social and Personal Needs; Curriculum;

Professional Programs: the twelve schools); Programs in the Arts and in Communications; Faculty Salaries, benefits, and outside activities; Student support; Adjuncts of Instruction and Research (contracts and grants); The Libraries; The University Press; The Language Laboratory; Neighborhood Problems and Physical Expansion.

During the work, in order to carry out the bulk of the Committee recommendations and build an administrative structure capable of stretching and adapting itself rapidly to the multiplying demands, the following offices, committees, faculties, and their accessories were planned and established, a number of them anticipating by a year or two (because of urgent need) the recommendations of the Committee.

It makes a quite substantial catalogue of innovations:

I. Offices
1. Coordinator of University Planning
2. Graduate Student Adviser
3. Director of Personnel (and Fringe Benefits)
4. Projects and Grants
5. Purchasing for Government Contracts and Grants
6. University Relations (including expanded News Office and new Office of Radio and Television)
7. University Publications (printing)
8. Space Utilization and Planning
9. New Construction
10. Consulting Architect (and drafting staff)
11. Health Physics (disposal of radioactive waste, etc.)
12. Staff decorator (receipt and distribution of gift furniture, maintenance, etc.)
13. Audio-Visual Aids to Instruction
14. Artistic Properties
15. National Alumni Program
16. Central Stores
17. Central Information (at campus entrance)
18. Community Affairs (including Campus Guide Service)
19. Administrative Data Processing (Facts and Figures)
20. Expansion of the Office of the Secretary for new faculty and visitor services
21. Neighborhood Services (including tenant relocation)

II. Central Administrative Committees
1. Advisory Committee of the Faculties

2. Cabinet (and subcommittee for administrative reports)
3. Budget Committee (recast, with subcommittees)
4. University Relations
5. Property Policy
6. Space Allocation and Building Alterations
7. Administrative Assistants
8. University Planning (current and future expansion)
9. Joint Committee on Student Life and Student Affairs

III. Reorganizations and Ancillary Changes

1. Alumni Records Center
2. Office of the Vice-President for Business and Finance
3. Office of the Controller (including recasting of Chart of Accounts)
4. Office of the Budget (including budget nomenclature and form)
5. Decentralization of eight Admissions Offices
6. Centralization of Expense Accounts for: furniture, equipment, faculty research in the arts and sciences, minor space alterations, travel, typing assistance, and miscellaneous "educational supplements"
7. Relocation and systematizing of the Columbiana Collection
8. Redesign of the academic costume
9. Creation of grade of Preceptor
10. Seven-year limit for the Ph.D.

IV. New or Modified Divisions of Instruction and Research (with associated services)

1. Faculty of International Affairs (unifying earlier programs and centers)
2. Faculty of Social Work (formerly an affiliate)
3. Faculty of the Arts (formerly a group of programs)
4. Restructuring of the Faculty of Architecture (to include enlarged instruction and research in Urban Planning)
5. School of Business brought to full-time and day-time instruction
6. Foreign Student Center (including instruction in American civilization and English for foreigners)
7. Graduate Students brought to full-time attendance and extended residence
8. Expanded Department of Astronomy

9. Union of Departments of Botany and Zoology as a Department of Biological Sciences
10. Language Laboratory
11. Computer Center
12. Institute of African Studies
13. Research Institute on Communist Affairs
14. Institute of Latin-American Studies
15. Institute of Southeast Asian Studies
16. Institute of Human Environment
17. Research Institute for the Study of Science in Human Affairs
18. International Fellows Program
19. Reid Hall (student and faculty residence in Paris)

V. Documents

1. Consolidation of Catalogues and Bulletins (redesign and condensation)
2. Graduate Student Guide (and ten others), 1957
3. Faculty Handbook, 1959
4. Administrative Guide, 1960
5. Personnel and Fringe Benefits Handbook
6. Telephone survey
7. Classification of users of the library
8. Classification of Visiting Scholars and other guests of the university
9. Rules Governing Travel Expense
10. Charts of Main Offices and Job Descriptions of Main Posts
11. Faculty Rules and Department By-laws (51 documents)
12. Inventory of University Property
13. Catalogue (in professional form) of Works of Art
14. Customs governing Oral Examinations and Prize Awards
15. List of tuition and other fees
16. Duties and Classification of Clerical Staff
17. Classification of Officers holding appointments, with their privileges
18. Short-form Annual Financial Report for public distribution
19. Annual report of the Coordinator of University Planning on the state of pending projects
20. Annual report on the outside activities of faculty members

    (N.B. The compiling of the annual Faculty Bibliography was dropped because of its excessive bulk and the difficulties of attaining even near-completeness.)

21. The Role of the Trustees, 1957
22. Graduate Study at Columbia (published volume by Hans Rosenhaupt, 1959)
23. Organization and Structure of Columbia University, with charts of administrative offices, 1963
24. Description of current activities (for foundation use), 1966
25. Provost's survey of departmental needs, 1967

Appendix D

Check List of Writings and Speeches by Jacques Barzun on Educational Subjects, 1926–1967

1. "Textbooks and Tediousness," *The Columbia Varsity,* October 1926.
2. "Irrelevant Maturity," *The Columbia Varsity,* December 1926.
3. (with R. Valeur) "Education in France: Its Theory, Practice, and Worth," *Redirecting Education,* ed. R. G. Tugwell and L. H. Keyserling, New York, 1935, vol II. (Fuller version), *Columbia University Quarterly,* December 1932.
4. "Teaching the Humanitics," *Columbia University Quarterly,* September 1938.
5. "The Humanities—Proper Study of Mankind," *English Journal,* October 1938.
6. "Read, Do Not Run," *Saturday Review,* March 9, 1940. (Review of M. J. Adler, *How to Read a Book.*)
7. "The College and the Citizen," Conference of University Administrators, Chicago, March 21, 1944.
8. "Are Teachers Escapists?," *Saturday Review,* Sept. 16, 1944.
9. "What Is Teaching?," *Atlantic,* December 1944.
10. *Teacher in America,* Boston and New York, 1945. (Anchor Books, 1954.)
11. "Distrust of Brains," *Nation,* Jan. 6, 1945.
12. "The Little Money," *Nation,* Feb. 3, 1945.
13. "Whom Shall We Teach?," *New Leader,* Feb. 24, 1945.
14. "Book Makers and Book Keepers," Fifth Annual Summer Conference for School Librarians, Geneseo, N.Y., July 31, 1945.

15. "Harvard Takes Stock," *Atlantic,* October 1945. (Review of Harvard University *General Education in a Free Society.*)
16. (with H. R. Steeves) *A College Program in Action,* New York, 1946.
17. Review of H. Craig *Literary Study and the Scholarly Profession,* in *American Historical Review,* January 1946.
18. "The Scholar Looks at the Library," *College and Research Libraries,* April 1946.
19. "Cross Currents in American Education," Voice of America broadcast, May 29, 1946.
20. "The Idea of a Career," *A Man's Reach: Some Choices Facing Youth Today,* ed. T. H. Johnson, New York, 1947.
21. "The Higher Learning in America," *Horizon,* London, October 1947.
22. "The Scholar Is an Institution," *Journal of Higher Education,* November 1947.
23. "Education," *The Lawrentian,* Spring 1948.
24. "The Backwardness of Present-Day Science Teaching," American Conference of Acdemic Deans, New York, Jan. 10, 1949.
25. "Calamophobia, or Hints Toward a Writer's Discipline," *The Writer's Book,* ed. H. Hull, New York, 1950.
26. "The Educated Man," *Life,* Oct. 16, 1950.
27. "Programs in the Humanities," Memorandum to the John Hay Whitney Foundation, Nov. 15, 1950.
28. "A Loyalty Oath for Scholars," *American Scholar,* Summer 1951. (Signed "Hippocrates, Jr.")
29. "John Henry Newman, the Educated Man," Newman Club, Columbia University, Feb. 20, 1951.
30. Review of *Chambers' Encyclopedia* and *The Columbia Encyclopedia,* Second Ed., *Herald Tribune Book Review,* Sept. 2, 1951.
31. "Literature in Secondary Education," *General Education in School and College,* Cambridge, 1952. (Remarks and memorandum to the Editorial Committee.)
32. Letter on "Examology," *Columbia Spectator,* Feb. 5, 1952.
33. "World Culture—Hope, Menace, or Illusion," Agnes Scott College, April 5, 1952; also University of Kentucky, April 8, 1952; also Fisk University, April 9, 1952.
34. "The Great Books," *Atlantic,* December 1952.
35. "The Language of Your Peers," School and College Conference on English, Barnard College, Feb. 21, 1953.

36. "English as She's Not Taught," *Atlantic,* December 1953.
37. "The Battle Over Brains in Democratic Education," *University of Toronto Quarterly,* January 1954.
38. "The Indispensable Amateur: Music in the Liberal Arts College," *Juilliard Review,* January 1954.
39. "The Ph.D. in Retrospect" and "The Dissertation Re-Defined," Ford Foundation Graduate Studies Meeting, Nov. 13–14, 1954.
40. "The Care and Feeding of the Mind," Phillips Exeter Academy, New Hampshire, Nov. 21, 1954. (Recording in Spoken Arts, No. 713 Distinguished Teachers' Series, Westminster Records, 1956.)
41. "The Scholar-Teacher and Our Respective Schools," Teachers College, Columbia University, Dec. 10, 1954.
42. "Adult Confusion and Adult Education," New School for Social Research, New York, Feb. 15, 1955.
43. "The College President in Theory and Practice," Institute for University Administrators, Cambridge, June 23, 1955.
44. (with others) "The Graduate School Today and Tomorrow," Fund for the Advancement of Education, New York, December 1955. (Report of the Committee of Fifteen.)
45. *Report of the Dean of the Graduate Faculties, 1955–56,* Columbia University, 1956.
46. "Who Ever Heard of Training College Teachers?," American Council on Education, Washington, D.C., Jan. 20, 1956.
47. "Teachers, Parents, and Money," *Harper's,* February 1956. (Anonymous.)
48. "Scholarship and Criticism," National Commission on the Humanities Report, April 5, 1956; also English Institute, Columbia University, Sept. 6, 1956.
49. (with others) "Report of the Educational Policies Committee of the Association of Graduate Schools," *Journal of Proceedings and Addresses,* October 1956.
50. "The Student at Grips with Time and Numbers," Graduate Faculties Convocation, Columbia University, Oct. 15, 1956.
51. *Report of the Dean of the Graduate Faculties, 1956–57*, Columbia University, 1957.
52. (editor) *A History of the Faculty of Philosophy, Columbia University,* New York, 1957.
53. (with H. Graff) *The Modern Researcher,* New York, 1957.
54. "The Oddest Profession in the World," *Expanding Resources for College Teaching,* Washington, D.C., 1957.

55. "The Ph.D. Octopus—Killed or Scotched?," Princeton University, April 5, 1957.
56. "Graduate Work Today—Why So Popular?," Columbia University Associates, New York, May 14, 1957.
57. (with others) "Doctors and Masters—Good and Bad," *Journal of Proceedings and Addresses of the Association of Graduate Schools,* October 1957. (Report of the Committee on Policies in Graduate Education, *New York Times,* Nov. 13, 1957.)
58. "Institutional Life and the Modern Student," Barnard College Convocation, Oct. 1, 1957.
59. "The Humanist Looks at the Business Man," Dean's Day, School of Business, Columbia University, Dec. 7, 1957.
60. *Report of the Dean of the Graduate Faculties, 1957–58,* Columbia University, 1958.
61. *The Graduate Student's Guide, 1957–58,* Columbia University, 1958.
62. "The Scholar-Critic," *Contemporary Literary Scholarship,* ed. L. Leary, New York, 1958.
63. "Paradox of Teaching: in Demand and in Disrepute," Berea College, March 26, 1958.
64. "Science vs. the Humanities," *Saturday Evening Post,* May 3, 1958.
65. (with others) "The Discovery and Encouragement of Humanists," Report of the American Council of Learned Societies Conference, May 16–17, 1958.
66. "On the Need of a Little Starch," Bennington College, June 27, 1958.
67. Preface to T. Caplow and R. McGee, *The Academic Marketplace,* New York, 1958.
68. (with others) "The Higher Degrees," Report of the Educational Policies Committee of the Association of Graduate Schools, December 1958.
69. "Research and Creativity," *Report of the Seventh Conference of the Association of Princeton Graduate Alumni,* Dec. 27–28, 1958.
70. *The House of Intellect,* New York, 1959. (Harper Torchbooks, 1961).
71. "The Tyranny of Idealism in Education," *The Woodrow Wilson Foundation Series,* No. 6, January 1959.
72. "The Place and the Price of Excellence," *Vogue,* Feb. 1, 1959.
73. "Facts and Fallacies in Language Teaching," Greater New York Teachers of French, New York, Feb. 21, 1959.

74. "Pride and the Engineer," School of Engineering Convocation, Columbia University, April 4, 1959.
75. "Communications—or Talking to Be Understood," CBS Fellows, Columbia University, May 12, 1959.
76. "Memoranda to the Old Dominion Foundation on Proposals for a Center for Humanistic Scholars," June 26 and July 14, 1959.
77. "Can Writing Be Taught?," Portland Writers' Conference, Portland, Ore., Aug. 12, 1959.
78. "Dangers To and From History," Blair Academy, Oct. 24, 1959.
79. "Publish or Perish. Scholarship and Security: An Uneasy Alliance," *The Times Literary Supplement,* Nov. 6, 1959. (Anonymous.)
80. "The Dangers of Professional Self-Worship," Engineering Convocation, Columbia University, Nov. 21, 1959.
81. "Intellect and Intelligence," French Graduate Students, Columbia University, Dec. 9, 1959.
82. *The Conduct of Oral Examinations* and *Scholarship and the Ansley Awards,* Columbia University, 1960.
83. "Statement on the Council for Basic Education," *Council for Basic Education,* Leaflet No. 2, January 1960.
84. "Academic Excellence in Liberal Arts Colleges," Association of American Colleges, Boston, Jan. 13, 1960.
85. "The Conditions of Success," *Vogue,* March 1, 1960.
86. "History—Antidote to Number," Graduate History Club, Princeton University, April 21, 1960.
87. "Educational Exchange—What Is the Gold Point?," State Department Meeting, Harvard University, April 30, 1960.
88. "University Work, Special Institutes, and the Clerical Revolution," Chancellor's Advisory Committee on an Institute for the Humanities, University of California, Berkeley, May 23, 1960.
89. "How Much Science in Our Mental Diet?," Industrial Indemnity Company, San Francisco, May 24, 1960.
90. "Education and Administration: Polar Opposites," Institute for University Administrators, Harvard Business School, May 31, 1960.
91. "The Nurse's Curriculum: Self-Knowledge and Mind-Reading," School of Nursing graduation ceremony, College of Physicians and Surgeons, June 2, 1960.
92. (with others) "American Education," *American Interviews,* Associate Television Limited, London, September 1960.
93. "Centering the Arts," *Columbia University Forum,* Winter 1960.
94. "Our Universities: Unguided Missiles," *Think,* November 1960.

95. "The American College in Double Jeopardy," *Proceedings of the American Philosophical Society,* vol. 104, no. 6, Dec. 15, 1960.
96. Foreword to S. Toulmin, *Foresight and Understanding,* Bloomington, Indiana, 1961.
97. "The College and Government," Van Am Society, Columbia University, April 20, 1961.
98. Review of R. Ulich, *The Education of Nations: A Comparison in Historical Perspective, Science,* April 28, 1961.
99. Preface to *Tomorrow's Illiterates: The State of Reading Instruction Today,* ed. C. Walcutt, Boston, 1961.
100. "The Advantages of Inconsistency," The Foundations Group, Ford Foundation, Sept. 28, 1961.
101. "Why Teach the History of Science?," History of Science Society, Washington, Dec. 29, 1961.
102. (with others) *The Education of Historians in the United States,* The Carnegie Series in American Education, New York, 1962. (Report of the Committee on Graduate Education of the American Historical Association.)
103. "Science and Public Opinion," Physics Teachers Institute, Columbia University, July 20, 1962.
104. Foreword to B. Hoffmann, *The Tyranny of Testing,* New York, 1962.
105. "What Is a University?," *College and University Journal,* vol. 1, no. 4, Fall 1962.
106. "Notes on the Making of a World Encyclopedia," *American Behavioral Scientist,* September 1962; and "Further Notes on Encyclopedias: The Organization of Knowledge," June 20, 1962. (Memoranda to the Board of Editors, Encyclopedia Britannica.)
107. "Money and the Man," American Historical Association, Chicago, Dec. 29, 1962.
108. "American Education," Downing College, University of Cambridge, May 12, 1963. (Public discussion with Lord [then Sir Charles] Snow.)
109. "The Library and the Born Reader," Cape Cod Writer's Conference, Craigville, Mass., Aug. 22, 1963.
110. "The Economics of Research," *Horizon,* September 1963. (See also *Church History,* vol. XXXII, no. 2, June 1963.)
111. "The Secondary School, Refuge of Liberal Education," Hill School, Pottstown, Pennsylvania, Sept. 17, 1963.
112. "Anthropology and the Humanities," Anthropology Seminar, Columbia University, Nov. 13, 1963.

113. "Intellectual History," History G6000 Seminar, Columbia University, Dec. 3, 1963.
114. "College to University—and After," *The American Scholar,* Spring 1964. (Originally, Dedication Address, Hofstra University, December 11, 1963.)
115. (with others) "Graduate and Professional Study," *Columbia University Forum,* Winter 1964.
116. "Fighting for Your Education," *Milton Academy Bulletin,* December 1964.
117. "What a University Alone Can Do with the Arts," Art History Advisory Council, Columbia University, Dec. 2, 1964.
118. "The New University," Charter Day Convocation, Columbia University, Jan. 9, 1965.
119. "Computers for the Humanities?," Yale University, 1965. (Record of conference on "Man and the Machine," Jan. 22–23, 1965.)
120. "Scientific Research and Public Affairs," Management Institute, Civil Service Commission, Washington, D.C., Feb. 3, 1965.
121. (with others) *Conflicts Between the Federal Research Programs and the Nation's Goals for Higher Education,* U.S. Government Printing Office, June 1965. (Response to inquiry by Subcommittee of the Committee on Government Operations.)
122. "The Liberal Arts—Shadow or Substance?," Gonzaga University, Spokane, Sept. 9, 1965.
123. "On the 'Relevance' of the Humanities," Aspen Institute, Colorado, Sept. 22, 1965.
124. "College Administration and Crime," 34th Annual Meeting of the Middle States Association of Collegiate Registrars and Officers of Admission, Atlantic City, Dec. 3, 1965.
125. "The Scholar in the Library," School of Library Service, Columbia University, Jan. 13, 1966.
126. "The University in the Swim," Alumni Association Midtown, Columbia University Club, Jan. 20, 1966.
127. "Fewer Facts: More Theory," Conference on Science and Society, Georgetown University, Feb. 22, 1966.
128. "Science as a Social Institution," *Proceedings of the Academy of Political Science,* April 1966.
129. "Scholar, Connoisseur, and Critic—What Do They Know of Art?," Walters Art Gallery, Baltimore, April 14, 1966.
130. "Art and Science—How Soon the Fatal Dose?," *Chancellor's Occasional Papers,* University of California, Berkeley, May 1966.

131. "The Humanities," New York School of Printing, New York, May 3, 1966.
132. "The University as the Beloved Republic," Convocation on "The University in America," Los Angeles, May 10, 1966.
133. "Intellectual Exchange—Illusions and Realities," Columbia Alumni Program, San Francisco, May 12, 1966; also Washington, D.C., Nov. 15, 1966.
134. "The Humanities Differ from the Arts," National Institute of Arts and Letters, New York, May 26, 1966.
135. "College—Under Discussion Now," Seminar for representatives of Southern Colleges, Columbia University Summer Session, July 13, 1966.
136. "The Idea of a Career," 39th Annual Conference of the Association of Eastern College Placement Officers, Lake Placid, N.Y., Oct. 4, 1966.
137. "The Decay of Liberalism and the Death of Liberal Education," Wesleyan University, Middletown, Conn., Nov. 2, 1966.
138. "The Graduate Student, the University, and the Government," Graduate Faculties Student Council, Columbia University, Dec. 6, 1966.
139. "Book or Machine—Which Is Dearer?," Union Club, New York, Jan. 18, 1967.
140. "On the Humanities," *The Sciences and the Humanities in the Schools after a Decade of Reform: Present and Future Needs,* Council for Basic Education Occasional Papers, April 1967. (Originally Address to the Council, Washington, D.C., October 21, 1966.)
141. "Love of Eden and All Our Woe," Seminar in Philosophy and Social Sciences, TF6001, Teachers College, April 18, 1967.
142. "The Intellectual Life and the School System," Aspen Institute on Education and Human Potential, Colorado, Aug. 15, 1967.
143. "Does Liberalism Fit the New Education?," Aspen Institute Seminar on Education and Human Potential, Colorado, Aug. 19, 1967.
144. "Museum Piece: 1967—The Curator as Scout and Teacher," Museum of the City of New York, New York, Oct. 10, 1967.

Notes

CHAPTER 1—THE NEW UNIVERSITY

1. *The University in America,* An Occasional Paper of the Center for the Study of Democratic Institutions, Santa Barbara, Calif., n.d. (1966), 29.
2. *Selected Letters,* Boston, 1933, 189, 3–5.
3. G. W. Allen, *William James,* New York, 1967, 153.

CHAPTER 2—SCHOLARS IN ORBIT

1. See the report "Academic Freedom and Tenure: Statements of Principle Endorsed by the Association of American Colleges and the American Association of University Professors." (Reprinted from the *Bulletin* of the latter association, vol. 39, no. 1, Spring 1953.
2. Paul Morand, *New-York,* Paris, 1930, 247, 249.

CHAPTER 3—STUDENTS OR VICTIMS?

1. *The Jefferson-Dunglison Letters,* ed. John M. Dorsey, Charlottesville, 1960, 40.
2. A. Lawrence Lowell, *What a University President Has Learned,* New York, 1938, 80.
3. "College Pressure—a Three-Part Series," *Life,* Jan. 8, 15, 22, 1965.
4. Julian Hall, *Alma Mater, Or The Future of Oxford and Cambridge,* London, 1928, 39–40, 44, 85–86.
5. Gertrude Stein, *Wars I Have Seen,* New York, 1945, 190.
6. Boswell's *Life of Johnson* under date of April 15, 1772.
7. A. L. Lowell, *op. cit.,* 30–31 and *n.,* and H. A. Yeomans, *Abbott Lawrence Lowell,* Cambridge, 1948, 525.

CHAPTER 4—ADMINISTRATORS ABOVE AND BELOW

1. Report of the President of Yale University for 1964–65, New Haven, 1965, 6.
2. *Teacher in America,* 2nd ed. (Anchor Books), New York, 1954, 158.
3. "Character of Mr. Pitt," *Political Essays, Works,* ed. Glover and Waller, vol. III, 347*n.*
4. Quoted in G. W. Allen, *William James,* New York, 1967, 363.

CHAPTER 5—FRIENDS, DONORS, ENEMIES

1. Address to the National Association of College Stores, June 1965.
2. *Timon of Athens,* Act I, Sc. 2.
3. *New York Times* editorial, "Uses of the University," Jan. 2, 1968.
4. Private communication, unsolicited.
5. Harold J. Seymour, *Designs For Fund-Raising,* New York, 1966, 43.
6. *Ibid.,* 45.
7. *Ibid.,* 15.
8. *Ibid.,* 165.
9. President Silberman of the Federation of Jewish Philanthropies, *New York Times,* Sept. 28, 1967.

CHAPTER 6—POVERTY IN THE MIDST OF PLENTY

1. "The Hardship of Accounting."
2. *Memo to a College Trustee,* Fund for the Advancement of Education, Ford Foundation, New York, 1959.
3. W. S. Brown, J. R. Pierce, J. F. Traub in *Science,* vol. 158, Dec. 1, 1967, 1153.
4. Martin Mayer, *The Lawyers,* New York, 1967, 450.

CHAPTER 7—THE HIGHER BANKRUPTCY

1. Private communication.
2. *The Free University News,* January 1966.
3. "The Cast-Iron University," *Kenyon Alumni Bulletin,* July–September 1965.
4. *Public Law and Government Newsletter,* February 1967.
5. "The Values of Youth and Accelerated Social Dislocation," *Modern Educational Developments: Another Look,* Report of the 30th Educational Conference of the Educational Records Bureau, New York, 1966, 3.

6. *The Office and Work of Universities,* ed. George Sampson, London, 1902, 206–207.
7. *Julius Caesar,* Act V, Sc. 5.
8. Adelphi Suffolk College, *Educational Trends,* vol. 4, no. 1, Spring 1967.
9. James P. Dixon, *Antioch Notes,* vol. 44, no. 8, May 1967.
10. Quoted from Appendix D, No. 142.
11. *New York Times,* Aug. 6, 1960.
12. *The Pilgrim Hawk,* New York, 1966, 15.
13. *Mission of a University,* ed. and trans. by Howard Lee Nostrand, Princeton, 1944, 57.
14. W. G. Carleton, "Letter to a New Ph.D.," *Teachers College Record,* December 1961, 199 ff.
15. "Graduate Students: New Style," *Journal of Higher Education,* vol. 35, November 1964, 443.
16. *Ibid.,* 445.
17. "Modern College Usage, Or What Is the Public Relations Office Saying?," *Columbia University Forum,* vol. II, no. 3, Spring 1959, 41.
18. John Weiss, "The University as Corporation," *New University Thought,* Detroit, vol. 4, no. 2, 1965, 37.
19. See note 5: *op. cit.,* 15.
20. "Quality in Higher Education," *Current Issues in Higher Education,* Association for Higher Education, New York, 1958, 8.
21. William J. Goode, *American Sociological Review,* vol. 32, no. 1, February 1967.
22. Robert M. Lukes, *Science,* vol. 159, Jan. 5, 1968.
23. "Icaromenippus," *Six Dialogues of Lucian,* trans. by Sidney T. Irwin, London, 1894, 19.

CHAPTER 8—THE CHOICES AHEAD

1. *Life and Letters of John Donne,* ed. Edmund Gosse, 1899, II, 84,
2. *Essays and Criticisms by Thomas Gray,* ed. C. S. Northup, Boston, 194, xix.
3. Mark Pattison, *Memoirs,* London, 1885, 53.
4. "On Legal Education," *Westminster Review,* X, July 1828, 84.
5. Written in 1859 and quoted in C. S. Dessain, *John Henry Newman,* London, 1966, 109.
6. "Address at the dedication of the Memorial Library," Notre Dame, May 7, 1964.
7. Condensed and paraphrased from Newman's *Office and Work of Universities,* ed. George Sampson, London, 1902, 15–16.
8. "William Pitt" (1861), *Complete Works,* ed. Forrest Morgan, Hartford, 1889, III, 126.

9. "Letter to Lord Halifax" (1701).
10. J.-B. L. Crevier, *Histoire de l'Université de Paris,* 1761, I, 57.
11. Frederic Lilge, *The Abuse of Learning: The Failure of the German University,* New York, 1948, 89. See also 86–8.
12. "An Address before the American Orthopsychiatric Association," Washington, D.C., March 23, 1967.
13. *Loc. cit.,* see note 6.
14. *Antioch Notes,* vol. 44, no. 5, February 1967.
15. *The Querist,* no. 405.
16. *New York Times,* July 15, 1967.
17. *Urban Extension: A Report on Experimental Programs Assisted by the Ford Foundation,* October 1966, 21.
18. George Pake, "Basic Research and Financial Crisis in the Universities," *Science,* vol. 157, Aug. 4, 1967, 519–20.
19. *New York Times,* Feb. 26, 1968; also: *Forbes* advertisement of demographic studies, *New York Times,* Nov. 3, 1967.
20. Letter to the *New York Times,* "Mini-Schools Opposed," Jan. 22, 1968.
21. American Broadcasting Company Program reported in the *New York Times,* April 8, 1966.
22. *New York Times,* Aug. 6, 1966, and Oct. 28, 1967.
23. *Ibid.,* July 22, 1967, and Aug. 8, 1967.
24. *Ibid.,* July 26, 1967.
25. Glenn T. Seaborg, "Time, Leisure, and the Computer," *The Key Reporter,* Spring 1967, 3.
26. Harry Malisoff, *The New York Statistician,* September–October, 1967, 1.
27. "Emerson Behind Barbed Wire," *The New York Review of Books,* vol. 10, no. 1, Jan. 18, 1968.
28. *New York Times,* June 15 and 28, 1966.
29. "On the art of conversation," Book III, Ch. 8.

Index